T5-BAR-951

Social Security:
Time for a Change

CONTEMPORARY STUDIES IN ECONOMIC AND FINANCIAL ANALYSIS, Volume 78

Editors: Robert J. Thornton and J. Richarad Aronson
Lehigh University

Contemporary Studies in Economic and Financial Analysis
An International Series of Monographs

Edited by **Robert J. Thornton** and **J. Richard Aronson**, *Lehigh University*

Volume 1 - ***Hunt, L.*** - Dynamics of Forecasting Financial Cycles

Volume 2 - ***Dreyer, J.S.*** - Composite Reserve Assets in the International Money System

Volume 3 - ***Altman, E.I., et al.*** - Application of Classification Techniques in Business, Banking and Finance

Volume 4 - ***Sinkey, J.F.*** - Problems and Failed Institutions in the Commercial Banking Industry

Volume 5 - ***Ahlers, D.M.*** - A New Look at Portfolio Management

Volume 6 - ***Sciberras, E.*** - Multinational Electronic Companies and National Economic Policies

Volume 7 - ***Allen, L.*** - Venezuelan Economic Developement: A Politico-Economic Analysis

Volume 8 - ***Gladwin, T.N.*** - Environment Planning and the Multinational Corporation

Volume 9 - ***Kobrin, S.J.*** - Foreign Direct Investment, Industrialization and Social Change

Volume 10 - ***Oldfield, G.S.*** - Implications of Regulation on Bank Expansion: A Simulation Analysis

Volume 11 - ***Ahmad, J.*** - Import Substitution, Trade and Development

Volume 12 - ***Fewings, D.R.*** - Corporate Growth and Common Stock Risk

Volume 13 - ***Stapleton, R.C.*** and ***M.G. Subrahmanyam*** - Capital Market Equillibrium and Corporate Financial Decisions

Volume 14 - ***Bloch, E.*** and ***R.A. Schwartz*** - Impending Changes for Securities Markets: What Role for the Exchange

Volume 15 - ***Walker, W.B.*** - Industrial Innovation and International Trading Performance

Volume 16 - ***Thompson, J.K.*** - Financial Policy, Inflation and Economic Development: The Mexican Experience

Volume 17 - Omitted from Numbering

Volume 18 - ***Hallwood, P.*** - Stabilization of International Commodity Markets

Volume 19 - Omitted from Numbering

Volume 20 - ***Parry, T.G.*** - The Multinational Enterprise: International Investment and Host-Country Impacts

Volume 21 - ***Roxburgh, N.*** - Policy Responses to Resource Depletion: The Case of Mercury

Volume 22 - ***Levich, R.M.*** - The International Money Market: An Assessment of Forecasting Techniques and Market Efficiency

Volume 23 - ***Newfarmer, R.*** - Transnational Conglomerates and the Economics of Dependent Development

Volume 24 - ***Siebert, H. and A.B. Anatal*** - The Political Economy of Environmental Protection

Volume 25 - ***Ramsey, J.B.*** - Bidding and Oil Leases

Volume 26 - ***Ramsey, J.B.*** - The Economics of Exploration for Energy Resources

Volume 27 - ***Ghatak, S.*** - Technology Transfer to Developing Countries: The Case of the Fertilizer Industry

Volume 28 - ***Pastre, O.*** - Multinationals: Bank and Corporation Relationships

Volume 29 - ***Bierwag, G.O.*** - The Primary Market for Municipal Debt: Bidding Rules and Cost of Long Term Borrowing

Volume 30 - ***Kaufman, G.G.*** - Efficiency in the Municipal Bond Market: The Use of Tax Exempt Financing for "Private" Purposes

Volume 31 - ***West, P.*** - Foreign Investment and Technology Transfer: The Tire Industry in Latin America

Volume 32 - ***Uri, N.D.*** - Dimensions of Energy Economics

Volume 33 - ***Balabkins, N.*** - Indigenization and Economic Development: The Nigerian Experience

Volume 34 - ***Oh, J.S.*** - International Financial Management: Problem, Issues and Experience

Volume 35 - ***Officer, L.H.*** - Purchasing Power Parity and Exchange Rates: Theory Evidence and Relevance

Volume 36 - ***Horwitz, B.*** and ***R. Kolodny*** - Financial Reporting Rules and Corporate Decisions: A Study of Public Policy

Volume 37 - ***Thorelli, H.B.*** and ***G.D. Sentell*** - Consumer Emancipation and Economic Development

Volume 38 - ***Wood, W.C.*** - Insuring Nuclear Power: Liability, Safety and Economic Efficiency

Volume 39 - ***Uri, N.D.*** - New Dimensions in Public Utility Pricing

Volume 40 - ***Cross, S.M.*** - Economic Decisions Under Inflation: The Impact of Accounting Measurement Error

Volume 41 - ***Kaufman, G.G.*** - Innovations in Bond Portfolio Management: Immunization and Duration Analysis

Volume 42 - ***Horvitz, P.M.*** and ***R.R. Pettit*** - Small Business Finance

Volume 43 - ***Plaut, S.E.*** - Import Dependence and Economic Vulnerability

Volume 44 - ***Finn, F.J.*** - Evaluation of the Internal Processes of Managed Funds

Volume 45 - ***Moffitt, L.C.*** - Strategic Management: Public Planning at the Local Level

Volume 46 - ***Thornton, R.J., et al.*** - Reindustrialization: Implications for U.S. Industrial Policy

Volume 47 - ***Askari, H.*** - Saudi Arabias Economy: Oil and the Search for Economic Technology Transfer in Export Processing Zones

Volume 48 - ***Von Pfeil, E.*** - German Direct Investment in the United States

Volume 49 - ***Dresch, S.*** - Occupational Earnings, 1967-1981: Return to Occupational Choice, Schooling and Physician Specialization

Volume 50 - ***Siebert, H.*** - Economics of the Resource-Exporting Country Intertemporal Theory of Supply and Trade

Volume 51 - ***Walton, G.M.*** - The National Economic Policies of Chile

Volume 52 - ***Stanley, G.*** - Managing External Issues: Theory and Practice

Volume 53 - ***Nafziger, E.W.*** - Essays in Entrepreneurship, Equity and Economic Development

Volume 54 - ***Lea, M.*** and ***K.E. Villani*** - Tax Policy and Housing

Volume 55 - ***Slottje, D.*** and ***J. Haslag*** - Macroeconomic Activity and Income Inequality in the United States

Volume 56 - ***Thornton, R.F.*** and ***J.R. Aronson*** - Forging New Relationships Among Business, Labor and Government

Volume 57 - ***Putterman, L.*** - Peasants, Collectives and Choice: Economic Theory and Tanzanias Villages

Volume 58 - ***Baer, W.*** and ***J.F. Due*** - Brazil and the Ivory Coast: The Impact of International Lending, Investment and Aid

Volume 59 - ***Emanuel, H., et al.*** - Disability Benefits: Factors Determining Applications and Awards

Volume 60 - ***Rose, A.*** - Forecasting Natural Gas Demand in a Changing World

Volume 61 - Omitted from Numbering

Volume 62 - ***Canto, V.A.*** and ***J.K. Dietrich*** - Industrial Policy and Industrial Trade

Volume 63 - ***Kimura, Y.*** - The Japanese Semiconductor Industry

Volume 64 - ***Thornton, R., Hyclak, T.*** and ***J.R. Aronson*** - Canada at the Crossroads: Essays on Canadian Political Economy

Volume 65 - ***Hausker, A.J.*** - Fundamentals of Public Credit Analysis

Volume 66 - ***Looney, R.*** - Economic Development in Saudi Arabia: Consequences of the Oil Price Decline

Volume 67 - ***Askari, H.*** - Saudi Arabias Economy: Oil and the Search for Economic Development

Volume 68 - ***Godfrey, R.*** - Risk Based Capital Charges for Municipal Bonds

Volume 69 - ***Guerard, J.B*** and ***M.N. Gu;ltekin*** - Handbook of Security Analyst Forecasting and Asset Allocation

Volume 70 - ***Looney, R.E.*** - Industrial Development and Diversification of the Arabian Gulf Economies

Volume 71 - ***Basmann, R.L., et al.*** - Some New Methods for Measuring and Describing Economic Inequality

Volume 72 - ***Looney, R.E.*** - The Economics of Third World Defense Expenditures

Volume 73 - ***Thornton, R.J.*** and ***A.P. OBrien*** - The Economic Consequences of American Education

Volume 74 - ***Gaughan, P.A.*** and ***R.J. Thornton*** - Litigation Economics

Volume 75 - ***Nafzinger, E. Wayne*** - Poverty and Wealth: Comparing Afro-Asian Development

Volume 76 - ***Frankurter, George*** and ***Herbert E. Phillips*** - Forty Years of Normative Portfolio Theory: Issues, Controversies, and Misconceptions

Volume 77 - ***Kuark, John Y.T.*** - Comparative Asian Economics

Social Security: Time for a Change

Edited by **KEVIN STEPHENSON**
Middlebury College

Greenwich, Connecticut *London, England*

Library of Congress Cataloging-in-Publication Data

Social security : time for a change/edited by Kevin Stephenson.
p. cm.—(Contemporary studies in economic and financial analysis : v. 78)
Includes bibliographical references.
ISBN 1-55938-933-8 (alk. paper)
1. Social security—United States. 2. Privatization—United States. 3. United States—Social policy—1993- I. Stephenson, Kevin. II. Series.
HD7125.S59944 1995
368.4'3'00973—dc20

95-44898

55 Old Post Road, No. 2
Greenwich, Connecticut 06836

JAI PRESS LTD.
The Courtyard
28 High Street
Hampton Hill
Middlesex TW12 1PD
England

ISBN: 1-55938-933-8

Library of Congress Catalog Card Number: 95-44898

Manufactured in the United States of America

CONTENTS

ACKNOWLEDGMENTS

I would first like to thank Willard Jackson, a Middlebury College trustee, who gets credit for the idea of hosting a conference on social security. David Colander and David Horlacher assisted in organizing the conference. Special thanks to David Horlacher for spending his "free" semester educating himself on the issues and getting this project off the ground. Sheila Cassin was instrumental in handling the conference logistics. I thank the authors for their participation in the Conference and their willingness to revise promptly. Justin Block assisted in formatting this volume. Lastly, I wish to thank Jones International for generously providing the resources for Middlebury College to host an annual conference on economic issues.

FOREWORD

Kevin Stephenson

The question of what to do about the social security system is one of the central policy questions facing the U.S. government. This volume covers the central issues in the policy debate and explores the privatizing solutions that have been put forward. The papers come from the April 1994 Middlebury College Conference on Economic Issues, at which experts on social security from government and academia discussed the social security system and what changes, if any, should be considered.

The volume is divided into four parts. Part I discusses the problems inherent in the current system. The first paper is an overview of our social security system and a brief discussion of some of the key issues. In the second paper, Barry Bosworth explains why the United States will face major increases in the cost of financing retirement pensions early in the next century. He then reviews the policy options which could finance these costs.

In the third paper, James E. Duggan discusses the impact of the projected social security deficits on U.S. debt policy and evaluates whether government fiscal policy is sustainable in the long run, in light of expected social security expenditures. The section ends with two shorter papers offering contrasting views from two social security specialists. In the first, Carolyn L. Weaver explains why social security is in need of genuine reform. In the second paper, Robert Myers argues that the social security system is essentially sound and requires only minor adjustments.

If there is to be reform, it is necessary to consider that reform in relation to the lessons provided by other countries. The retirement systems of other nations are examined in Part II. In the first paper, John Turner and David M. Rajnes discuss the pension systems in Japan and the United Kingdom. In the second paper, David M. Rajnes examines the retirement systems emerging in Eastern Europe, with an emphasis on those characteristics that might become part of the reform legislation in the United States. In these countries, companies that meet certain criteria may opt out of the public retirement system and provide their own retirement plans for their workers. The most successful foreign experience has been in Chile, but experts disagree about whether that experience is relevant to the United States. A highly positive assessment of the Chilean social security system is offered by Marco Santamaria in the next paper. He argues that Chile is a possible model for the United States and that a Chilean-type system can be implemented in the United States. Santamaria's views are not shared by all. In the final paper of this section, Robert Myers voices concerns over using Chile as a model for other nations, arguing that many features of the Chilean system are unique to Chile and the lessons do not carry over.

The U.S. social security system currently has annual surpluses which are placed into a trust fund. One way to alleviate the expected future social security deficits would be to earn a higher rate of return on these surplus funds. The Social Security Trust Fund investment policy is examined in Part III. In the first paper, Carolyn L. Weaver updates and expands her 1990 testimony before the Social Security Advisory Council. Her testimony explains our current investment policy and examines alternative policies. She specifically cautions against investing government-controlled funds in the private sector. Next, a contrasting view is presented by Robert C. Perez. Perez argues that the precarious condition of the system today results from the historical reliance on a "Treasuries-only" investment policy for the Trust Fund. He contends, from a rate-of-return point of view, that the Trust Fund should be invested in private securities, with an emphasis on common stock.

Corporate pension plans and individual retirement accounts (IRAs) earn contributors a much higher rate of return, on average, than their social security contributions. Can and should the U.S. social security system incorporate some of the aspects of our private retirement systems? Partial privatization schemes are examined in Part IV. Yung-Ping Chen outlines the major issues surrounding the privatization debate. He discusses the freedom of choice issue, compares defined benefit plans with defined contribution plans, and examines the impact of privatization on fiscal policy and interest rates.

Any reform measure must take into account the relevant political considerations. In the second paper, Representative John Edward Porter of Illinois discusses his bill to establish mandatory IRA-type retirement accounts using part of an individual's social security taxes. He highlights the major advantages of moving toward a partially privatized system and offers a firsthand look at the politics involved in the social security reform movement. Peter J. Ferrara goes one step further and advocates moving much closer to a completely privatized system. Specifically, workers would be allowed to make larger contributions to an IRA-type account and would receive full income tax credit for their contributions.

To conclude, given the demographic time bomb built into the U.S. social security system, it is evident that changes need to be made. Social security experts examine several possible solutions in this volume. Although the magnitude of the necessary changes is controversial, there is a consensus that action needs to be taken soon. It is hoped that this volume will provide an impetus to such action.

PART I

WHAT'S WRONG WITH OUR SOCIAL SECURITY SYSTEM?

AN OVERVIEW OF THE U.S. SOCIAL SECURITY SYSTEM:

PROBLEMS AND OPTIONS

Kevin Stephenson, David Horlacher, and
David Colander

INTRODUCTION

Privatization of prisons, telecommunications and education has been much in the news in the 1980s and 1990s. One area that has been little discussed since the early 1980s, but in which calls for privatization continue to be made, is the provision of social retirement insurance. This paper is a very brief introduction to some unresolved issues behind those cries for change.

In the United States, retirement security is based on a triad composed of private savings, employment-related pensions, and a publicly financed system of social insurance. A number of proposals have been made to change the relative weights within this mix, increasing the proportion that is privately supplied and decreasing the proportion which is publicly supplied. This volume considers these proposals, asking such questions as: Is the current system financially sound? Does privatization make economic sense? Does it make political sense? What will it cost?

There can be no definitive answers to such questions; most involve value judgments on which reasonable people can, and often will, differ. Hence, the goal of this volume is not to arrive at an agreement on specific policy proposals but rather to clarify the issues and to narrow the range of disagreement.

In that context, this paper provides some background for the debate and introduces the topics that will be discussed in greater depth throughout this volume. We begin with a brief introduction to the social security system. Next, we review arguments for the public provision of retirement insurance. We then discuss arguments for changing the current system, especially the implications of the decline in the worker-retiree ratio. Finally, we discuss the issues surrounding two very different proposals for privatizing the social security system.

THE SOCIAL SECURITY SYSTEM

The Social Security Act, a centerpiece of President Roosevelt's New Deal, was enacted in 1935 and amended many times thereafter. In 1939, it was expanded to provide benefits to the dependents of deceased workers. Amendments in 1956 and 1958 provided benefits to disabled workers and their dependents. Together, these income maintenance programs have come to be known as Old Age, Survivors and Disability Insurance (OASDI). In 1965, the Medicare program for the aged and disabled was established; this included hospital insurance (HI). The complete program is referred to as OASDHI. However, this paper will not address the complex issue of health insurance for the elderly, a subject that is now part of a much larger national debate.

The tax rate for Old Age Survivors Insurance (OASI) is 5.6% of the first $60,600 of gross salary and wages and the tax rate for Disability Insurance is 0.6%, making a total of 6.2% of taxable wages up to $60,600. This amount is matched by employers. About 95% of all American workers pay social security taxes. If it is assumed that the employer's contribution reduces the wages that otherwise would have been paid, then over 70% of all taxpayers pay more in social security taxes than in personal income taxes.

In 1993, OASDI provided benefits totaling approximately $308 billion to 42 million Americans. The typical retiree currently receives about $8,100 per year.

Although the system was initially designed to accumulate a large fund that would earn significant interest income which would pay for a substantial portion of total benefits, Congress converted the social security system to a pay-as-you-go (PAYG) basis in 1939. Under that system, taxes paid by workers in a given period would be used to pay benefits to retirees in the same period. Although it included a small trust fund as a contingency reserve, the system was to be essentially a mechanism for making intergenerational transfers at any given point in time.

From a financial standpoint, a pay-as-you-go public system stands in direct contrast to a private actuarially based system, where each family funds its own retirement benefits from accumulated savings out of its own earnings. However, from a social point of view, both pension systems are similar in that both involve a transfer of real goods and services from the families of those who are working to the families of those who are retired. What is different in the two cases is the financing used to effect the real transfer.

ARGUMENTS FOR A PUBLIC SOCIAL SECURITY SYSTEM

Since retirement security can be provided by private savings and employment-related pension plans, is there any reason why a compulsory federal old-age retirement scheme is required? A number of justifications have been offered. Most have been based on the need for government to rectify market failures and to provide a social safety net for those who would otherwise be indigent.

Market Failures

Laurence Kotlikoff (1987) observes that an important rationale for compulsory social security is the failure of private insurance markets to offer appropriately priced annuities that provide a specified level of real income until death. Because of adverse selection, moral hazard, and related problems, it is not possible for insurance companies to sell such annuities at an actuarially fair price. By requiring everyone to purchase its annuities, the social security system avoids this problem.

In the United States, private insurance companies are unable to sell annuities indexed against inflation because the government does not sell inflation-indexed bonds (Munnell, 1982). However, the social security system can provide inflation-adjusted annuities because of its pay-as-you-go nature. Inflation increases the nominal value of the wage base of social security taxes at the same time as it raises nominal benefit levels.

Private insurance companies are also unable to guarantee that they will meet their obligations in the event of mass unemployment and business failures, such as occurred in the Great Depression.1 Finally, private markets cannot sell insurance to enable the sharing of risks between current and unborn generations. For example, insurance companies cannot pool good and bad economic times across generations.

Altruism

Another rationale suggested by Kotlikoff is what he called "self-serving altruism." If individuals were concerned about the welfare of others, then transfers to the poor elderly could raise the general welfare. But a voluntary system of savings would tempt some to undersave since they could then count on the generosity of others to supplement their savings.

It can be assumed that individuals would only benefit if their generosity went to the "truly needy" elderly. However, this category is best determined by the government, which is in a position to know the incomes and assets of the beneficiaries. Similarly, Inman (1987) observed that many people would want to help only the "deserving poor" elderly but cannot distinguish the "deserving" from those who have been profligate, eschewing savings for luxurious consumption. Government can force the potentially profligate to save.

Though many households would inadequately save due to myopia, misinformation, and miscalculation, that is an argument merely for a compulsory savings scheme, not necessarily a public pension scheme. A compulsory minimum payment to a private pension scheme could also assure that people saved, thus protecting the society as a whole.

Over the life cycle, the social security system redistributes income from those who were high-wage workers to those who were low-wage workers.[2] Although this may be in accord with the altruistic desires of the population, such a redistribution requires the power of compulsion. Otherwise, high-wage workers would opt out of the program, gaining the psychic benefits of public altruism while benefiting financially as "free riders" (Aaron, Bosworth, and Burtless, 1989).

ARGUMENTS FOR ALTERING THE PRESENT SOCIAL SECURITY SYSTEM

The social security system has been criticized as financially unsound due to the declining worker-retiree ratio. It also has been criticized for providing a low rate of return to its participants and for lowering the national savings rate.

The Declining Ratio of Workers to Retirees

An argument advanced in favor of proposals for the privatization of retirement insurance is that they may better deal with the effects of the projected decline in the ratio of workers to retirees, especially the effects of the projected retirement of the "Baby Boom" generation sometime early in the next century. The latter has been referred to as a "demographic time bomb" within the social security system. In 1950, there were 16 workers for every social security recipient. As the system matured, greater and greater portions of retirees became covered. Because of this maturation, an increase in life expectancy, and a trend toward early retirement, that ratio has now fallen to about three workers for each retiree.

Clearly, a three-to-one ratio is eminently supportable since the social security system is currently running sizable annual surpluses. However, because of the large number of persons born in the two decades after World War II and the decline in birth rates that began in the 1960s, that ratio is projected to gradually decline to two workers for every retiree. At that time, projected revenues will fall short of projected benefit payments. In the absence of a policy change, the two-to-one ratio would deplete, and ultimately exhaust, the Trust Fund.

Critics of social security have likened a pay-as-you-go retirement system to a "Ponzi" or "pyramid" scheme—a system that pays off the early contributors with the money paid in by later contributors—a scheme that must ultimately crumble if the flow of new contributors is not maintained.

The implications of the changing dependency ratio as the population ages was recognized by the Congress in 1983. On the recommendation of the Greenspan Commission, social security taxes were raised to build a reserve that would fund liabilities for payments to future beneficiaries.[3]

That fund totaled $378.3 billion at the end of 1993 (Board of Trustees, 1994) and is projected to continue growing for the next two decades, to reach a maximum of approximately $12 trillion (Greenspan, 1990). Although it was projected that the measures taken in 1983 would maintain a positive balance in the Trust Fund until at least 2060, recent projections indicate the current growth of the Trust Fund is not sufficient to offset projected shortfalls.

The Board of Trustees of the Social Security Trust Fund annually makes long-range projections of the actuarial status of the fund based on three alternative sets of assumptions about economic and demographic trends. The intermediate assumptions that are the basis for the "Alternative II" projection reflect the Trustees' best estimate of what the future experiences of the Trust Fund will be. These estimates for the OASI and OASDI Trust Funds are shown in Figure 1. In 1993, OASDI contributions totaled $355.6 billion and total expenditures were $308.8 billion, yielding an annual surplus of about $47 billion. Starting in about 2010, however, the OASDI cost rate (the outgo from the trust fund expressed as a percentage of taxable income) will increase rapidly as the Baby Boom generation begins to rise. Beginning in about 2013, the cost rate will exceed the income rate. If nothing is done to alter the projection, the OASDI Trust Funds will be exhausted in 2029.[4] Thereafter, the system will have to borrow to cover the shortfall if it is to avoid defaulting on its obligations.

Though these are merely projections, the broad outline of the problem is clear. If the assumptions underlying Alternative II are correct, either benefits will have to be reduced or income (i.e., taxes and interest) will have to be increased.

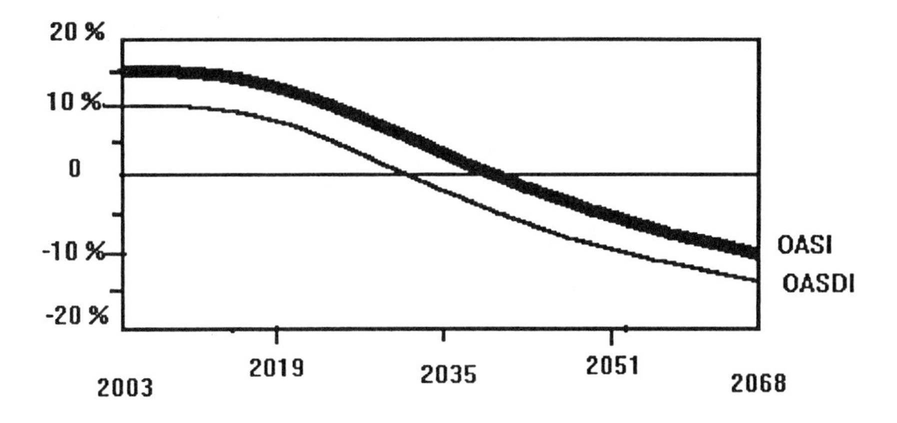

Source: Social Security Bulletin, Spring 1994, p. 55.

Figure 1. Actual Balance as a Percentage of Summarized Cost Rate and Long-range test Close Actuarial Balance

Avoiding the Potential Shortfall

The potential shortfall could be avoided by increasing the labor force participation of women and the elderly. However, increasing the labor force participation of women will only delay the problem until they retire. David Colander has proposed that the OASDI retirement age be linked to the worker-beneficiary ratio, raising it for large cohorts and lowering it for small ones. Carolyn Weaver (1990c) proposes raising the retirement age to 68 or 70 and indexing the retirement age to longevity. However, in all industrial countries, activity rates for the elderly are declining due to the incentive effects of pensions and increasing unemployment of the elderly (Marchand and Pestieau, 1991).

The trend toward increasing dependency rates could also be offset by reducing benefit rates. Weaver (1990c) suggests that indexing benefits to prices rather than wages would generate very large savings.

Under a PAYG system, the tax rate must be equal to the replacement ratio (the ratio of pension income to wage income) multiplied by the dependency rate. If it is not possible to reduce the dependency rate or the replacement ratio, then payroll taxes must be raised. Munnell and Ernsberger (1990) observe that under a PAYG system, social security taxes would have to be raised between one and two percentage points each for employers and employees starting in 2018 to offset the projected deficits, hence avoiding any decline in the $12 trillion Trust Fund.[5] They claim that such a tax increase is "completely manageable" in view of the fact that real wages will have doubled by that time.

Barry Bosworth (1990) argues that the social security system is in sound condition, with current taxes on workers close to the level required to finance their future benefits.[6] Furthermore, as noted by Robert Myers (1992), if financial difficulties arise in the social security program, small adjustments in contribution rates and/or benefit provisions can easily be made to rectify the situation. In short, the demographic time bomb can be diffused without any great difficulty.

Rate of Return to the Trust Fund

By law, the Trust Fund must hold its assets in the form of U.S. obligations. The Secretary of the Treasury invests the assets of the Trust Fund in special-issue securities which earn interest at a rate equal to the average market yield on long-term U.S. government bonds; they are redeemable at par and maturities are set with "due regard" for the needs of the Trust Fund.[7] Interest is becoming an increasingly important source of income for the Trust Funds. According to Weaver (1990b), interest earnings now account for 6% of income to the OASDI Trust Fund. They are projected to account for 15% in 2000 and to rise to 24% in 2020.[8] Robert Perez (1993) notes that social security deficits can also be reduced by improving the system's investment performance. Perez and Hammerbacher (1993) claim that had social security used the same portfolio mix as private pension plans in the 1980s, it would have grown to $343 billion instead of $280 billion, a difference of 22%.

Rate of Return to Individuals

As the social security system has matured, the rate of return on contributions has declined. For example, a worker and nonworking spouse retiring in 1980 received a 5.5% rate of return, compared with a projected 2.1% for workers retiring in 2010 (Weaver, 1993).[9] Social security offers today's young workers, on average, a real return of about 1% to 2% (the growth rate of real wages), which is substantially below the real rate of return on private capital. Returns also vary among individuals, given the redistributive nature of the system. David Boaz (1990) estimates that the most young workers can expect when they retire ranges from a 1.5% real rate of return for low-income workers to a negative real rate of return for upper-income participants.

Peter Ferrara (1986) notes that if young workers entering the work force today could invest all their social security money, including the employer's share, in IRAs and earn a 6% real rate of return, which is somewhat less than the average return earned in the stock market over the last 60 years, most would receive three to six times the retirement benefits promised under social security, while at least matching the other types of benefits offered under the program. At a 4% real rate of return, most would receive two or three times the retirement benefits promised by social security.[10]

Altering the Balance Between Public and Private Expenditures

A number of observers have expressed concern over the impact of the current social security surpluses on the size of government expenditures. Recall that those surpluses are currently used to purchase Treasury securities, the proceeds of which are then used to fund general government expenditures. James Buchanan (1990) and others have argued that government expenditures have increased because of the availability of these funds. That is, the government uses these surpluses to expand outlays rather than to replace funds previously borrowed from the private sector. Buchanan argues that if this continues, claims will accumulate in the social security account against the Treasury and, hence, taxpayers. However, there will be no increase in future income which would allow these claims to be easily settled through taxation or debt issues.

Munnell and Ernsberger (1990) point out, however, that not all government spending is consumption; the building of roads, bridges, and other types of infrastructure by government is investment just as much as the construction of a factory.

Reducing the National Savings Rate

There is widespread concern that the growth of American living standards has been slowed by an inadequate rate of saving. In the 1980s, the United States had an average savings rate of only three percent of income, or about half the savings rate of prior decades (Bosworth, 1990). According to James Poterba (1990), this low saving rate exposes our economy to the unpleasant choice of low investment and slow productivity growth or heavy reliance on capital flows from foreign investors.

As Greenspan (1990) observes, if retirees' living standards keep pace with those of workers and they become relatively more numerous, they will consume a growing proportion of total output in the future. The goods and services that retirees buy can only come from the output of active workers. Since the consumption of retirees must cut into what is available to the rest of the population for consumption and investment, the only way to make things better for future workers is to raise output by raising the rate of capital formation. Although the saving of today will not reduce the share of GNP that will be transferred to the retirees of tomorrow, current capital formation would help to ensure that incomes in the future would be large enough to provide benefits to retirees without cutting the living standards of their children. Noting that the social security reserves are merely a bookkeeping entry within the federal sector, Greenspan argues that their size matters only to the extent that they lead to smaller federal budget deficits and, thus, to more national saving.

Mathiasen (1990) also observes that the economic well-being of individuals at the time the baby boom retires will be determined by how much total output there is, which in turn will depend on the amount of savings between now and then.

If social security surpluses do not alter government fiscal policy, and households do not respond to these surpluses by reducing their own savings (in anticipation of lower future taxes), then the surpluses must increase the rate of capital formation. As the Trust Fund "buys" securities from the Treasury, there would be a dollar-for-dollar reduction in federal securities purchased by the private sector. This would increase the funds available to purchase private sector securities, thereby driving up their prices and lowering the cost for borrowers wishing to purchase real assets. Hence, the build-up of a trust fund should increase the investment rate, which in a closed economy would equal the savings rate.

If, as many suggest, social security surpluses encourage the government to spend more or tax less, the effect of those surpluses on savings rates would depend on the savings response of households. Households might foresee higher future taxes and, therefore, increase their savings rate to offset the future consequences of increased government borrowing. However, most households may not foresee far-off tax increases. If so, government borrowing and spending of the surplus would reduce the national savings rate.

While Alan Blinder (1990) argues that social security surpluses are important as a way to raise the rate of capital formation and to ease the burden on future generations, John Makin (1990) questions the goal of increasing savings rates, noting that a higher savings rate means transferring resources from current to later generations. He maintains that the government has no better knowledge of how resources should be allocated among generations than the private sector.

Intragenerational Income Transfers

The benefit structure of the social security system is highly progressive, giving low rates of return to high-wage earners and high rates of return to low-wage workers. For some observers, this is a significant disadvantage of the system. Gary Becker (1993) maintains that social security should provide retirees with benefits that strictly depend on their contributions while they worked. Benefits would be based solely on total contributions, retirement age, and marital status of family members. Though Becker acknowledges that some retired workers would not receive enough to enjoy a decent standard of living and would require supplemental benefits paid out of general revenues, he estimates that only one in five families would need these supplemental benefits.

Buchanan (1990) observes that the redistributive aspects of the social security system violate most of the traditional principles of fiscal equity. Taxes imposed on currently productive young workers finance payments to pensioners who may be financially better off than the taxpayers. Kotlikoff (1987) maintains that the redistribution across one-and two-earner couples is quite capricious, paying discriminatory low returns to two-earner couples, workers without children, and single workers. Ferrara (1986) points out that black Americans tend to receive lower returns than white Americans because they live fewer years in retirement, yet they are subject to the same taxes during their working lives. Moreover, black Americans as a group are younger than white Americans and, since social security discriminates against younger workers, it disadvantages black Americans.

PRIVATIZING THE ASSETS OF THE SOCIAL SECURITY TRUST FUND

We first consider proposals to allow the Trust Fund to purchase nongovernmental securities.

The Perez Proposal

A recent study (Aaron, Bosworth, and Burtless, 1989) claims that a one percentage point increase in the earnings rate on social security reserves over 75 years would effectively substitute for an increase of a 0.43 percentage point in the payroll tax rate. Robert Perez and Irene Hammerbacher advocate allowing the Trustees of the Social Security Trust Fund to use modern asset allocation techniques to increase the rate of return earned on the Trust Fund. Their 1993 study incorporates the Trustee's projections of future annual surpluses with various asset combinations to project an expected future value of the surplus, using historical rates of return for various securities. Depending on the assumptions used, adding equities to the Trust Fund's assets would either add several years to the Trust Fund's expected date of exhaustion or extend that date indefinitely.

To those who claim that investment in stocks is too risky, Perez and Hammerbacher (1993) reply that in only two decades (1929 through 1938 and 1930 through 1939) did investors lose money. In all other 10-year periods, stocks have provided a positive return, far greater than bonds. With time on their side, the social security trustees can wait for equities to produce superior future results despite the fact that they are riskier than bonds in the short run. In support of this position, Marco Santamaria (1992) observes that in 1988, private pension funds invested over 47% of their assets in corporate equities.

Effects on the Savings Rate

If the government now were to factor into its taxing and spending decisions the ease of borrowing social security surpluses, then allowing the Trust Fund to purchase nongovernment securities could have an impact on the national savings rate. If, however, the surpluses do not alter federal fiscal policy, then allowing the Trust Fund to invest in private securities is not likely to alter savings rates. Funds will merely be shuffled between assets, with private investors now purchasing the Treasury securities that would otherwise have been sold to the Trust Fund, and vice-versa.

Effect on the Cost of Government Borrowing

It is probable that under the Perez proposal, the cost of government financing would rise somewhat. However, given the size of global financial markets and the relative ease with which capital flows between countries, the shifting of Trust Fund assets from Treasury securities to other securities would be unlikely to significantly alter the interest rates paid on federal securities. The likelihood that the Trust Fund would continue to keep a substantial portion of its assets in Treasury obligations reinforces this view.

Effect on Securities Markets

The Social Security Trust Fund currently owns about $380 billion of Treasury securities, or about 10% of the total outstanding. This is not enough to cause any turmoil in the government securities market if the Trust Fund were to sell a portion of its holdings. Even if the social security system were to sell all its current holdings and use the proceeds to purchase private securities, such a shift would not be likely to disrupt financial markets unless it were done precipitously or narrowly. On the contrary, since the Social Security Trust Fund would be a long-term investor, including equities in the Trust Fund asset mix should reduce the overall volatility of the stock market while simultaneously providing a more reliable source of equity financing for the expansion of business.

Some observers, including Carolyn Weaver (1990a), have expressed concern that government ownership of corporate stock could lead to political manipulation. The total capitalization of the companies listed on the New York Stock Exchange is just over $4 trillion, an amount close to the maximum value of the assets that the Trust Fund is scheduled to amass (expressed in current dollars). The fear has been expressed that if the revenues of a fully funded social security system were invested in the equity market, the ultimate result could be public ownership of the means of production—in a word, "socialism."

A similar argument can be made regarding corporate bonds. For the next two decades, corporate bond issues will be about one-quarter of a percent of GNP; while annual social security surpluses will be about one-and-a-quarter percent of GNP for two decades (Blinder, 1990). Hence, the Social Security Trust Fund would be able to purchase a large share of the corporate bond market. However, the fear that this might happen is unwarranted since much of the Trust Fund would probably be kept in Treasury securities. Furthermore, a well diversified portfolio would include such assets as state and municipal securities and foreign securities. Although the Trust Fund at its peak would be very large, its size during much of the buildup and drawdown phases would be only a small fraction of the expected total capitalization of the entire securities market.

Carolyn Weaver (1990a) argues that expanding the discretion of the federal government to manage Social Security Trust Fund investments would have adverse results. She maintains that if the power to control such an enormous portfolio were delegated to a government entity, investment decisions would not be made in the same way as they would by private portfolio managers in a competitive market. Instead, Weaver argues, investment decisions would be politically determined and resources would flow to politically favored projects. Since large public portfolio managers would have the capacity to influence individual firms and to concentrate the ownership of corporations, a policy of government-directed investments would put tax dollars at risk and distort the allocation of capital in the economy.

Perez and Hammerbacher (1993) and Weaver (1990a) suggest that bias or conflict of interest could be avoided by requiring that the equity portion of the Trust Fund be invested in some broad market index, such as the Standard and Poor's 500 Stock Index. The social security system could then maintain the mix by allocating the fund's assets automatically among individual securities in line with the market index utilized. Since the use of index funds representing certain asset classes might subsidize particular industries in the corporate sector, several indexes, representing an array of asset classes, could be used.

Replacing Social Security with Individual Retirement Accounts

Proposals

Two closely related proposals for replacing social security with individual retirement accounts have been offered by Congressmen John Porter of Illinois and Peter J. Ferrara of the National Center for Policy Analysis. They are briefly described below.

The Porter Plan

In April 1991, Illinois Representative John Porter introduced legislation calling for a partial privatization of social security. Workers would continue to pay the same payroll taxes as before, but a portion of their FICA taxes, instead of being sent to the Social Security Trust Fund, would be paid to an IRA-type account, called an Individual Social Security Retirement Account (ISSRA). Participation in the ISSRA program would be mandatory and funds placed in the ISSRA could not be withdrawn prior to retirement. Benefits based on contributions and interest would be paid directly out of the proceeds of these accounts. The ISSRAs would be managed by financial institutions, according to specific investment guidelines. The rest of an individual's FICA taxes would go toward funding the existing system.

The plan would be implemented over a period of decades, since the current obligations of the system need to be met. Hence, the social security program would have a public and private component. One tier would offer an adjusted payment from the Social Security Trust Fund, reduced to compensate for the second-tier benefit levels, while the second component (the ISSRA) would provide an earnings-related payment, financed on a fully funded basis. By design, there would be no surplus receipts to be managed by the federal government and the government would not have to pay any second-tier benefits (Weaver, 1990c).

Porter (1991) points out that his plan would prevent Congress from borrowing social security surpluses. He argues it would also reduce the disproportionate reliance on the payroll tax to finance the federal government and would help build a substantial base of domestic savings and investment in the U.S. economy.

The Ferrara Plan

Peter Ferrara (1985) has proposed that workers be given the option of substituting "Super IRAs" for at least part of their social security. Though they would continue to pay the full social security tax, they would be allowed to contribute additional amounts to their IRAs, up to some reasonable limit. In return for these contributions, workers would receive a 100% income tax credit, equal to the amount of such contributions. If employers made the contribution, they would get the tax credit. Workers who bought Super IRAs would have their future social security benefits reduced to the extent that they did so. For example, if a worker put an amount equal to 20% of his or her social security taxes into an IRA, the worker's social security benefits would be reduced by 20%

The tax credits would give workers their money back to the extent they agreed to forego future social security benefits and rely on their own Super IRAs. Since the credits would be taken against income taxes, social security payroll tax collections would not be reduced and would continue to flow into the program to finance benefits for today's elderly. The Super IRA would simply result in a loss of income tax revenues. The government could make up this loss by decreasing spending or raising other taxes, in which case savings would be increased. Otherwise, the government could make up the revenue loss with increased borrowing. The revenue loss would eventually be offset by reduced social security expenditures and by new revenues generated from increased investment through IRAs.

The plan could gradually be phased in, perhaps beginning with the Social Security Survivors Insurance (SI) program. Ultimately, each worker would have complete freedom to choose how much to rely on Super IRAs and how much to rely on social security. The Supplemental Social Security Income (SSI) program would continue to provide means-tested, welfare benefits to the elderly poor, financed from general revenues.

Among the advantages of the Ferrara proposal are that it would give workers an enforceable claim on their pensions, it would end the use of compulsory savings as a redistributive device, and it would provide retirees with a higher rate of return on their savings.

Criticisms of IRA-type Proposals

Equity

If participation in an IRA-type program were made mandatory, low-income workers would be required to exchange a benefit structure that is progressively related to earnings for benefits that were proportional to earnings.[11] By eliminating the possibility of paying extra benefits to workers whose earnings had been low, the result might be an increase in the number of applicants for welfare or other means-tested benefits, which are not cost effective and which involve substantial general revenue financing. This increased burden on general revenues might also negate the gains to upper-income groups from IRAs.

If, on the other hand, the choice to leave social security and set up an IRA-type account were optional, high-income earners would probably leave the system while low-income earners would be likely to stay. The result would be a deficit in the social security system because the reduction in revenues would be proportionately larger than the reduction in benefits. In that event, it would be necessary to raise payroll taxes on those who remained or to cut their benefits. In either case, the results would be a further exodus. It would destroy the viability of the social security system and its capacity to redistribute income.

Increased Volatility of the Equity Markets

As discussed earlier, investing part of the trust fund in private securities would probably reduce the volatility of stock markets, since the government would likely hold a stable asset portfolio. However, if workers instead had IRA-type accounts and could adjust their asset allocation, they might attempt to sell equities following a sudden market drop, with the myopic view that stocks are "too risky." This behavior pattern was observed following the fall in stock prices in 1987.

Government Supervision

Any IRA-type plan requires a substantial amount of federal government supervision over the retirement account trustees. This could be costly and there are likely to be vast differences over what role the government should take in regulating this system.

Inflation

Neither the Porter plan nor the Ferrara plan make any provision for enabling retirees to convert their individual retirement accounts into inflation-indexed annuities. Retirees are forced to run the risk that their retirement incomes would be seriously eroded by unexpected episodes of inflation. Furthermore, because stock returns have historically been negatively related to inflation, periods of high inflation could result in significantly lower retirement benefits from IRA-type accounts than from social security.

Lack of Political Support

Perhaps the biggest obstacle to privatizing the Trust Fund or creating an IRA-type system is that despite statements in the media that social security is in trouble, there exists no large constituency in favor of tinkering with OASDI. The social security system enjoys overwhelming political support, making it very difficult to modify the system. However, much of this support may come from a uninformed public, raising hopes that support for a change could arise if the general public was made more aware of the problems expected to arise with the current system.

CONCLUSION

If no changes are made to the U.S. social security system and the expected demographic and economic trends of the next few decades materialize, social security will be technically insolvent in about 2029. This means that unless the system is structurally altered, a combination of tax increases and benefit cuts will need to be implemented.

• Several nations facing similar demographic problems, including Chile and Sweden, have altered their public retirement systems to allow for investment in private securities. Proposals have emerged in the last decade advocating that the United States adopt similar changes, either by allowing the U.S. Social Security Trust Fund to invest in private securities or moving to a fully funded system where individuals are required to contribute to IRA-type accounts. However, there is wide disagreement over whether such measures are necessary and/or desirable. This paper has outlined those proposals, offering arguments for and against their implementation, in the hopes of laying a groundwork for this, Middlebury's Sixteenth Annual Conference on Economic Issues.

NOTES

1. However, as Carolyn Weaver has noted, the social security system has never been tested against an economic downturn like that of the Great Depression.

2. Social security replaces about 65% of after-tax income for low-income earners and about 25% of after-tax income for high income earners (Mandel, 1993).

3. The 1983 amendments did not greatly alter the treatment of current elderly recipients. It significantly affected the baby boom generation by: (1) advancing the normal social security retirement age from 65 to 67, (2) raising payroll taxes, and (3) subjecting a growing fraction of future social security benefits to taxation.

4. The projected year of exhaustion under Alternative III is about 2020. Under Alternative I, it is never exhausted (Board of Trustees, 1994).

5. If Congress were to wait until 2036 to take action, it would require an increase in OASDI portion of the payroll tax from 6.2% to about 7.7% (an increase of 25%) to eliminate the shortfall in income (Weaver, 1993).

6. According to Herman Leonard (1990), an important source of income not included in the social security projections is that under the 1983 amendments, taxes on social security benefits are credited to the Social Security Trust Fund. Social security currently receives $5 billion annually from this provision. Benefits are taxable for individuals with adjusted gross incomes over $25,000 (or $32,000 for couples). The thresholds are not adjusted for inflation and, thus, will decline over time in real terms. Whereas in 1990, roughly $23 billion of social security benefits were taxable, in 2050 in constant 1990 dollars, over $253 billion will be taxable (Lindsey, 1990).

7. Because it must be used to purchase Treasury obligations, the Trust Fund is to some degree an illusion since one government promise to pay is backed by another government promise to pay.

8. These projections are made on the assumption of a 2% real rate of return. Bosworth (1990) argues that this assumption is too conservative.

9. The first benefit check paid by social security went to Ida May Fuller of Ludlow, Vermont, whose lifetime contributions to social security totaled $20.33. Prior to her death at the age of 100, Ms. Fuller received over $22,000 in social security benefits.

10. For similar calculations, see Perez and Hammerbacher (1993), Becker (1993), Boaz (1990), and Gennetski (1993).

11. Low income workers tend to be less educated about investment opportunities. If higher income participants choose investment strategies which earn a higher long-run return than low income participants, then benefits are actually regressively related to earnings under an IRA-type system.

REFERENCES

Aaron, H.J., B.P. Bosworth, and G. Burtless. 1989. *Can America Afford to Grow Old?* Washington, DC: The Brookings Institution.

Becker, G.S. 1993. "How to Secure Social Security's Future." *Business Week* (July 12): 18.

Blinder, A.S. 1990. "Political Effects of the Social Security Surpluses." In C. Weaver (ed.), *Social Security's Looming Surpluses: Prospects and Implications.* Washington, DC: The American Enterprise Institute, pp. 79-82.

Board of Trustees for the Social Security and Medicare Trust Funds. 1994. "Actuarial Status of the Social Security and Medicare Programs." *Social Security Bulletin* 57(1, Spring): 53-59.

Boaz, D. 1990. "Privatize Social Security." *New York Times* (March 21): A27.

Bosworth, B. 1990. "Social Security, Budget Deficits and National Saving." In C. Weaver (ed.), *Social Security's Looming Surpluses: Prospects and Implication.* Washington, DC: The American Enterprise Institute, pp. 29-33.

Buchanan, J.M. 1990. "The Budgetary Politics of Social Security." In C. Weaver (ed.), *Social Security's Looming Surpluses: Prospects and Implications.* Washington, DC: The American Enterprise Institute, pp. 45-56.

Ferrara, P.J. 1985. "Super IRA: A Populist Proposal." In P.J. Ferrara (ed.), *Social Security: Prospects for Real Reform.* Washington, DC: Cato Institute, pp. 193-220.

________. 1986. "Intergenerational Transfers and Super IRA's." *Cato Journal* 6 (1, Spring-Summer): 195-220.

Genetski, R. 1993. "Privatize Social Security." *Wall Street Journal* (May 21): 10.

Greenspan, A. 1990. "Statement to the U.S. Senate Committee on Finance, February 27, 1990." *Federal Reserve Bulletin* 76 (4, April): 222-226.

Inman, R.P. 1987. "Justifying Public Provision of Social Security: Comment." *Journal of Policy Analysis and Management* 6(4, Summer): 689-692.

Kotlikoff, L.J. 1987. "Justifying Public Provision of Social Security." *Journal of Policy Analysis and Management* 6(4, Summer): 674-689.

Leonard, H.B. 1990. "In God We Trust—The Political Economy of the Social Security Reserves." In C. Weaver (ed.), *Social Security's Looming*

Surpluses: Prospects and Implications. Washington, DC: The American Enterprise Institute, pp. 57-73.

Makin, J.H. 1990. "The Ineffectiveness of Trust Fund Surpluses." In C. Weaver (ed.), *Social Security's Looming Surpluses: Prospects and Implications.* Washington, DC: The American Enterprise Institute, pp. 39-42.

Marchand, M. and P. Pestieau. 1991. "Public Pensions: Choices for the Future." *European Economic Review* 35 (2-3, April): 441-453.

Mathiasen, D.G. 1990. "Fiscal Policy and Politics." In C. Weaver (ed.), *Social Security's Looming Surpluses: Prospects and Implications.* Washington, DC: The American Enterprise Institute, pp. 75-77.

Munnell, A. and N. Ernsberger. 1990. "Foreign Experience with Public Pension Surpluses and National Saving." In C. Weaver (ed.), *Social Security's Looming Surpluses, Prospects and Implications.* Washington, DC: The American Enterprise Institute, pp. 85-118.

Myers, R. 1992. "Chile's Social Security Reform After Ten Years." *Benefits Quarterly* (Third Quarter): 41-55.

Perez, R. 1993. "Let Social Security Earn More Money." *New York Times.*

Perez, R. and I. Hammerbacher. 1993. "Looking Towards a Sounder Social Security System." *Review of Business* 14(3, Spring): 30-34.

Porter, J.E. 1991. "Social Security Can Work for Us All." *The Chicago Tribune* (April 6): 16.

Poterba, J.M. 1990. "Boosting National Savings through U.S. Fiscal Policy." In C. Weaver (ed.), *Social Security's Looming Surpluses: Prospects and Implications.* Washington, DC: The American Enterprise Institute, pp. 35-38.

Santamaria, M. 1992. "Privatizing Social Security: The Chilean Case." *Columbia Journal of World Business* (Spring): 38-51.

Weaver, C. 1990a. "Social Security Investment Policy." Testimony before the Social Security Advisory Council, March 9.

________. 1990b. "Introduction." In C. Weaver (ed.), *Social Security's Looming Surpluses: Prospects and Implications.* Washington, DC: The American Enterprise Institute, pp. 1-13.

________. 1990c. "Controlling the Risks Posed by Adverse Funding—Options for Reform." In C. Weaver (ed.), *Social Security's Looming Suprluses: Prospects and Implications.* Washington, DC: The American Enterprise Institute, pp. 167-178.

________. 1993. "Baby-Boom Retirees, Destined to Go Bust." *The Wall Street Journal* (August 23): A10.

THE POLICY RESPONSE TO AN AGING POPULATION

Barry Bosworth

INTRODUCTION

Public discussions of social security are always a bit unbalanced. On the one hand, the program has been highly successful in providing the cornerstone of retirement income for the elderly. Expansion in coverage and increases in benefits for workers at the bottom of the wage distribution have succeeded in sharply cutting poverty among the elderly to a rate slightly below that of the population as a whole. The creation of social security has had profound effects on work and retirement patterns and the structure of families. On the other hand, there are concerns about its future. After remaining on a plateau for about 30 years, the number of beneficiaries per worker is projected to rise sharply early in the next century, raising the tax on workers required to maintain the current ratio of benefits to wages. The precise magnitude of the increase is uncertain because it depends on future birth and death rates and immigration, but under the most reasonable assumptions the ratio of beneficiaries to workers will rise by two-thirds or more, from about 30 per hundred workers to 50 or more in the middle of the next century. The aging of the population combined with reduced expectations of future growth in real wages raises the near certainty of large future deficits in the social insurance fund unless benefits are reduced or taxes increased.

Currently, the United States provides for retirement needs with a mixture of public and private programs. The basic purpose of this volume is to discuss whether some of the above problems of an aging society can be better met by a shift toward greater reliance on the private pillar of the retirement system, scaling back social security to rely more heavily on the private component. Given the old adage that one should not put all of one's eggs in one basket, a mixed system has substantial merits. The risks associated with public pensions—mainly political—are substantially different than those associated with a privately funded program, although not necessarily less. The precise balance between private and public programs, however, is not easy to resolve, and many of the current concerns about the future of social security exist for private pensions as well.

The public pillar exists to meet several perceived problems. First, many aspects of social security are forms of insurance in providing funds to meet uncertain contingencies, such as disability or early death of the income earner in a household or the uncertain life spans of the elderly. Given a determination that everyone should be required to have such insurance, it can be more efficient to provide it on a public basis so as to avoid the costs associated with the adverse risk selection inherent in private programs. Second, the retirement program incorporates a major element of redistribution. Some of this redistribution is quite straightforward in that low-wage workers will receive a larger retirement benefit in relation to their contribution than high-wage workers. While the tax is regressive in representing a larger burden on low than high-wage workers, the benefit formula is sharply skewed toward providing a higher return to low-wage workers.[1] That aspect can also be viewed as an insurance program: even if individuals do not do well during their working life, they will still receive a pension during retirement that is designed to provide at least a poverty-level income. Other elements of the redistribution are less straightforward, however. For example, married couples with a single earner do better than dual-income households. Third, an added argument for a universal retirement program results from the myopic behavior of some individuals who fail to provide for their own retirement. This could represent a burden on the rest of society if humanitarian concerns create strong pressures to provide them with some benefit in spite of their own folly.

The distribution issues have long been subjects of controversy and differing perceptions of what constitutes equitable treatment. Americans have strongly varying views of the extent to which some problems should be dealt with collectively or left to the individual, and their views are influenced by the extent to which they can foresee their own future. The controversy influences the debate over public versus private programs because most private programs do not incorporate redistribution. I have little to add to that debate and will focus, instead, on the future financing problems.

The following section provides some background information on the financial outlook for social security. It is followed by a discussion of several proposals for privatizing all or a portion of the current system and the extent to which they could resolve or ameliorate some of the financial concerns.

SOCIAL SECURITY PROJECTIONS

The trustees of the Old-Age and Survivors Insurance and Disability Insurance Trust Funds (OASDI) provide annually a set of projections of the financial condition of the funds for a period of 75 years into the future. The projections are relevant because they describe the dimensions of a demographic and economic problem of an aging society that must be managed by any retirement program, public or private. Because of the wide uncertainty surrounding such estimates, the trustees provide three alternatives based on grouping the different demographic and economic assumptions in terms of their favorable or unfavorable impact on the trust funds.

The intermediate projection is widely interpreted as representing the actuaries' best guess of the future and the 1993 projections for income, outgo, and reserves, all expressed as a percent of taxable wages. Some aspects of this forecast are shown in Figures 1A and 1B. On that basis, the funds will run substantial surpluses until a significant number of the baby-boom generation begin to retire. Tax income will fall short of benefit costs in about 2020. The fund can then continue to operate for about another 15 years on the basis of the accumulated reserves. Without additional tax increases or benefit reductions, the fund will be exhausted in 2035.[2]

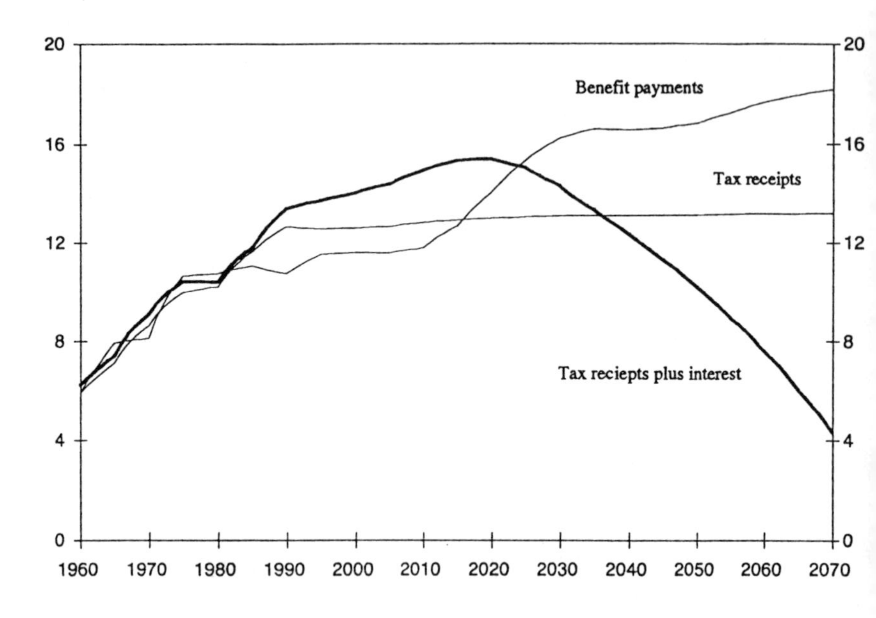

Figure 1A. Income and Expenditures of the Social Trust Funds, Intermediate Case, 1960-2070 Percent of Taxable Wages

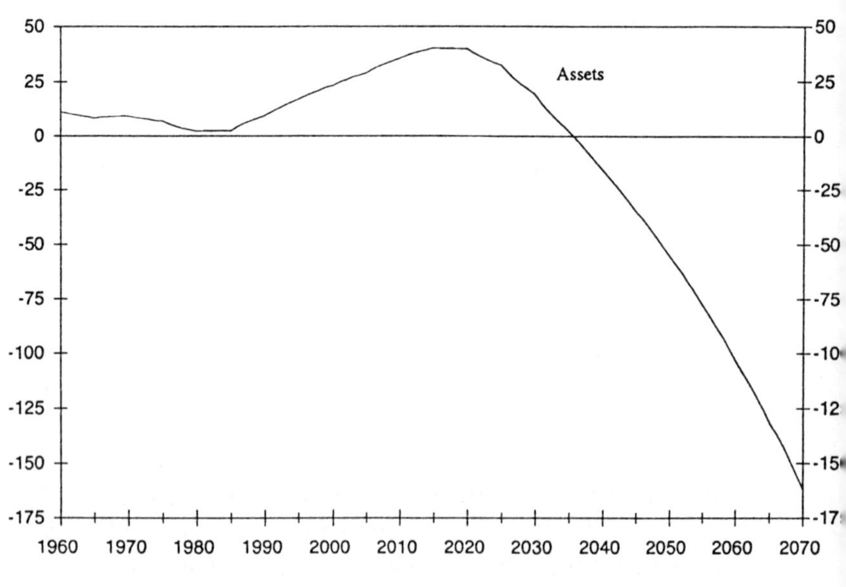

Figure 1B. Reserves of the Social Security Trust Funds, Intermediate Case, 1960-2070 Percent of taxable wages

The 1993 trustees' report concluded that the system did not meet the criteria of close actuarial balance over the full 75-year projection period. They so notified the Congress; but the latter, focusing on the large near-term surpluses, chose not to act. Future trustee reports are likely to show a continuing deterioration of the long-run conditions of the fund as their economic assumptions are revised down in line with the most recent trends.

One major point to emphasize about the projections is the wide range of uncertainty. For example, under the optimistic scenario the fund would run surpluses throughout the 75-year period, while the pessimistic version implies an exhaustion of the fund in 2015. One problem with the trustee's projections is that the intermediate projections cannot really be interpreted as the mean expectation, and the pessimistic and optimistic projections cannot be regarded as equally likely alternatives on each side of the mean.[3] Most analysts seem to believe that the intermediate forecast is too optimistic and that the optimistic projection is less likely than the pessimistic one.

The range of uncertainty is illustrated in Figures 2A, 2B, and 2C by decomposing the cost rate (CR), the ratio of expenditures to taxable wages, into two components: the dependency rate (DR) and the benefit rate (BR).

$$CR = DR \cdot BR.$$

The dependency rate, the ratio of beneficiaries to covered workers, reflects largely the role of demographic factors and changes in the legal retirement age. The benefit rate, the ratio of the average benefit to the average wage, is reflective more of changes in economic factors.[4] The initial benefit is based on a worker's wage history, indexed to the average economy-wide wage. Thus, the ratio of the average benefit at time of retirement to the average wage can be treated as fixed by legislation. However, in subsequent years the benefit is adjusted only for price inflation. Thus, high rates of real wage growth lower the benefit ratio. The pessimistic projection, with a long-run real wage growth of 0.6% annually, has a benefit rate about 13% higher than that of the optimistic projection with 1.7% growth.

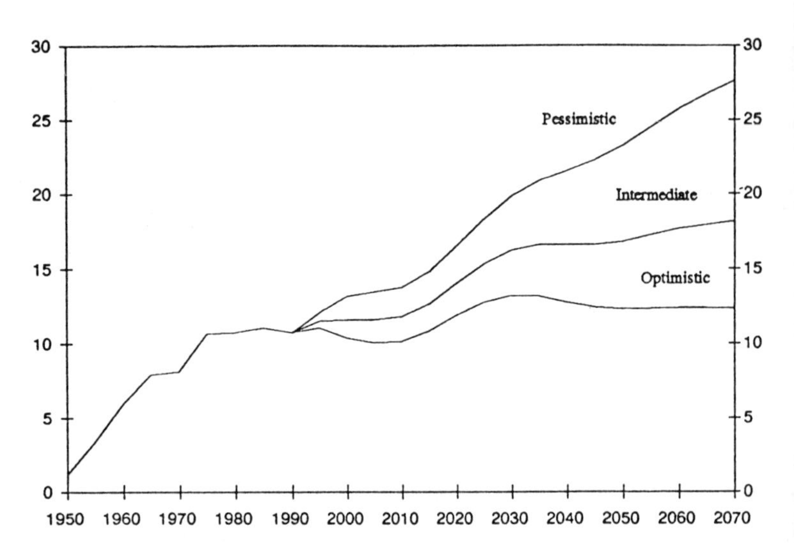

Figure 2A. The OASDI Cost Rate Under Three Alternative Scenarios, 1950-2070—Total Outlays as a Percent of Taxable Wages

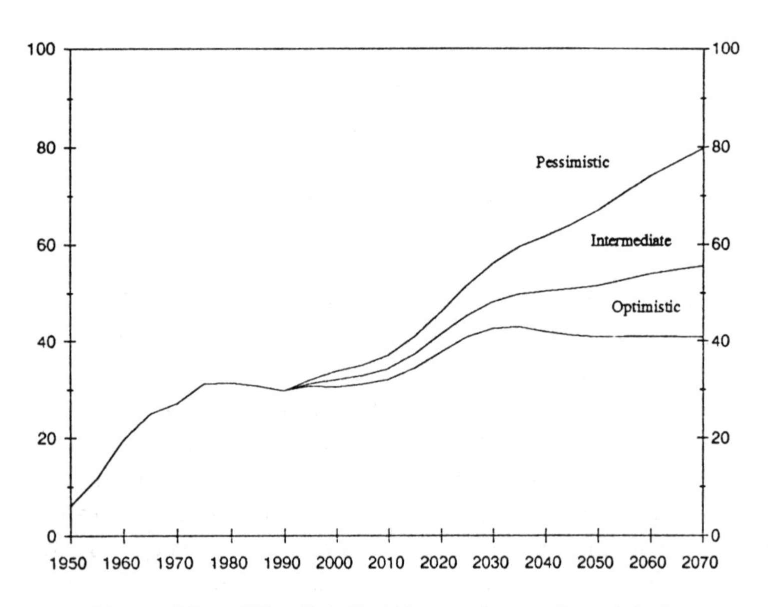

Figure 2B. The OASDI Dependency Rate Under Three Alternative Scenarios, 1950-2070—Beneficiaries per 100 workers

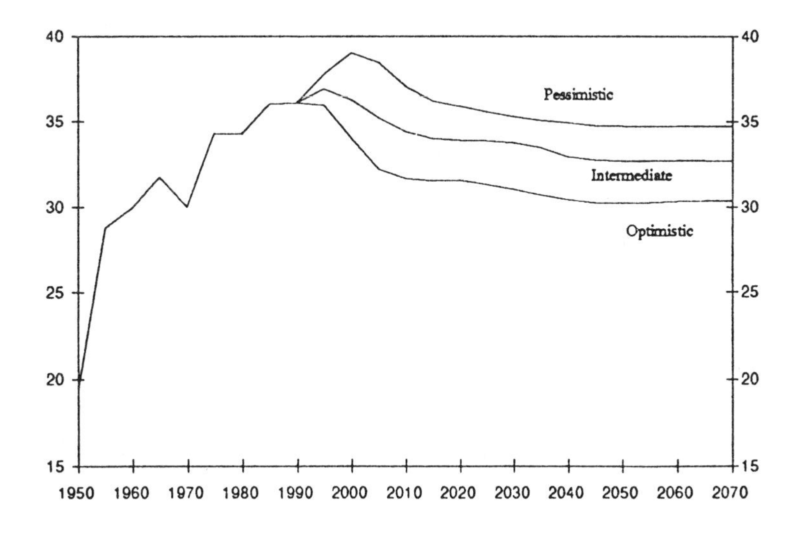

Figure 2C. The OASDI Benefits Rate Under Three Alternative Scenarios, 1950-2070—Average benefits as a percent of the average wage

Despite the tendency in recent years to focus on revisions in the economic outlook, particularly the growth of real wages, both the sharp increase in the cost rate and the uncertainty in the long-run projections are dominated by variations in the assumed demographic trends. This reflects uncertainty about future trends in birth rates, mortality, and immigration. The dependency rate is projected in the intermediate projection to rise by 80% between now and 2070, while the benefit rate remains essentially unchanged. Furthermore, the average dependency rate over the full 75-year period varies between the optimistic and the pessimistic projections by 37%, compared to 13% for the benefit rate.

The cost rate is a convenient means of summarizing many of the future trends in the financing of OASDI. It is, for example, equivalent to the tax rate under a strict pay-as-you-go financing system. It is not, however, very useful as a means of measuring the burden that the system places on future generations of workers. It represents the share of wage earnings that must be set aside to finance the retired, but it says nothing about the level of real wages out of which those benefits must be paid. For example, a one-shot increase in the level of labor productivity would raise the real wages on which future benefits are based and add to the future outlays of the social security system. Yet, the burden of the system on future workers would be less because the wages out of which the benefits must be paid would have increased far more than the added retirement costs. From this perspective, a focus on the cost rate understates the importance of changes in the growth of productivity and real wages in measuring the future costs. If the current generation could prescribe a means of sharply raising the incomes of future generations, its retirement would not represent an increased burden, even though the cost rate might rise very sharply.

BASIC STRUCTURE OF THE OASDI PROGRAM

By international standards, the U.S. social security system has a relatively sound technical structure. Complete records on the contributions of workers are maintained on an individual basis, and a worker's full wage history is used in computing the basic retirement benefit as an incentive not to evade paying into the system. At age 62, a worker's retirement benefit is computed by adjusting past taxable earnings through age 60 for wage inflation and computing an average indexed monthly earnings (AIME). The primary insurance amount (PIA) is then determined using a progressive rate structure of 90% of earnings up to the first "bend point," 32% of the next interval, and 15% for the excess over the second bend point. In 1993, the bend points of the AIME were $401 and $2,420, and they are indexed for future change in the wage index. This is the primary source of the income redistribution present in the OASDI program.

The PIA is the basic benefit paid to an individual at the normal retirement age, but there are numerous adjustments to fit varying circumstances. For example, married couples may receive a benefit equal to 150 percent of the PIA and the amount is actuarially reduced for early retirement and increased for those who postpone retirement. After retirement, subsequent benefit adjustments are based on changes in the consumer price index with a one-year lag.[5] Compared to the situation in many other countries, the cost of the U.S. system is largely unaffected by variations in inflation: it affects the cost rate only to the extent that there are differing lags in the indexation formulas.

The U.S. system also offers frugal public retirement benefits compared to benefits offered in other countries. The replacement rate, the initial benefit as a percent of final year's earnings, averages about 40% in the United States for a 65 year-old worker and is projected to decline in the future because of an increase in the retirement age to 67. Because of the redistribution inherent in the formula, the replacement rate for a low-wage worker is about twice that of a worker at the taxable maximum. The average replacement rate is below that of most other OECD countries. More than most countries, the United States already relies on private pensions for a significant portion of retirement income. The basic benefit will put many low- and even moderate-wage retirees at the threshold of poverty. If they want to enjoy more comfortable retirement incomes, they need to make additional provision on their own.

POLICY OPTIONS

The above discussion is meant to highlight two dimensions of the problem faced by an aging society that are relevant to the design of an optimal retirement policy. First, under most reasonable assumptions, the costs of retirement are likely to rise substantially over the next century; second, the magnitude of the increase is extremely uncertain. The first emphasizes the importance of doing something now unless current generations wish to place a great deal of trust in the altruism of future generations, and the second emphasizes the importance of designing a retirement system that is flexible in adjusting to changing future conditions.

It is possible to respond to these problems by continuing with heavy reliance on a pay-as-you-go (PAYG) public program. The magnitude of increase in the cost rate, however, does imply a major increase in the burden on future generations, and current workers should be concerned about the risk that those future generations might refuse to finance such a program. A sudden reduction in the benefit, if that were the response to the financing problems, would encounter strong opposition from those approaching retirement, because it would leave them no time to adjust their own saving behavior as an offset to the loss of future retirement income.

The more likely outcome is that future workers will block any increase in the tax rate and the retired will prevent any reduction in the benefit. In that case, the system would simply run a deficit and Americans would borrow in the international capital market to sustain expenditures, much as they are doing today to sustain the nonretirement budget. Future generations of Americans would pay not through higher taxes but through the inheritance of a smaller stock of net assets.

A reduction in the promised benefit offers the most straightforward method of reducing costs. It is often pointed out that the current poverty rate among the retired is less than that of the population of working age. Between 1970 and 1992, the poverty rate among those 65 and older was cut in half, from 25% to 13%, while the rate for those under age 65 rose from 11.3% to 14.7%. A larger portion of the elderly than of the general population, however, are clustered near the poverty threshold. The poverty rate also tends to increases with age, so the suggestion of less-than-complete price indexation of benefits, which implies a decline in the real benefit with age, would seem less attractive than a reduction in the initial benefit amount. Benefit costs could also be reduced by introducing the increase in the retirement age from 65 to 67 sooner than its planned phase-in after 2002. Such a change would be consistent with the steady increase in life expectancy—the life expectancy at age 65 of males rose from 13 years in 1970 to 15 in 1990 and is projected to reach 17 in 2040. A lengthening of the retirement age would have a large effect on future benefit costs, but it does run counter to the recent trend toward earlier retirement.

One alternative suggestion is to means test social security benefits. In that case, the transfer of resources would be concentrated initially more within a given generation; also, by reducing the overall cost of the system, the transfer across generations would be reduced. However, if we assume, as seems reasonable, that the well-off respond to the loss of such benefits by drawing down their own assets rather than reducing retirement period consumption, future generations would still lose through a smaller inheritance. Second, means-testing of a retirement benefit can have strong implications for saving. If the test is based on income during retirement, as opposed to lifetime income, the incentive to save for retirement would be severely eroded: Why save for retirement if it simply leads to an offsetting reduction in OASDI benefits?[6] On the other hand, means testing on the basis of lifetime income implies a even greater skewing of benefits toward low-wage workers than is embodied in the current formula for computing the PIA, but there must be limits to the extent of such redistribution, and the negative returns that it implies to high-wage workers, before it leads to a collapse of support for the program.

Without a reduction in benefits, the increased burden of an aging population on future generations can only be truly reduced through an increase in today's saving so as to provide them with a larger stock of wealth and income out of which the consumption of the retired would be financed. As long as we view the problem as a collective problem, the issue is one of increasing national saving, not just the private saving of the current generation. Thus, in evaluating policy options other than those that aim to reduce the consumption of the future retired, the major criteria should be whether they have a positive impact on the current and near-term rate of national saving. In what follows, I examine several options in terms of their implications for national saving.

Partial Funding of OASDI

Up to now, the United States has relied on a PAYG system. Under such a method of financing, the first generation receives a large wealth transfer, while the last generation gets a raw deal—but they will have other problems. As long as the ratio of retirees to workers remains constant, all intermediate generations should be largely indifferent between a PAYG system and one that is fully funded.[7] Furthermore, during the work life of the first generation, the nation may have lost out on an increment to national saving and wealth that would have occurred under a fully funded system. Whether the decision to provide the first generation with a benefit for which they had not fully contributed was wise or not, it is difficult to reverse today. Few would support a large reduction in the benefit to the currently retired at a time that they have no opportunity to offset its consequences by adjusting their own saving. Nor is it easy to convert in midstream to a fully funded pension system because the transitional generation of workers would have to pay twice: once for their own retirement and a second time for the retirement of their parents.

However, the issue arises again today because the ratio of retirees to workers will not remain constant. Current workers support a smaller population of retirees for a shorter period of time than will be the case when they retire. This added cost, due to a rise in the dependency rate, could be managed either under a continuation of the PAYG principle or through an advanced funding of the added costs. If the return to society on the added capital equals the rate of increase in the pension benefit, there would be no increased burden on future workers associated with a rise in the dependency rate. In fact, under most plausible assumptions, they would gain.

In a 1989 study, Henry Aaron, Gary Burtless, and I evaluated the economic consequences of a modified rule for social security in which the social security tax rate would be increased in any year for which the 75-year projection of the trustees showed the fund to be out of actuarial balance.[8] Also, the resulting surpluses would be added to national saving by adopting a fiscal rule for the rest of the federal budget that prevented an offsetting rise in deficit of the non-OASDI funds. The focus on a 75-year horizon provides a means of adjusting social security tax rates and benefit promises gradually to a changing outlook, and also at a sufficiently early point in workers' careers to allow them to adjust their own saving behavior as an offset to any changes in the future OASDI benefit. In effect, the increase in the cost rate, beyond the current level, would be funded.

In a growth accounting exercise, we found that the resulting additions to national wealth were sufficient to finance the added cost associated with the rise in the cost rate over the next century, while avoiding any increase in the burden on future workers beyond current levels.[9] Such a funding arrangement does relatively little to reduce the magnitude to the tax rate increase that future workers must bear; but, because the tax is being paid out of a higher real wage, they do not suffer any reduction in their levels of consumption.

As long as domestic and foreign rates of return are equal, it makes little difference whether the added saving is invested domestically or abroad. If the investment is domestic, the higher saving raises the capital stock and, thus, the wages of future workers out of which the OASDI benefits are paid, while reducing interest rates and, thus, the return to owners of old capital. If the added saving is modeled as being invested in a global economy, there is no appreciable increase in wages or reduction in interest rates—domestic income is largely unchanged—but there is a much larger flow of capital income from abroad. In many respects, that study was quite reassuring because it suggested that the problem of an aging population could be resolved by a relatively modest increase in national saving as long as the nation acted well before the onset of the increase in the dependency rate.

For several years, the OASDI fund did operate in a fashion consistent with maintaining actuarial balance, and there were substantial annual surpluses and an appreciable buildup of the reserve. However, it is argued that the policy failed because there is no sense in which we can say that the annual surpluses of OASDI did pass through into a higher level of national saving. Instead, it would appear that the current generation simply offset larger OASDI surpluses with larger deficits in the non-OASDI portion of the federal budget, using surpluses (saving) in one account to finance deficits (current consumption) in another (see Table 1), thus avoiding the necessity of raising taxes or cutting expenditures in the nonretirement budget.[10] Furthermore, Congress has failed to act to adjust the program in recent years when the inclusion of more deficit years at the end of the forecast horizon has begun to move the fund out of actuarial balance.[11] Equally alarming, there has been a general decline in the private saving rate at a time that we might expect it to rise in anticipation of greater retirement costs.

Such a situation is potentially more dangerous than continuing with a strict PAYG system since it implies the use of a highly regressive wage tax to finance current government outlays. Also, it may establish a future political situation in which retirees claim that the surpluses of the OASDI system represent past saving to which they are entitled. Future generations will face a lower employment tax, but their income taxes will need to increase to finance the repurchase of treasury debt from the OASDI system as its reserve is drawn down.

On the other hand, we may be too quick to conclude that the existence of a surplus in the OASDI accounts is an important cause of the large deficits in the federal nonretirement accounts since 1980. Many factors have contributed to the emergence of a large deficit and the difficulties of taking action to reduce it. Mistakes were made in the early 1980s in combining a buildup of defense with a tax reduction; also, the expected positive effects of supply-side economics on economic growth and, thus, federal revenues never materialized. In addition, the opening of international

Table 1. Federal Budget Balance With and Without Retirement Trust Funds, Fiscal Years 1960-2004

	Annual Averages					
	Actual			*Projected*		
	1960-1969	*1970-1979*	*1980-1989*	*1990-1994*	*1995-1990*	*2000-1904*
			Billions of Dollars			
Total Federal Budget	-6	-35	-157	-252	-181	-292
Less Surplus in:						
Social Security (OASDI, off-budget)	1	0	12	53	78	116
On-Buget Balance	-7	-35	-169	-305	-259	-407
Less Surplus In:						
Medicare (HI)	0	1	7	9	9	9
Federal Employee Ret.	1	4	16	28	43	47
Non-Retirement Balance	-8	-41	-192	-342	-311	-464
			Percent of GDP			
Total Federal Balance	-0.8	-2.3	-4.1	-4.2	-2.3	-2.9
Less Surplus in:						
Social Security (OASDI, off-budget)	0.1	0.0	0.3	0.9	1.0	1.2
On-Budget Balance	-1.0	-2.3	-4.4	-5.1	-3.3	-4.1
Less Surplus in:						
Medicare (HI)	0.0	0.1	0.2	0.1	0.1	0.1
Federal Employee Retirement Fund	0.2	0.3	0.4	0.5	0.5	0.5
Non-retirement Balance	-1.2	-2.6	-5.0	-5.7	-4.0	-4.6

capital markets dramatically altered the channel through which budget deficits affect the economy and, thus, the public's perception of their costs. In earlier decades, large sustained deficits would have led to excess aggregate demand and pressure on either interest rates or higher rates of inflation, outcomes which the public opposed. With open capital markets, however, many of the effects spill out into the global economy and the public is less aware of the costs. For example, a current account deficit does not affect daily life in the same way as higher inflation or higher interest rates. As a result, deficits are more sustainable than in the past.

Moving OASDI Off-budget

There have been several proposals aimed at making more clear to the Congress and the public the need to set aside the OASDI surplus and allow it to flow through as an increment to national saving. In the early 1980s, the OASDI program was reclassified as off-budget, but all public presentations, as well as the Gramm-Rudman-Hollings deficit reduction act, continued to include the programs—inventing a new term, total deficit, as a substitute for the unified budget deficit.[12]

Other proposals have gone further in suggesting that social security be moved further away from the budget, perhaps as a government-sponsored enterprise managed by an independent Board of Trustees. But it is doubtful that the problem is simply one of presentation. It is not evident that reporting the budget deficit, completely free of the social security surplus, would have any effect on public attitudes toward fiscal policy when it involved no change in the near-term economic consequences. It is true that, under a more complete system of separation, the annual public issues of Treasury securities would be about $100 billion larger, but on the other side of the capital market, there would be a $100 billion increase in total demand. The restructuring would, through the elimination of private placements of Treasury debt, represent a change in financial intermediation, but there would be little or no change in interest rates, national saving, or GDP unless the reorganization led to a smaller deficit in the non-OASDI budget deficit. If voters are unwilling to accept tax increases or cuts in expenditures in the face of reported budget deficits of $200 billion, it is not clear that telling them that the deficit is $300 billion would change their attitudes appreciably.

It is important to understand that the issue of saving the surplus is beyond the control of the managers of OASDI. The fund is near actuarial balance and the OASDI trusties are reinvesting the current surplus. The problem is in the nonretirement budget where expenditures (consumption) are running far in excess of revenues, negating any rise in national saving whether it arose from an increase in the surplus of social security or private saving.

Investing in Private Securities

It is sometimes suggested that some of the future financing problems could be reduced if the OASDI fund were free to invest in private securities on which it could earn a higher rate of return.13 From the perspective of society as a whole, however, this is largely a false issue. It would make the financing position of the OASDI system appear stronger, but it would not, in itself, increase national saving. As a simple thought experiment, imagine that the OASDI system sold off $1 trillion dollars of Treasury securities and replaced them in its portfolio with an equal number of private securities paying a higher rate of return. The higher return would presumably reflect the higher degree of risk inherent in the private debt. However, a simple swap of public and private debt between the OASDI trust fund and private markets would have no appreciable effect on total saving, the stock of physical capital, or output. The trust fund would report a higher rate of return, while the private sector would hold the lower-yield Treasury securities previously held by the fund. The total return to society would remain the same. Thus, it would not significantly change the resources out of which the consumption of retirees must be financed in the future.[14]

Society as a whole does not benefit from having the OASDI fund hold a larger proportion of the outstanding stock of risky assets, unless there are barriers to portfolio diversification in private markets[15] Interest rate differentials are largely a reflection of the risk characteristics of various financial assets, not the relative magnitudes outstanding in the market. The interest rate differential, for example, between government and corporate securities of equivalent maturity show little relationship with their relative quantities. Furthermore, asking the fund managers to make decisions among private assets with varying degrees of risk raises significant problems of determining the basis on which those decisions are to be made. In private markets, individuals can shop among mutual funds in choosing the degree of tradeoff between risk and return with which they feel most comfortable. Public fund managers would undoubtedly be widely condemned should they err, and the potential for congressional investigation seems unlimited.

In open international markets, Americans could decide as a society to adopt a more aggressive investment strategy, purchasing higher-risk, higher-return foreign assets. But that seems to be a rather dubious strategy for managing the costs of a permanently more-aged society.

Privatizing Retirement Saving

I would identify three major arguments in favor of greater reliance on the private sector to meet the costs of an aging population. The first is that some individuals do not approve of the redistribution within a given age cohort that is typical of public programs. As I mentioned earlier, I am not going to address this issue though I think it is important.

Second, many countries have encountered severe problems managing a public program in which benefit promises far exceed the financing capability of the system. These systems often create strong incentive for workers to avoid the system for much of their working lives by remaining in the informal sector. The systems are then forced to impose very large taxes on a small proportion of the workforce to maintain solvency. There are very large and often capricious redistributions of income within a given age cohort, often induced by inflation. Private pension funds are often seen as less sensitive to political risk and management incompetence, although the actual record on this score is not clear-cut. These difficulties are particularly evident in developing countries. I do not believe these problems have turned out to be severe within the U.S. system. Its administrative costs are very low, and the benefit commitments are modest by international standards. Many Americans appear to approve of a basic pension program that prevents severe poverty among the elderly but leaves retirement income above the poverty level as a responsibility of the individual.

The third argument is that a public PAYG system, combined with the future aging of the population, implies an unacceptable degree of intergenerational transfers. While this problem could be met with a full or partially funded public program, there are grave doubts that such an outcome could be guaranteed, given the myopic behavior of public officials. A funded retirement program would raise the national saving rate prior to the onset of a demographic shift and provide through increased wealth the resources to finance future retirement costs. On the other hand, private programs also have often been underfunded, as witnessed by the number of private pension programs that are in financial difficulty, and arbitrary rules often have been used to deny benefits.

Much of the discussion of public versus private programs actually revolves around the distinction between defined-contribution and defined-benefit programs. Historically, public and most private pensions in the United States have been defined-benefit programs. In such plans, the benefit is tied to the worker's wage and number of years of service, and the manager of the fund, typically the employer, is responsible to ensure that contributions are sufficient to maintain it on a sound basis. Some private defined-benefit plans have been funded and some unfunded, and the measure of what constitutes an adequate degree of funding depends upon government regulations. Defined-contribution plans, in contrast, are by their nature funded programs, and they have been of rapidly growing importance in the private sector. Under these plans, an individual's pension depends only on his contributions and subsequent investment earnings: the individual bears all of the investment risk. Defined-contribution plans eliminate any concern with the degree of funding since the retirement benefit is automatically scaled up or down in line with the accumulation of retirement saving. Defined-contribution plans also have the advantage that they are more easily portable from job to job. The major disadvantage of a defined contribution plan is that all of the uncertainty of future economic outcomes is reflected in a revision of the benefit rather than an increase in the contribution rate. It is not evident that simply adjusting pension benefits is the optimal response to unforeseen economic changes—particularly for those for whom the change occurs close to the date of retirement.

One suggested change would be to substitute a mandated defined-contribution program, such as that of Chile or Singapore, for all or part of the present defined-benefit public plan. The Chilean system has attracted particular attention because it combines the defined contribution option with private management of the investment funds and purchase of a private annuity at time of retirement. It was instituted in the early 1980s as a replacement for a public system that was in complete disarray.[16] The old system was highly vulnerable to changes in the overall state of public finances, and the structure of benefit payments was highly inequitable and distorted by inflation. Noncompliance was a major problem and in some cases the contribution rates (including medical care) exceeded 50%. The Chilean experience demonstrates both the advantages and potential problems of conversion to a private system.

First, Chile managed the problem of the transition through a dramatic increase in the general government budget surplus to about 5% of GDP prior to the conversion. It issued bonds in proportion to past contributions to active workers who switched to the new system. The cost of continuing retirees was also shifted to the regular budget. In both cases, the government has financed the payments out of current revenues, by generating a large primary budget surplus. This was possible because the major portion of the transition was done under a dictatorship that cut other government programs to pay for the transition.

Under the new system, workers are required to contribute a flat 10% of wages to retirement saving, but they are free to chose among several privately managed funds that also provide disability insurance. At retirement, they can chose between the purchase of an indexed annuity or a phased withdrawal. The government guarantees a nonindexed minimum pension which is financed out of general revenues if the account of the individual worker is insufficient. No other redistribution is attempted.

The system has been popular from its beginning because participants have earned a phenomenal rate of real return, averaging about 15% since its inception, even though the vast bulk of the initial assets were invested in public and private bonds.[17] These high returns were made possible by the economic conditions in Chile at the time of conversion. Because of a past financial collapse and lack of public confidence, real rates of interest were between 10% and 20% through much of the early period of the conversion. Thus, while the current generation of workers has earned a high return in their pension accounts, they have paid dearly in taxes to pay the interest on public debt. Real rates of interest have declined considerably in recent years, and the regulations on investments are gradually being liberalized to allow a larger degree of investment in equities and foreign assets. At present, the composition of pension fund assets is spread among government bonds (40%), corporate bonds (10%), bank liabilities (25%), and equities (25%).

One surprising result is that the management fees are extremely high in comparison to a public system. Recently, the administrative costs have stabilized at about 3% of average taxable earnings, or nearly 30% of the annual contribution. These costs are about 10 times higher than those under a public program such as that of the United States.[17] They reflect both the costs of managing a large number of small accounts and a fairly substantial level of advertising expense.

A second problem of the Chilean system involves the difficulty of establishing an efficient market for the purchase of annuities. A universal public system can provide annuities at a common community-rated fee. But, once individuals are given a choice among competing annuities or are offered the right to lump-sum withdrawals as an alternative to an annuity, there are severe problems of selection risk. The insurance companies will try to attract the better risks, while individuals will use information about their own health in choosing between annuities and lump-sum withdrawals. The market for annuities is notoriously inefficient even in the United States. The implicit average return on privately-offered annuities is about 2.5 percentage points below the return on government-issued debt (Friedman and Warshawsky, 1990).[18] With workers restricted to a single opportunity to convert to an annuity at time of retirement, they also face substantial risks that retirement will coincide with a time of low-valuation of their portfolio.

The social security reforms have been highly successful in Chile in resolving some of the political risk of pension systems. The program has also had a major benefit for Chile of spearheading the development of a substantial capital market. The funds have contributed the equivalent of about 3% of GDP to annual national saving. There is little evidence that this saving has been offset by increased government dissaving: Chile has had budget surpluses since the mid-1980s.[19] The effects on private saving are more indeterminant because of difficulties of specifying what saving would otherwise have been, given the extreme volatility of the Chilean economy in the 1980s.

However, it should be recognized that the Chilean reforms were a response to a different set of problems than those faced by the United States. From the latter's perspective, the major attractions are the incentives to fund the system and the reduced probability that the surpluses will be appropriated to finance other government programs. Against those potential benefits must be set the higher administrative costs of a privately managed system, the shift of the risk of unforeseen future economic changes from the public sector to the individual, and the costs of the transition. Some observers will find the lack of a redistributional element a plus; others, a negative.

CONCLUSION

There should be little question that the United States will face major increases in the cost of financing retirement pensions early in the next century. Given the required magnitude of tax increase required under strict PAYG financing of the OASDI system, current workers ought to be concerned about the risks that their benefits might be scaled back in the future, as future generations may rebel at the costs. It is important to understand, however, that the only effective means of reducing the burden on those future generations of workers, other than through a reduction of benefits, is through an increase in today's rate of saving. By increasing the stock of capital provided to future workers, the increase in the burden beyond current levels can be offset. The required magnitude of increase in the national saving rate is on the order of about 2% of national income annually.

Various proposals to reorganize the OASDI system, such as privatization, will succeed in reducing the burden on future generations of a given amount of retiree consumption only to the extent that they result in a higher rate of the national saving. It is not enough to increase the rate of saving within the retirement system, if the response to that increased saving is a higher rate of dissaving in the rest of the public sector or a decline in private rates of saving.

At present, the effort to fund a portion of future retirement costs has encountered two problems. First, the Congress has been unwilling to act to increase taxes in response to warnings of an increasingly severe degree of underfunding of future liabilities. Second, it is not evident that the saving that is currently taking place within the OASDI system is providing an increment to national saving. Many observers argue that the surplus is being used as an offset to larger deficits in the non-OASDI portion of the federal budget.

While I sympathize with the frustrations of those who advocate a higher current rate of national saving as a means of financing

Table 2. Net Saving and Investment As A Share Of Net National Product, 1951-1993

	Percent of Net National Produt					
Catagory	*1951-1970*	*1971-1980*	*1981-1990*	*1991*	*1992*	*1993*
Net savings[a]						
Private saving[b]	8.9	9.8	8.1	7.1	7.2	6.9
Government savings	-0.7	-2.0	-4.3	-5.0	-6.1	-5.0
Total national saving-investment	8.3	8.1	3.8	2.3	1.5	2.3
Net domestic investment	7.8	7.9	5.9	2.2	2.6	3.9
Net foreign investment	0.5	0.2	-2.1	0.1	-1.0	-1.6
Addenda:						
Capital consumption allowances[c]	8.6	10.0	11.4	10.9	10.9	10.6
Household saving**d**	6.8	7.7	6.2	4.8	5.3	4.0

Notes: [a] Net saving and investment equal the gross flow minus capital consumption allowances. Net National Product equals Gross National Product minus capital consumption allowances The sum of the savings components differs from the total by the amount of the statistical discrepancy.

[b] Business and household saving. Employee pension funds of state and local governments are allocated to household saving to match the treatment of private pension funds.

[c] Percent of Gross National Product.

[d] Percent of disposable income.

Source: U.S. Department of Commerce, Bureau of Economic Analysis, *United States National Income and Product Accounts.*

future retirement costs, I do not believe that privatization of retirement security in any of its various options is automatically an effective solution. In the long run, the greater degree of funding would probably translate into an increased level of national saving; but during the transition period, the effect is potentially negative. On the other side, the costs of such a major change in the structure of the system seem very high. The costs of the transition to current workers are substantial, and a private program is likely to be less efficient in management costs and in the provision of annuity income. Nor is it evident that absorbing all of the risks of future economic changes through an adjustment of benefits, as envisioned in the defined-contribution feature of most privatization proposals, is a desirable reform.

Further, it should be emphasized that there is nothing special about OASDI in that it is part of a broader issue that any reduction in today's rate of saving can be viewed as a burden on future generations in the form of a lower inheritance. In that sense, the rising costs of OASDI are no more serious than the large current deficit of the nonretirement budget or the decline in the private saving rate (Table 2). All imply a cost to future generations. Furthermore, in a debate over the structure of retirement saving, we should not forget the more immediate problem of financing the health care of the retired, where costs are rising sooner and even more rapidly.

Finally, the whole focus on saving as conventionally measured may be too narrow a basis for discussion. Of perhaps greater importance to future generations will be the magnitude of investment in their education as well as technical progress, as reflected in current efforts in R&D. Neither of these forms of saving and investment are reflected in the conventional accounting concepts. Yet, most efforts to broaden the definition conclude that the current decline in national saving and investment is even greater than that of the conventional measure. It provides no basis for comfort.

ACKNOWLEDGMENT

The author is indebted to Hillary Sheldon for research assistance.

NOTES

1. The system is less progressive than it might appear on the surface because low-wage workers generally live a shorter period of time in retirement (see Hurd and Shoven, 1985). On the other hand, they are more likely to make use of the disability program, so the precise distributional effects are debatable. Such problems arise with both public and private pensions. There are substantial differences in life expectancy by sex, race, and socioeconomic group, but the courts have generally ruled in the case of private pensions that individuals should not be penalized, in the form of lower annual benefits, for having a higher life expectancy.

2. The recent release of the 1994 Trustees Report indicates a substantial increase in the estimated magnitude of the funding deficit. Because of time constraints, I have continued to use the data from the 1993 report.

3. Suggestions on how to deal with the inherent uncertainty of social security projections in a more structured fashion are discussed in Burtless (1993).

4. This is not completely true, because the benefit ratio will vary in response to changes in the length of retirement and the proportion of workers who take early retirement with an actuarially reduced benefit. Because post-retirement benefits are indexed only for price inflation, the benefit rate will decline as the average number of years of retirement rises.

5. This is a simplified presentation of the benefit computation. More complete details are provided in Myers (1989).

6. An alternative outcome might be that well-to-do households would hide their assets prior to retirement or make early bequests to their children. This sort of fraud is well illustrated by the problems that currently plague the Medicaid nursing care program.

7. The current tax rate of OASDI is close to that which would be required under an equivalent funded program providing the same level of future benefits.

8. One could just as well substitute a reduction in promised benefits for the increase in taxes; but, since we were interested in supplying the same magnitude of resources to future retirees, the changes were modeled as an increase in taxes and saving.

9. That analysis referred only to the OASDI program. There are other costs of the retired, such as Medicare and nursing homes, for which the costs are rising more rapidly.

10. It is virtually impossible to prove whether the nonretirement budget deficit would have been smaller or unchanged in the absence of an OASDI surplus. But, it is notable that virtually all statements and analysis of the Administration's economic advisors refer to a budget balance that incorporates the OASDI accounts as a regular part of the budget.

11. Using the assumptions of the 1993 projections, the tax rate would need to be increased by about 1.5 percentage points under the intermediate projection, and by 5.5 percentage points under the pessimistic alternative, to restore the trust fund to a positive position at the end of the 75-year horizon.

12. In part, the budgetary treatment of OASDI reflects a dispute as to whether it is a retirement program, separate from other budgetary functions with the need to save the surplus, versus an interpretation that it is a transfer program that simply should be included with other similar functions within the overall budget. However, if the latter view is to hold, serious questions arise as to the use of a regressive wage tax to finance it.

13. Currently, the trust fund is invested in special nonmarketable issues of the Treasury, and the fund receives the average rate of interest on marketable debt with a maturity in excess of four years.

14. A policy of investing in assets earning a real rate of return three percentage points higher than the assumed 2.3% rate of the intermediate forecast would extend the period in which the trust fund was exhausted from 2035 to 2065. For the pessimistic alternative, a higher interest rate assumption actually worsens the fund position over the full 75-year period because it increases the costs of deficit finance in later years of the period.

15. Aaron, Bosworth, and Burtless, (1989), pp. 101-104.

16. My understanding of the Chilean system is drawn from a recent study by Diamond and Valdes-Prieto (1994).

17. The rate of return on the Singapore fund has been quite low because the government credits the accounts with the equivalent of a bank deposit rate. The assets are heavily invested in foreign securities, on which the government is believed to have earned a high return, but those gains have not passed through to the retirement accounts.

18. These costs are not unique to Chile. The administrative costs of life insurance companies in the United States generally run 12% to 14% of annual benefit payments.

19. It is also interesting to note that they found that individuals who chose private annuities systematically live longer than those who do not chose them. This adverse selection factor is responsible for about half of the 30% load factor charged on annuities.

20. The budget balance did shift from a large surplus in 1980 to significant deficits during the first few years of the reform. But this shift can be traced largely to the economic depression that hit Chile in 1981 and drove unemployment to about 25 percent of the workforce. The large surplus of 1980 can be attributed in part to an effort to build up a reserve to finance the transition.

REFERENCES

Aaron, H.J., B. Bosworth, and G. Burtless. 1989. *Can America Afford to Grow Old?* Washington, DC: The Brookings Institution.

Board of Trustees of the Federal Old-Age and Survivors Insurance and Disability Insurance Trust Fund 1993. *The 1993 Annual Report.* Washington DC: U.S. Government Printing Office.

Burtless, G. 1993. "The Uncertainty of Social Security Forecasts in Policy Analysis and Planning." Paper prepared to the Public Trustees of the Social Security and Medicare Boards of Trustees, Washington, DC, December 28.

Diamond, P. and S. Valdes-Prieto. 1994. "Social Security Reforms." In B. Bosworth, R. Dornbusch, and R. Laban (eds.), *The Chilean Economy: Policy Lessons and Challenges.* Washington, DC: The Brookings Institution, pp. 257-320.

Friedman, B.M. and M.J. Warshawsky. 1990. "The Cost of Annuities: Implications for Saving Behavior and Bequests." *Quarterly Journal of Economics* 105: 135-154.

Hurd, M.D. and J.B. Shoven. 1985. "The Distributional Impact of Social Security." In D.A. Wise (ed.), *Pensions, Labor, and Individual Choice.* Chicago: University of Chicago Press, pp. 193-215.

Munnell, A. 1989. "Public Pension Surpluses and National Saving: Foreign Experience." *New England Economic Review* (March): 16-38.

Myers, R.J. 1989. *Summary of the Provisions of the OASDI System, the HI System, and the SMI System.* Washington, DC: Mercer Meidinger Hansen Inc.

SOCIAL SECURITY AND FISCAL SUSTAINABILITY IN THE TWENTY-FIRST CENTURY

James E. Duggan

INTRODUCTION

During the decade of the 1980s, significant attention was given to two aspects of government finance: a rapid increase in government debt held by the public and growing surpluses in the Social Security trust funds. The U.S. public debt as a proportion of Gross Domestic Product (GDP) increased from 26.8% at the end of 1980 to 51.6% at the end of 1993.[1] Most OECD countries also experienced an increasing debt burden during the 1980s, though for many the debt/GDP ratio had already begun to rise during the 1970s (Buiter, 1993). A continuously rising debt/GDP ratio means that the interest burden on government debt becomes increasingly burdensome, creates uncertainty over the form of future government financing (Masson, 1985), ultimately leads to an acceleration of inflation (Bispham, 1987), and portends adverse long-run consequences for output and consumption (Tobin, 1986). These concerns led to, *inter alia*, new efforts at measuring fiscal deficits (Blejer and Cheasty, 1991) and at defining appropriate indicators of the sustainability of fiscal policy (Blanchard, 1990; Blanchard, et al., 1990; Buiter, 1993).

Since the mid-1980s, the combined Old-Age, Survivors, and Disability Insurance (OASDI) program has been generating substantial surpluses, amounting to $47 billion in fiscal year 1993. The OASDI trust fund held $366 billion in assets at the end of 1993 and is projected to continue accumulating assets for the next 20 years, rising from 6.1% of GDP in 1993 to 13.2% of GDP in 2013 (see Figure 1). Thereafter, continuous deficits are projected to deplete the fund by 2029.[2] The prospect of large swings in the OASDI trust fund balances has motivated analyses of the potential effects on saving and economic growth (Anderson, et al., 1988; Munnell, 1988; Aaron, et al., 1989), intergenerational equity (Hambor, 1987), trust fund investment policy (Burtless, 1988; Weaver, 1990), and implications for the long-run public debt (Duggan, 1991).

Until the late 1980s, Social Security income and outgo were approximately in balance. The rising debt/GDP ratio over the 1980s was due to large non-Social Security deficits.[3] Over the past few years, significant efforts have been made toward controlling federal deficits, notably in the budget enforcement laws passed in 1990 and 1993. In the future, however, government fiscal policy will face unprecedented challenges. Anticipated demographic changes will eventually turn

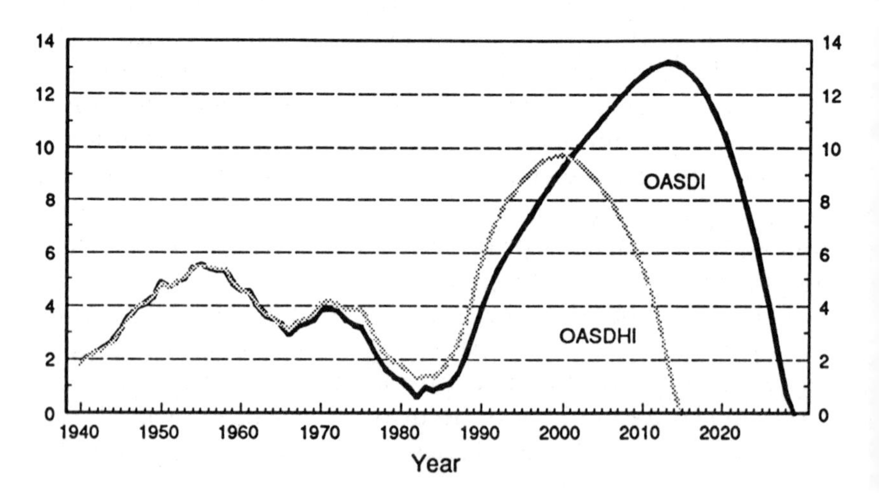

Source: U.S. Government (1994a) for historical data U.S. Congress (1994a) for projected data; Health Care Financing Adminstration, author's calculations for projected HI data.

Figure 1. OASDI and OASDHI Trust Fund Assets (percent of GDP)

OASDI surpluses into deficits that are projected to rise to 2% of GDP before 2070. More importantly, the same demographic conditions are expected to cause sizeable deficits in the health care part of the Social Security program, namely, Medicare. Part A of Medicare (Hospital Insurance (HI)) is already incurring deficits that are projected to rise to almost 3.5% of GDP by 2070. Part B of Medicare (Supplementary Medical Insurance (SMI) is expected to ultimately absorb over 4% of GDP.

What do the projected Social Security deficits imply for U.S. debt policy? An earlier paper (Duggan, 1991) showed that, in the absence of rare fiscal restraint, long-run social security deficits could result in very high and unstable debt/GDP ratios. Adjustments will be required if the United States is to carry a sustainable fiscal policy into the 21st century. Sustainability in this paper means a policy that is consistent with a present-value borrowing constraint. Violation of that constraint signals that, sooner or later, taxes and/or expenditures will have to be adjusted. Later means a larger correction, and failure to make a correction could lead to the problems described above. The magnitude of such adjustments, given projected Social Security imbalances, is the focus of the present paper. Using the framework suggested by Blanchard (1990) and Blanchard et al. (1990), present value tax-expenditure changes are computed that would result in a sustainable fiscal policy. Potential changes are computed for the separate Social Security programs and for the combined federal budget that would result in a sustainable fiscal policy. The purpose is to provide an empirical perspective of the *total* fiscal burden on the federal budget of social insurance for the elderly. This contrasts with the more typical focus on individual Social Security programs, which are generally considered outside the context of an intertemporal budget constraint.

The analysis presented here indicates that the OASDI program, by itself, presents a comparatively small concern for fiscal sustainability. Over the standard valuation period used to judge the financial status of Social Security (75 years), a potential fiscal sustainability gap due to OASDI alone could be closed with a relatively modest, though significant, adjustment in contributions or expenditures. The adjustment is modest when compared to what would be required for the non-OASDI accounts, though it may be regarded as burdensome when considered *in addition* to the required (for fiscal sustainability) non-OASDI adjustments. The HI program, for example, portends a significant fiscal sustainability problem. The SMI program presents the same difficulties as HI. Closing the overall fiscal sustainability gap will require extraordinary fiscal discipline.

The second section of this paper reviews the relationship between the trust funds and the federal budget, characterizes the nature of debt accumulation, and presents historical and projected data on deficits and debt. The third section describes the concept of sustainability. The fourth section presents evidence on sustainability and discusses the implications of fiscal sustainability gaps, and the fifth section concludes.

SOCIAL SECURITY, THE FEDERAL BUDGET, AND THE PUBLIC DEBT

Trust Funds and the Budget

Social Security includes four separate social insurance programs, each with its own trust fund: two cash-benefit, retirement programs—Old-Age and Survivors Insurance and Disability Insurance (taken together, OASDI)—and two health benefit programs—Hospital Insurance (HI) and Supplementary Medical Insurance (SMI) for physician services (taken together, Medicare). The compulsory OASDI and HI programs share a similar financing basis and, in the past, interfund borrowing has occurred when one of the funds faced a financial shortfall. The voluntary SMI program is three-quarters financed from federal general revenues and one-quarter financed by individual premiums. Emphasis is given here to the combined OASDHI programs, due to their common financing and mandatory features. Some data presented later show that, by excluding SMI, the fiscal sustainability gaps computed in this paper should be regarded as conservative.

The relationship between the Social Security trust funds and the rest of the federal budget is crucial to federal government finance. That relationship is suggested by the following:

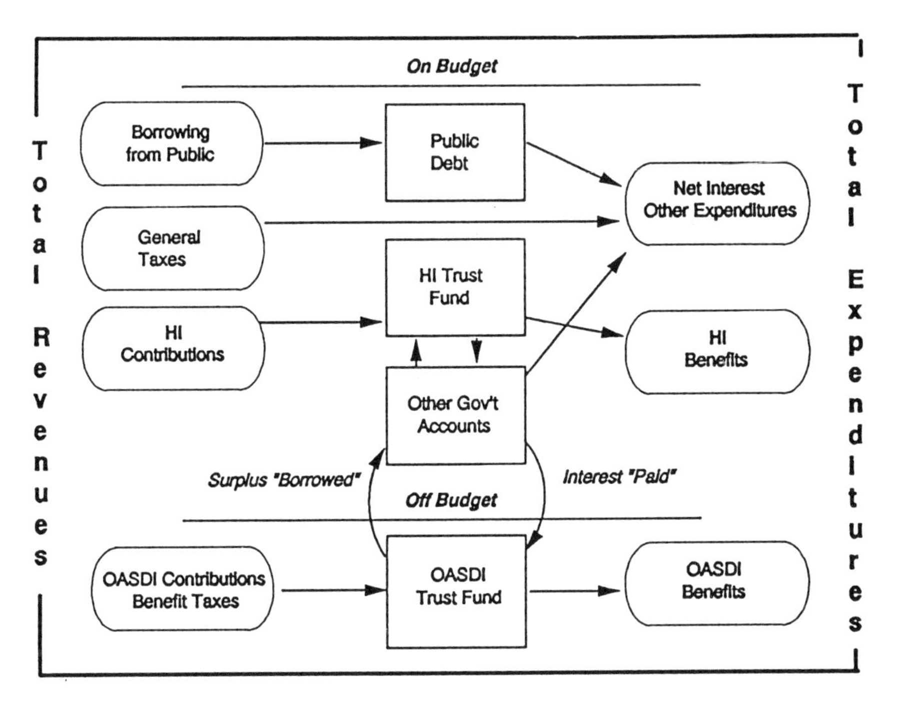

Figure 2. Unified Federal Budget

> The assets of the trust funds are generally invested in special securities of the U.S. Treasury. The initial accumulation of assets will result in a substantial cash flow from the trust funds to the general fund of the Treasury, and the amount of special securities held by the combined trust funds will increase. The subsequent redemption of securities will cause this cash flow to reverse. The magnitude and pattern of these cash flows have important public policy and economic implications that extend beyond the operation of the OASDI program itself (U.S. Congress, 1994, p. 5).

Figure 2 attempts to capture, in simplified form, the essential flow of funds in the federal budget that is of interest to the present discussion. The unified budget has two major components, the general fund ("on-budget") accounts and the OASDI ("off-budget") account; the HI trust fund is on-budget.[4] When OASDI (and/or HI) income exceeds benefit payments, the surplus is "borrowed" by the general fund and used to finance other government expenditures. In turn, the general fund pays interest to the trust funds. This transaction is recorded nearly exclusively through the issuance of special interest-bearing public debt obligations for purchase by the trust funds.[5] The interest payment is an outlay from the general fund, reducing its balance, and it is income to the trust fund accounts, increasing their balances. This is an internal transaction that, for the HI trust fund, cancels within the on-budget balance and, for the OASDI trust fund, cancels when off-budget and on-budget accounts are combined in the unified budget. When Social Security benefit payments exceed current income, expected to first occur around 2013 for OASDI (already occurring for HI), the trust funds begin to redeem the special issue bonds, thereby imposing new financing requirements on the general fund.

The Nature of Debt Accumulation

Let D_t = the public debt in period t, G = government expenditures on goods and services, T = general taxes (income, corporate, excise), r = the real interest rate on government debt, OAB = OASDI benefits, $OATF$ = OASDI trust fund, HIB = HI benefits, $HITF$ = HI trust fund, $OAPC$ = OASDI payroll contributions (less benefit taxes), and $HIPC$ = HI payroll contributions. Corresponding to Figure 2, the total budget deficit in period t is the sum of the non-Social Security and Social Security balances:

$$D_t - D_{t-1} = (G_t - T_t + rD_{t-1} + rOATF_{t-1} + rHITF_{t-1}) + (OAB_t - OAPC_t - rOATF_{t-1}) + (HIB_t - HIPC_t - rHITF_{t-1}) \quad (1a)$$

$$= (G - T)_t + (OAB - OAPC)_t + (HIB - HIPC)_t + rD_{t-1} \quad (1b)$$

The first set of parentheses in Equation (1a) represents the non-Social Security accounts and shows the interest payments ($rOATF_{t-1}$, $rHITF_{t-1}$) paid by these accounts to the trust funds. The first three sets of parentheses on the right side of Equation (1b) represent the total value of noninterest federal spending less taxes and payroll contributions. This is typically referred to as the primary deficit (or surplus), and measures the balance between current spending and currently collected taxes. The total (interest-inclusive) deficit defines the borrowing requirements of the Federal Government.

In a growing economy, the one-period budget constraint in equations (1a) and (1b) is more meaningfully written in terms of ratios to Gross Domestic Product (GDP). Let Y_t = GDP in period t and define $d = D/Y$, $g = G/Y$, $oab = OAB/Y$, $hib = HIB/Y$, $t = \tau/\mathbf{Y}$, $oapc = OAPC/Y$, $hipc = HIPC/Y$, and n = the rate of growth in GDP. Then, equation (1b) can be expressed as:

$$d_t - d_{t-1} = (g - \tau)_t + (oab - oapc)_t + (hib - hipc)_t + (r - n)d_{t-1}. \quad (2)$$

Equation (2) captures the essential elements of government debt accumulation. It makes clear that the evolution of the debt/GDP ratio depends upon the primary deficits and the product of the difference between the interest and growth rates and the accumulated debt. The chief components of the primary deficit are the two Social Security account balances (OASDI and HI) and the remaining (non-Social Security) accounts. The interest rate-growth rate difference is crucial in this context and is discussed below. A positive difference means that a constant debt/GDP ratio requires a primary surplus.

Historical Deficits

Past income and expenditure patterns are the starting point for assessing future government fiscal policy. Table 1 summarizes the historical and expected U.S. fiscal situation. Clearly, the burden of net interest has grown over time, especially during the 1980s when, compared to the 1970s, net interest doubled as a percent of GDP. Beginning in the 1960s, total noninterest receipts grew at about the same rate as GDP, while total noninterest spending increased to an average of 20% of GDP during the 1980s. Excluding OASDI, noninterest spending has been fairly stable since the 1950s, edging up somewhat in the 1980s. However, corresponding receipts declined, particularly during the last decade. Non-Social Security fiscal discipline seems to have worsened considerably during the 1980s: the ratio of receipts to spending fell, on average, from .92 to .82. The consequence for the public debt is illustrated in Figure 3, which shows the debt/GDP ratio over the period 1940 to 1993. The debt ratio averaged 41.3% of GDP over the entire period, ranging from 82.4% in 1950 to 24.5% in 1974. The reason for the growth in this ratio during the 1980s is made apparent in Figure 4, which charts the components of the primary deficit ($g_t - \tau_t$ and $(oab - oapc)_t + (hib - hipc)_t$) over the historical period, 1950-1993.

Table 1. The U.S. Fiscal Situation, 1950-1999 (percent of GDP)

Fiscal Category	*1950-1959*	*1960-1969*	*1970-1979*	*1980-1993*	*1994-1999*
Total Spending	18.0	19.1	20.6	23.0	21.6
Total Receipts	17.6	18.3	18.5	18.8	19.1
Balance	-0.4	-0.8	-2.1	-4.2	-2.5
Net Interest	1.4	1.3	1.5	3.0	3.0
			Excluding Net Interest[1]		
Spending	16.7	17.8	19.1	20.0	18.6
Receipts	17.2	17.8	17.8	17.7	18.2
Balance	0.5	0.0	-1.5	-2.3	-0.5
Spending less OASDI	15.6	15.2	15.2	15.4	13.9
Receipts less OASDI	15.9	15.2	14.0	12.9	13.0
Balance	0.3	-0.0	-1.2	-2.5	-0.9
Spending less OASDHI	15.6	15.1	14.5	14.2	12.3
Receipts less OASDHI	15.9	15.0	13.3	11.7	11.6
Balance	0.3	0.0	-1.2	-2.5	-0.8

Sources: U.S. Congress (1994); 1994-1999 figures are those projected for the Clinton Administration 1995 budget.

Note: [1]Net interest is deducted from spending (outlays) and estimated receipts from taxes on interest paid are deducted from receipts, assuming an average 25% tax rate; Federal Reserve Deposits are also deducted from receipts.

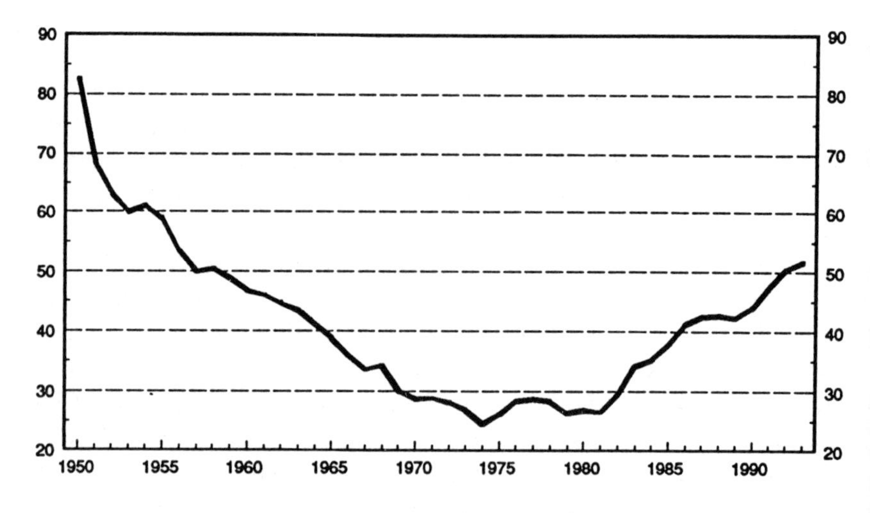

Figure 3. U.S. Public Debt/GDP Ratio 1950-1993

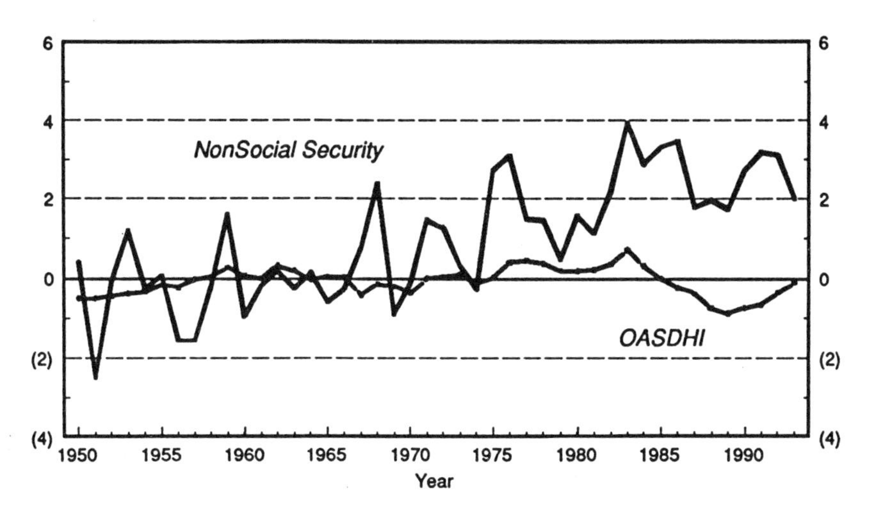

Source: U.S. Government (1994a).

Figure 4. Primary Deficits/Surpluses
NonSocial Security and OASDHI, 1950-1993
(percent of GDP, deficit: +, surplus: −)

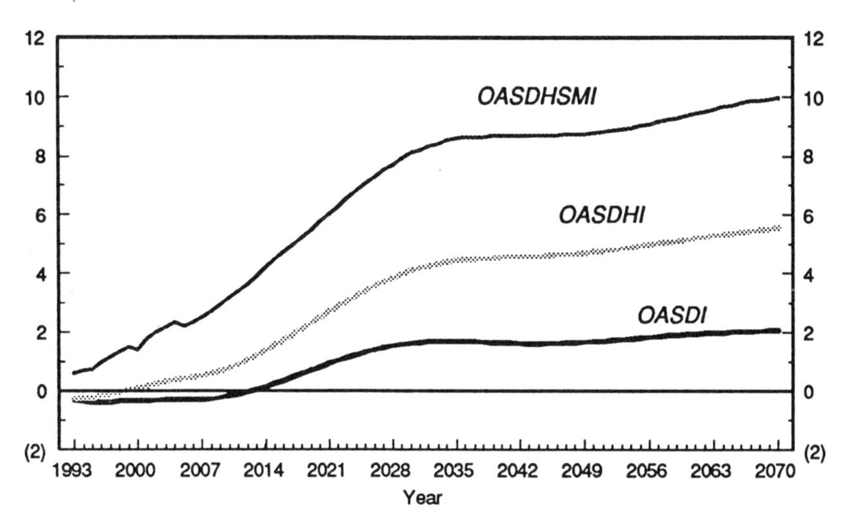

Source: Social Security Administration and Health Care Financing Administration

Figure 5. OASDI, OASDHI, and OASDHSMI
Noninterest Balances, 1993-2070
(percent of GDP, deficit: + surplus: −)

Future Deficits

Figure 4 makes clear that, except for the second half of the 1980s, the OASDHI balances played a relatively minor role in the U.S. postwar deficit and debt experience. Figure 5 shows how this will change in the future. OASDI surpluses $(oab - oapc)$ averaging 0.3% of GDP are expected until the year 2013, followed by rising deficits until about 2030 to about 1.6% of GDP, after which the deficits level off for about 15 years and then rise gradually to about 2% of GDP. The Social Security deficit outlook changes dramatically when the HI program is taken into account. The middle line in Figure 5 shows the combined OASDHI balances $[(oab - oapc) + (hib - hipc)]$ in Equation (2)). Deficits begin in 1999 and rise rapidly to 4.5% of GDP before 2040, ultimately reaching 5.6% of GDP by the end of the projection period. Finally, the top line in Figure 5 adds SMI expected costs. The ultimate Social Security deficit for all four trust funds is almost 10% of GDP.

Projected Social Security imbalances of the magnitude shown in Figure 5 would severely strain future fiscal policy. If the Social Security programs were unchanged, the non-Social Security accounts would have to maintain significant surpluses in order to keep the overall budget balance close to the historical average. This suggests that current fiscal policy is not sustainable, a suggestion supported by the empirical evidence presented below. First, however, the concept of sustainability requires more precise definition.

THE CONCEPT OF SUSTAINABILITY

Definition of Sustainability

Sustainability refers to the feasibility of government fiscal policy. Is a policy of running permanent deficits, for example, feasible or are there constraints that prevent a government from pursuing such a policy? Hamilton and Flavin (1986) originated work in this area by posing the question: does a government deficit in one period imply a promise to creditors of a surplus in some future year? If so, then the government is subject to a present-value borrowing constraint in the sense that the current market value of government debt is equal to the discounted value of the sum of expected future surpluses. For a government subject to this constraint, permanent fiscal deficits are not feasible.

This leads to an intuitive definition of sustainability (Wilcox, 1989). Namely, a fiscal policy is sustainable if it results in a series of deficits and debts that satisfy the present-value borrowing constraint. This can be seen through equation (1b). Let PD_t be the primary deficit—that is, $PD_t = (G - T)_t + (OAB - OAPC)_t + (HIB - HIPC)_t$. If the equation holds in all periods 1 through m, then the current value of debt can be expressed as the sum of discounted surpluses and the discounted value of outstanding debt:

$$D0 = -\Sigma^{m}{}_{1}\, PD_t(1 + r)^{-t} + D_m(1 + r)^{-m}. \tag{3}$$

Equation (3) is an accounting identity and will not constrain government fiscal policy without an additional assumption. Following Hamilton and Flavin (1986), the important economic issue with respect to equation (3) is what creditors expect to happen to the second term on the righthand side of the equation. If the expectation of that term goes to zero, then the current value of debt will be equal to the sum of expected noninterest surpluses (deficits), which is the present-value borrowing constraint. That is, creditors (reasonably) expect the government to make good on its promises of loan repayment. Otherwise, the public (and foreigners) will become less willing to buy government debt. Thus, the condition for this constraint to hold is that the limiting value of the second term in equation (3) is zero, which means that the debt cannot grow faster than the interest rate (though the stock of debt could continue to grow subject to this condition).[6]

To extend the present-value sustainability framework to a growing economy, an alternative assumption is needed, whereby creditors expect a limit on the debt/GDP ratio.[7] In that case, defining $pd_t = PD_t/Y_t = (g - \tau)_t \mid (oab\ '' \ oapc)_t \mid (hib\ ''\ hipc)_t$, the current value of the debt/GDP ratio can be expressed as the sum of discounted primary deficit/GDP ratio and the discounted outstanding debt/GDP ratio:

$$d0 = -\Sigma^{m}{}_{1}\, pd_t(1 + r - n)^{(-t)} + d_m(1 + r - n)^{-m}. \tag{4}$$

The required condition for the present-value budget constraint to hold is, as above, that the discounted value of debt goes to zero. In equation (4), the second term on the righthand side must tend to zero as m approaches infinity. If this condition holds, then a sustainable fiscal policy is defined as one in which the present discounted value of primary surplus/GDP ratios is equal to the current level of debt to GDP:8

$$d0 = -\Sigma^{m}{}_{1}\, pd_{t}(1 + r - n)^{(-t)}. \quad (5)$$

Thus, if the government has existing outstanding debt, then at some point surpluses must be run to satisfy equation (5). If the primary budget is in balance, those surpluses have to be large enough to cover interest growth in the extant debt.

Components of Sustainability

If fiscal sustainability were viewed solely in general terms as a concern about overall government spending ($g + oab + hib$) in relation to overall government receipts ($\tau + oapc + hipc$), then equation (4) can be solved for the tax or expenditure adjustment that will satisfy the present-value condition. For example, assume that annual spending projections are available for each of the three components over the period 1 to m. Then, following Blanchard (1990) and Blanchard *et al.* (1990), assume that $d_m = d0$ and solve for the constant tax rate, $\varnothing_m$, that will return the debt/GDP ratio to its initial level:

$$\varnothing^{m} = (r - n)\{q\Sigma^{m}{}_{1}\, [g + oab + hib]_{t}(1 + r - n)^{(1-t)} + d\}^{0}. \quad (6)$$

Equation (6) says that the sustainable tax rate is equal to the discounted value of spending (Social Security and non-Social Security) plus the interest-growth change in the base period debt ratio.[9] When $\varnothing^{m}$ is compared to the current total receipt rate ($\tau + oapc + hipc$), the result is what Blanchard (1990) suggests for an index of sustainability ($\varnothing^{m} - [\tau + oapc + hipc]$) and is essentially equivalent to Buiter's (1993) permanent primary gap. If the constant tax rate is higher than the current rate, then taxes *and/or expenditures* will have to be adjusted at some point. The index gives the size of the required adjustment if it were made today. Any delay will cause the size of the adjustment to increase.

In the present context, the fiscal sustainability problem has three components:

$$\varnothing^{m} = \tau^{*} + oapc^{*} + hipc^{*}, \tag{7}$$

where the three terms on the righthand side of equation (7) are the constant tax/contribution rates that will satisfy the present value constraint for each of the three principal components of government spending. Clearly, the initial debt/GDP ratio is sustainable if the net (income less outgo) present discounted value of each of the three components of the primary deficit is zero and income is sufficient to cover debt service. For the Social Security components, this would imply fully funded programs such that discounted benefits equaled discounted payroll contributions. We saw in Figure 5, however, that large imbalances in those programs are expected in the next century, suggesting that sustainability gaps arise when $oapc^{*}$ is compared to $oapc$ and when $hipc^{*}$ is compared to $hipc$. For the non-Social Security component, we saw in Figure 4 that, especially since the late 1970s, the primary deficit has been well above zero. If that were to continue, then a sustainability gap would also arise when τ_{m} is compared to τ. In order to achieve a sustainable fiscal policy in the future, fiscal gaps in each of the three components must be addressed. The potential size of these gaps is calculated in the next section. It must be emphasized that the constant tax rate adjustments are equivalent to constant expenditure adjustments of opposite sign. Fiscal sustainability would presumably be achieved through both types of adjustments.

EVIDENCE ON FISCAL SUSTAINABILITY

Sustainability Gaps

Our interest is in evaluating long-term fiscal sustainability, given the projected Social Security expenditures described earlier. Combining those projections with an assumption about the future path of non-Social Security expenditures implies a specific federal fiscal policy. Adding assumptions about future interest and growth rates, the framework described above can be used to evaluate the sustainability of that policy. The evaluation is based on the assumption that a reasonable long-term fiscal objective is one in which, over the target period, fiscal policy eventually returns the current debt/GDP ratio. A more stringent objective would require a reduction in the debt/GDP ratio.[10]

In what follows, the initial value for ***d0*** is set equal to the 1993 U.S. debt/GDP ratio of 51%. This is higher than the 1950-1993 postwar average debt ratio of 41% and even higher than the 1960-1993 average of 36%. Thus, from an historical perspective, the 1993 value is a conservative choice. Assumptions about future non-Social Security expenditures are guided by the data underlying Table 1, particularly data for the most recent time period. For interest rates and growth rates, we initially assume that the differential is 1% but examine alternatives later.

Next, consider the noninterest budget data in Table 1 that exclude OASDHI. The expenditure/GDP ratio has been fairly stable over the past two decades, just above 14%. Tax rates have fallen to below 12% of GDP, however. If noninterest, non-OASDHI expenditures were to continue indefinitely at, say, 14.2% of GDP and if the tax rate were held at 11.7%, then, ignoring future OASDHI imbalances, the debt/GDP ratio could proceed on a path like the one shown in Figure 6 (labeled "Non-Social Security Deficit"). The debt ratio would reach 100% of GDP in about 15 years. Such a path would be unprecedented in peacetime experience and seems as unlikely as it is unacceptable.

The first column in Table 2 relates to the scenario just described. The constant tax rate, τ, that would satisfy the present-value constraint over the period 1993-2070 is 14.7%. Thus, the fiscal sustainability gap in the absence of Social Security is 3% of GDP. If the tax rate were raised by this amount, the result would be a debt/GDP ratio of 51% in the year 2070. Naturally, part of the adjustment could be made on the expenditure side for a more balanced correction. In fact, as Table 1 shows, the current administration's budget would reduce non-Social Security expenditures by 1.9% of GDP, on average, over the next five years, closing much of the non-social-security sustainability gap shown in Table 2.

The second column in Table 2 adds projected OASDI expenditures. The required contribution rate (or expenditure

Table 2. Present-value Tax-Expenditure Adjustments for Alternative Social Security Expenditure Scenarios, 1993-2070 (percent of GDP)

	Expenditure Scenarios			
	No Social Security	*OASDI*	*HI*	*Total*
Projected				
Expenditure Rate	14.2	14.2+*oab*	14.2+*hib*	14.2+*oab*+*hib*
Current Tax/ Contribution Rate[1]	11.7	4.8	1.2	17.7
Constant Tax Rate	14.7	5.7	3.4	23.8
	(τ*)	(*oapc**)	(*hipc**)	(∅*)
Sustainability Gap	3.0	0.9	2.2	6.1

Note: [1] The numbers in this row are from Table 1. For example, under the OASDI column, 4.8 ′ 17.7 ″ 12.9.

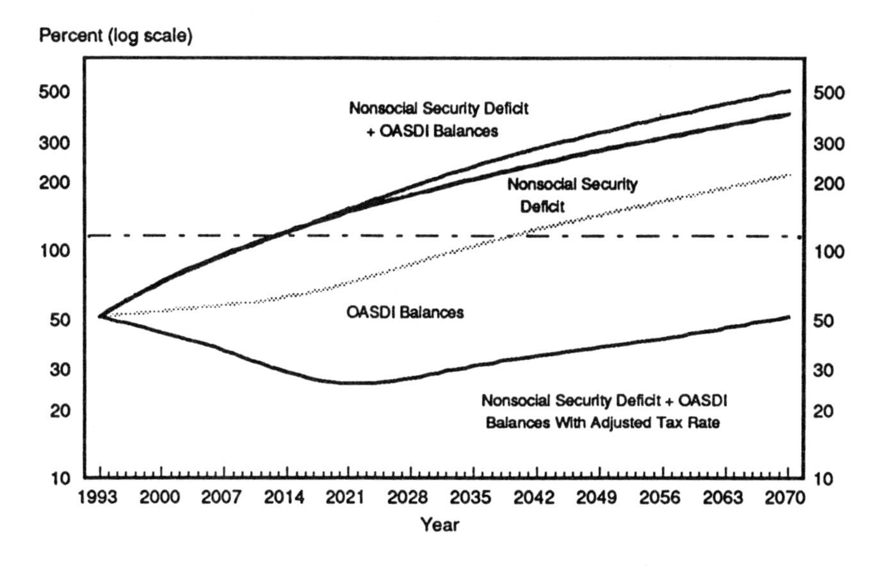

Figure 6. Debt/GDP Paths for OASDI and NonSocial Security 1993-2070

decrease) for fiscal sustainability in the OASDI program is 5.7%, which is 0.9% higher than the current contribution rate of 4.8%. This gap is small relative to the gap for the case that ignores Social Security expenditures and, as seen in Figure 6, the debt/GDP paths are, at least for the next 35 years, very close. Nevertheless, a 0.9% constant annual contribution-expenditure adjustment is significant. As shown in Figure 6, the debt ratio path due to this gap rises to 200% of GDP by the end of the projection period. The key policy issue is the manner in which the gap would be closed. Presumably, the marginal gap due to OASDI would be closed through an adjustment to that program. If the total (non-Social Security and OASDI) sustainability gap of 3.9% of GDP were closed, the debt ratio could, over the next 75 years, follow the path of the bottom line in Figure 6.

The third column of Table 2 adds to the non-Social Security expenditure rate (*g*) the projected HI expenditures (*hib*). The sustainability gap for the HI program is 3.4% of GDP, 2.2% higher than the current contribution rate, *hipc*. As shown in Figure 7, even if the rest of the budget were in balance (i.e., the 3% gap were closed), the debt ratio due to HI imbalances alone will rise to 100% of GDP in about 25 years. If the rest of the budget were not in balance, that ratio would be reached in about 12 years.

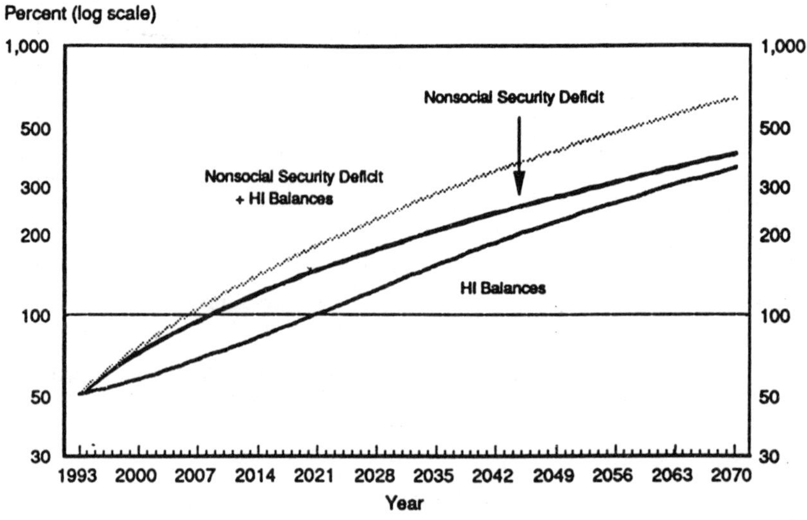

Figure 7. Debt/GDP Paths for the Hospital Insurance and NonSocial Security, 1993-2070

Finally, the last column of Table 2 combines the projected expenditures from the first three columns. The total fiscal sustainability gap is 6.1% of GDP. This is the adjustment that, if made today through some combination of tax-expenditure adjustments across the non-Social Security, OASDI, and HI accounts, would achieve fiscal sustainability over the period 1993-2070.[11]

Implications of Fiscal Unsustainability

Table 2 shows a substantial fiscal sustainability gap. From a macroeconomic perspective, such a gap could lead to the problems suggested in the first paragraph of the paper. As the debt/GDP ratio continued to grow, uncertainty over the form of government financing could convert even a stable debt path to an unstable one. Continuous deficit financing could lead to higher interest rates through higher uncertainty premia as investors became concerned about a government policy that appeared unresponsive to the prospect of large, continuing deficits. The problems worsen, the longer the deficits persist.

Nevertheless, those concerns do not lead to the conclusion that the sustainability gap should be closed by raising the general tax rate or lowering the expenditure rate on goods and services. Rather, the gap signals that policy changes will be required in the three major components of the primary budget. If the Social Security programs currently have the desired benefit structure, then their financing structure needs to be rationalized. For example, the OASDI sustainability gap in Table 2 (0.9% of GDP) could be closed by a 2.1% increase in the payroll contribution rate or equivalent reduction in the OASDI expenditure rate. For HI, financing the current benefit structure over the next 75 years would require a roughly 5.2% increase in the payroll contribution rate. Thus, the total required OASDHI adjustment is quite large, which points to the reason resource allocation decisions must consider the combined programs. The OASDI adjustment may not be regarded as modest when considered on top of the HI adjustment.

CONCLUSION

The four Social Security trust funds account for about 30% of total federal government expenditures, and that percent is expected to increase significantly in the future as the baby-boom generation reaches retirement age. Imbalances in the combined OASDHSMI programs could reach 10% of GDP by the middle of the next century. This paper has provided an indication of the extraordinary fiscal restraint that will be required in order to meet current-law commitments to these social insurance programs while maintaining a sustainable fiscal policy in the 21st century. If made today, fiscal adjustments (tax and/or expenditure) could exceed 6% of GDP, particularly if the SMI program is considered. If official Social Security projections are realized, the magnitudes will continue to increase the longer the delay in making adjustments. Moreover, when the baby-boom generation begins to retire, deficits in the social insurance programs will grow rapidly, suggesting that delay could be highly disruptive.

Federal initiatives, such as health care reform, that could substantially alleviate financial difficulties in the health care programs, which account for most of the projected growth in federal financial liabilities. Initiatives aimed at specific programs can be thwarted, however, if fiscal discipline is not imposed on the non-Social Security programs. A major point of emphasis in this paper is that the retirement and health care portions of Social Security should be viewed jointly, with adherence to an intertemporal budget constraint, in deciding on total resource allocation to social insurance for the elderly.

ACKNOWLEDGMENTS

The views expressed in this paper are those of the author's alone and do not necessarily reflect those of the Department of Treasury. The author thanks Robert Gillingham, John Greenless, and John Hambor for comments.

NOTES

1. These figures refer to the marketable public debt and do not include debt held by the Social Security trust funds. The U.S. public debt/GDP ratio averaged 41% during 1950-1993, ranging from 24.5% in 1974 to 82.4% in 1951; the 1960-1993 average was 36%. All historical data used in this paper are from U.S. Congress (1994).
2. Unless otherwise noted, all projected data used in this paper are from U.S. Congress (1994).

3. In the absence of Social Security surpluses in the late 1980s, the current debt ratio would be slightly higher.

4. The OASDI fund was moved off-budget by the 1985 Gramm-Rudman-Hollings Act, which nevertheless set five-year deficit targets that included OASDI balances (the targets were reset in 1987). The Budget Enforcement Act of 1990 established the requirement that the official budget figures exclude the off-budget accounts. Official budget documents show both on- and off-budget totals and the combined balance of the unified budget, which defines federal borrowing requirements. Beginning with fiscal year 1989, the postal service fund was placed off-budget, making the OASDI and postal service funds the only two accounts with off-budget status. For a thorough pre-1985 history of these relations, see Munnell (1985).

5. The special issue bonds bear interest at a rate equal to the average market yield on all marketable interest-bearing public debt obligations that are not due or callable for four years. The special issues are always redeemable at par value and so bear no market risk.

6. Hamilton and Flavin (1986), Wilcox (1989), and a number of subsequent papers report on empirical tests for violations of the constraint. Bohn (1991) proposes a sustainability test that does not rely on this condition.

7. Equation (3) is expressed in level form and, therefore, puts no constraint on the behavior of the debt/GDP ratio. If the interest rate exceeds the growth rate of GDP, then, in the absence of an additional assumption, the ratio could increase without bound.

8. This condition for sustainability is necessary only if the interest rate exceeds the growth rate. Such an assumption is not obviously the case. The relationship between the interest rate and growth rate is theoretically indeterminate and unsettled empirically. With $r > n$, there is no limit to the debt/GDP ratio unless the government eventually runs surpluses. On the other hand, if $r < n$, then a debt/GDP limit is well-defined and the government can run primary deficits indefinitely and still achieve sustainability.

The literature provides little guidance on this issue. Blanchard, *et al.* (1990) assume a positive $(r - n)$ relationship. Similarly, Buiter says that "prudence calls for working with a one to two percentage points per annum number for $(r-n)$" (Buiter, 1993, p. 11). On the other hand, Abel et al. (1989) and Bohn (1991) assume a negative $(r - n)$ differential. The data are also not much help in deciding on the long-run relationship. Until the 1980s, the growth rate exceeded the interest rate, but this reversed during the 1980s. The 1993 OASDI trustees' report assumes a $(r - n)$ differential of about 1% in the long run, the assumption used in Table 2 of this paper.

9. In Equation (6), q is a normalization factor that makes the weights on expenditure/GDP ratios sum to one: $q = [1 - (1 + r - n)^{-m}] - 1$. See Blanchard (1990) or Blanchard, *et al.* (1990) for further details.

10. If the total (interest-inclusive) budget is continuously balanced at zero, the debt/GDP ratio will fall continuously according to the rate of growth in GDP.

11. The sustainability gaps also depend upon the interest rate-growth rate differential. Because the non-Social Security expenditure rate is assumed to remain constant, the gap increases for larger values of $(r - n)$. For the social security components, program deficits rise later in the projection period, resulting in smaller fiscal sustainability gaps for larger values of $(r - n)$.

REFERENCES

Aaron, H., B. Bosworth, and G. Burtless. 1989. *Can America Afford to Grow Old?* Washington, DC: The Brookings Institute.

Abel, A., N.G. Mankiw, L.H. Summers, and R.J. Zeckhauser. 1989. "Assessing Dynamic Efficiency: Theory and Evidence." *Review of Economic Studies* 56: 1-20.

Anderson, J., R. Kuzmack, D. Jorgenson, D. Moran, and G. Schink. 1988. *Study of the Potential Economic and Fiscal Effects of Investment of the Assets of the Social Security Old-Age and Survivors Insurance And Disability Trust Funds.* Final Report to the Department of Health and Human Services. IFC, Inc., May.

Bispham, J.A. 1987. "Rising Public-Sector Indebtedness: Some More Unpleasant Arithmetic." In M.J. Boskin, J.S. Fleming, and S. Gorini (eds.), *Private Saving and Public Debt.* New York: Blackwell.

Blanchard, O. 1990. "Suggestions for a New Set of Fiscal Indicators." Working Paper No. 79, OECD Department of Economics & Statistics, April.

Blanchard, O., J. Chouraqui, R. Hagemann, and N. Sartor. 1990. "The Sustainability of Fiscal Policy: New Answers to an Old Question." *OECD Economic Studies* 15(Autumn): 7-36.

Blejer, M.I. and A. Cheasty. 1991. "The Measurement of Fiscal Deficits: Analytical and Methodogical Issues." *Journal of Economic Literature* 29(December): 1644-1678.

Bohn, H. 1991. "On Testing The Sustainability of Government Deficits in a Stochastic Environment." Rodney White Center for Financial Research Working Paper, University of Pennsylvania.

Buiter, W.H. 1993. "Public Debt in the USA: How Much, How Bad, and Who Pays?" NBER Working Paper No. 4362. Washington, DC: NBER, May.

Burtless, G. 1988. "Investment Policy for the Social Security Trust Funds" In J. Gist (ed.). *Social Security and Economic Well-Being Across Generations.* Washington, DC: American Association of Retired Persons, pp. 89-112.

Duggan, J.E. 1991. "Social Security and the Public Debt." *Public Finance* 46(3): 382-404.

Hambor, J.C. 1987. "Economic Policy, Intergenerational Equity, and the Social Security Trust Fund Buildup." *Social Security Bulletin* 50: 13-18.

Hamilton, J. and M. Flavin. 1986. "On the Limitations of Government Borrowing: A Framework for Empirical Testing." *American Economic Review* (September): 808-819.

Masson, P.R. 1985. "The Sustainability of Fiscal Deficits." *Staff Papers* (International Monetary Fund) 32(December): 577-605.

Munnell, A.H. 1985. "Social Security and the Budget." *New England Economic Review* (July/August): 5-18.

———. 1988. "Social Security and National Savings." In J. Gist (ed.), *Social Security and Economic Well-Being Across Generations.* Washington, DC: American Association of Retired Persons, pp. 63-88.

Tobin, J. 1986. "The Monetary-Fiscal Mix: Long-Run Implications." *American Economic Review, Papers and Proceedings* 76(May): 213-218.

U.S. Congress, House Committee of Ways and Means. 1994. *1994 Annual Report of the Trustees of the Federal Hospital Insurance Trust Fund.* 104th Congress, Washington, DC, April.

U.S. Governemnt, Office of Management and Budget. 1994a. *Hostorical Tables-Budget of the United States Government-Fiscal Year 1995.* Washington, DC.

U.S. Government, Office of Management and Budget. 1994b. *Budget of the United States Government-Fiscal Year 1995.* Washington, DC.

Weaver, C. 1990. "Controlling the Risks Posed by Advance Funding—Options for Reform." In C. Weaver (ed.), *Social Security's Looming Surpluses, Prospects and Implications.* Washington, DC: American Enterprise Institute, pp. 167-178.

Wilcox, D. 1989. "The Sustainability of Government Deficits: Implications of the Present-Value Borrowing Constraint." *Journal of Money, Credit, and Banking* 21(3, August): 291-306.

IS OUR PUBLIC PENSION SYSTEM BEYOND REPAIR?

Carolyn L. Weaver

To the question "Is our public pension system beyond repair?" my answer is no, but it sure is in need of repair! Social security promises substantially more in benefits to baby-boom retirees and future generations than can be financed with the structure of taxes now in the law; it redistributes income and wealth in perverse, if unintended, ways and distorts individuals' decisions regarding work and saving; and it no longer offers young people being asked to support the system in the years ahead the expectation that they will fare as well as they would have if they had invested their taxes privately. The system must be reformed if it is to meet the challenges and the opportunities of the 21st century.

This should come as no surprise. After all, social security is close to 60 years old itself! The system was created during the depths of the Great Depression, before the development of modern financial markets and institutions, before the great expansion of employer-provided pensions and other sources of retirement income, and before the great expansion of social safety-net programs that have brought cash assistance and medical care to all of the nation's elderly poor. Plenty of work needs to be done to ensure that the system accommodates these developments, is compatible with long-term economic growth, and is capable of meeting the needs of both present and future retirees.

First, the financing problem. According to the government's official projections (see Board of Trustees, OASDI, 1994, intermediate projections), social security will be technically insolvent—unable to meet monthly payments on time—in 2029, just 35 years from now, when today's college-age students will be in their peak earning (and tax-paying) years and beginning to contemplate retirement, and most of their retired baby-boom parents will be alive, drawing social security benefits, and hoping to continue drawing benefits for the rest of their lives. The surpluses we hear so much about today are projected to give way to cash-flow deficits in 2013. Thereafter benefits can be met only by drawing on interest payments from the federal Treasury and, ultimately, by redeeming all of the bonds now being credited to the trust funds. Social security's long-range deficit amounts to $59 billion annually (in constant 1994 dollars) over the next 75 years, or close to $2 trillion in present-value terms. Under the government's more pessimistic assumptions, deficits are much larger and the projected date of insolvency (2014) is much sooner.

Long-range insolvency is nothing new for social security. The system was plagued by deficits in the 1970s and early 1980s and, in spite of the much-applauded 1983 reform legislation which raised the social security retirement age and temporarily resolved the long-range financing problem, the system has been plagued by deficits ever since. The average annual deficit over the next 75 years has increased fivefold since 1985. The long-range deficit today is actually *larger* than it was in the early 1980s when the system was widely viewed as being in dire financial straights.

To get a feel for the relative magnitude of the long-range deficit: if Congress were to act within the next three or four years to raise the retirement age from 65 to 70, effective for people born in 1952 or later (instead of to age 67 for people born in 1960 or later, as scheduled in the law), this would close just two-thirds of the current funding gap, leaving one-third to be met in other ways.[1] To get a feel for the importance of dealing with the financing problem sooner rather than later: it would take a 10% or 15% reduction in the growth of *future* benefits, if enacted today, to close the long-range gap, whereas it would take a 25% reduction in benefits *for those on the rolls* if enacted when the program is finally insolvent.

Of course, the picture is much bleaker if the Medicare portion of social security is factored in. According to the government's projections, the long-range Medicare (hospital insurance) deficit is twice as large as the social security (old-age, survivors, and disability insurance) deficit (see Board of Trustees, FHITF, 1994; see also Board of Trustees, OASDI, 1994). Without any changes in benefits, the government's projections imply that meeting the cost of social security and Medicare would ultimately require a payroll tax on the order of 25%-30% (employee and employer rates combined), up from 15.3% today. Under the government's more pessimistic assumptions, the tax rate would reach 45%-50%!

While some complain about mentioning Medicare's financial woes in the same breath with social security's, the programs rely on the same cohorts of workers for their sustenance and transfer this sustenance to the same cohorts of retirees. It is impossible to think seriously about the long-term reform of one without being cognizant of the pressures that will come to bear on the other.

Finances are not all that ails social security, and it is for this reason that real reform is so important. Tinkering adjustments in taxes and benefits are unlikely to be satisfactory on a long-term basis. Whereas the system once offered huge wealth transfers to retirees, it offers today's young workers a real return on taxes of no more than about one percent on average (the growth rate of real wages), which is substantially below the real return on private capital. Social security is a system of largely unfunded benefit promises (i.e., debt) backed up by government IOUs rather than by real capital.[2] Society would benefit from a system built on real capital investment.[3] Little wonder that younger workers show increasing interest in proposals that promote private retirement savings.[4]

In part because of declining returns, there is increasing concern about the way social security treats people with different family, work, and savings patterns. Social security contains complex redistributive features, allowing some people (not always the ones we expect) to fare much better than average and some to fare much worse. For example, it is well known that the weighted benefit formula subsidizes people with low earnings at the expense of those with higher earnings. The same feature of the law, however, produces sizable windfalls to people who work in covered employment for relatively brief periods, even at substantial earnings. In addition, the 50% benefit supplement for spouses that subsidizes the once-traditional family—one breadwinner and a nonworking spouse—does so at the expense of single people and the now-traditional two-earner couple. In fact, the marginal return on taxes for the secondary earner in a couple (generally the wife) is negative until his or her earnings reach a significant fraction of the couple's combined earnings. Even then, the couple's expected return on taxes remains below that of the single-earner couple (see Boskin et al., 1987).

Finally, various features of the system—including the retirement earnings test and actuarial adjustments for early or delayed retirement—subsidize people who retire at age 65 (and possibly earlier) at the expense of those who retire later,[5] while the taxation of benefits, which applies only to people with adjusted gross incomes above certain thresholds, subsidizes people who do not save (or work) to generate private retirement incomes in excess of the thresholds at the expense of those who do.

These cross-subsidies, and others like them, create perverse (and often unintended) wealth transfers. They also distort individuals' decisions regarding work versus leisure or retirement, saving versus consumption, and even marriage. The compromise inherent in social security between paying benefits based on earnings or contributions (as in a pension plan) and paying benefits based on ill-defined social criterion (for purposes of income redistribution) limits the ability of the system to perform either function well.[6]

The 1983 legislation dealt only a glancing blow to these problems. Despite years of analyses and the clear need for reform, no serious consideration was given to proposals to rationalize the system for individuals in different family patterns, to eliminate work and savings disincentives, or to privatize any of the functions of social security.

Proposals that attempt to deal with these more fundamental issues often involve, as a first step, separating the pension component of social security (monthly payments to workers in amounts based on past earnings or contributions) from the income redistributive elements (net transfers to particular individuals and families who may or may not be poor). For example, some have argued for moving toward a two-tiered system in which one tier provides means-tested income assistance to the elderly poor—and any other groups deemed socially deserving—and the other tier provides a pension based on contributions plus interest.[7] Under such an arrangement, the first tier—perhaps an expanded

Supplemental Security Income program—would be financed on a current-cost basis from the general fund of the Treasury.[8] The second tier could continue to be payroll-tax-financed and, since assets would equal accruing liabilities, it would be fully funded; with no redistributive elements, taxes could be channeled directly into individualized private savings accounts, possibly along the lines of individual retirement accounts, and benefits could be paid directly from the proceeds of these accounts. In effect, the retirement program would amount to a compulsory law to save for retirement, such as proposed by Nobel Laureate James Buchanan over 25 years ago, not a vehicle (or subterfuge) for income redistribution (see Buchanan 1968).

From a fiscal standpoint, this arrangement would be attractive because it would create a substantial pool of investable funds, allowing for real saving to help lighten the burden of retirement payments in the next century. It would do so, moreover, without involving the federal government in the direct management and control of vast sums of private resources. In addition, the cost of such a system, including the pension and transfer components, would likely be lower than our current system because the income transfers now hidden in social security's complex maze of benefit rules and eligibility criterion would be made explicit and would be limited to people who were in need.[9]

From the standpoint of retirement income policy more generally, this arrangement would be attractive because it would give workers control over a major portion of their retirement savings—the portion channeled through social security. Empowered (within limits) to make their own investment decisions,[10] workers would assume the risks associated with return on investment. In exchange, they would gain contractual rights to future benefits, thus eliminating an important source of political risk in the present system.[11] Such a system would foster individual choice and competition where it does not presently exist.

A number of other difficulties with the current system could be rectified within this two-tiered approach. For example, retirement pensions could be made payable regardless of work status, eliminating the need for the (antiquated) earnings test. In addition, the tax contributions of married couples could be divided equally between spouses, ensuring that individuals and couples with the same lifetime taxes were eligible (ex ante) for the same benefits, while ensuring that nonworking spouses and secondary earners in two-earner couples gained protection that survived the divorce or death of their spouses.[12]

As with any major reform, the question arises of how people who are already retired or near retirement would be affected. Under the Buchanan proposal and other more recent adaptations, outstanding benefit promises would be met in full.[13] This would be an expensive proposition, of course, because it would involve paying some portion of benefits even to younger workers who may have little or no expectation that the current schedule of benefits can be met. While one can conceive of other less generous guarantees that might gain broad support, the problem of meeting past liabilities and current expectations is a problem of transition that can and should be seen as distinct from the problem of designing a new system that could better meet the needs and aspirations of future generations.

ACKNOWLEDGMENT

This paper draws on the author's previous publications (Weaver 1993a, 1993b and 1994).

NOTES

1. Calculated from data contained in Office of the Actuary (1992) and Board of Trustees, OASDI (1994).

2. For a more complete discussion of the way social security is financed and its assets are invested, see Weaver (1990), Aaron et al. (1989), and Weaver (1995).

3. For more on this, see Feldstein (1976).

4. In a November 1992 survey by the Gallup Organization for the Employee Benefit Research Institute, 58% of respondents agreed that they would like to contribute half of their social security taxes to an IRA and take a smaller social security benefit when they retire. The percentages ranged from (a surprising) 37% of those ages 55 and older to 61% of those ages 35 to 54 reported in Roper Center, 1994, p. 33.

In a separate survey, conducted in March 1994 by the Employee Benefit Research Institute and the Gallup Organization for the National Academy of Social Insurance, 74% of respondents agreed that most people could make more money investing retirement funds in the private sector than they get from social security (reported in Friedland, 1994, p. 20).

5. For an excellent discussion of retirement incentives, see Quinn et al. (1990; see also Steuerle and Bakija, 1994).

6. For more on this point, see Buchanan and Campbell (1966) and Buchanan (1968).

7. Boskin (1986) would retain government supply of retirement income whereas I have argued (Weaver, 1995, this volume) for privatizing the pension component of social security in a two-tiered system. Note that this discussion pertains only to the retirement and survivors insurance components of social security, not to disability insurance or Medicare.

8. The first tier could also be designed to accommodate non-means-tested income transfers if deemed socially worthwhile. For example, nothing would prevent the government from supplementing retirement accounts for low-income workers. However, such transfers should be made explicitly as add-ons to retirement pensions; they should be closely monitored, and they should be financed from the general fund of the Treasury.

9. This statement relates to the comparative cost of the systems for future workers, excluding the cost of transition, as discussed below.

10. Presumably, as with IRAs, the government would authorize a range of allowable investments.

11. As some indication of the risks that people recognize, in the EBRI/Gallup poll cited above, more people (56% as compared to 30%) were confident that their personal savings would be available throughout their retirement than that their social security would be. Of the respondents, 43% were not confident that social security would be there, as compared to 19% who were not confident about their personal savings (survey results for February 1994; see Friedland, 1994, p. 23).

12. Individuals who wished to provide protection to their survivors, over and above that available through the balances in their retirement accounts, could make additional contributions for the purchase of life insurance.

13. The federal government would issue bonds (general purpose national debt) to all workers and retirees in the amount of the benefits they had earned (or, more accurately, been promised) but had not yet been paid—in effect, making the government's implicit debt explicit. These bonds would be redeemable at retirement. The debt, and the interest thereon, would be repaid from the general fund of the Treasury (see Buchanan, 1968).

REFERENCES

Aaron, H.J., B. Bosworth, and G. Burtless. 1989. *Can America Afford to Grow Old?* Washington DC: The Brookings Institution.

Board of Trustees of the Federal Hospital Insurance Trust Fund (FHITF). 1994. *1994 Annual Report.* Washington, DC: U.S. Government Printing Office.

Board of Trustees of the Federal Old-Age and Survivors Insurance Trust Fund and the Federal Disability Insurance Trust Fund (OASDI) 1994. *1994 Annual Report.* Washington, DC: U.S. Government Printing Office.

Boskin, M. 1986. *Too Many Promises: The Uncertain Future of Social Security.* Homewood, IL: Dow Jones-Irwin.

Boskin, M., L.J. Kotlikoff, D.J. Puffert, and J.B. Shoven. 1987. "Social Security: A Financial Appraisal Across and Within Generations." *National Tax Journal* XL(1, March): 19-34.

Buchanan, J.M. 1968. "Social Insurance in a Growing Economy: A Proposal for Radical Reform." *National Tax Journal* (December): 386-395.

Buchanan, J.M. and C.D. Campbell. 1966. "Voluntary Social Security," *The Wall Street Journal* (December 20): 14.

Feldstein, M. 1976. "The Social Security Fund and National Capital Accumulation." In *Funding Pensions: Issues and Implications for Financial Markets.* Boston, MA: Federal Reserve Bank of Boston, pp. 32-65.

Freidland, R.B. 1994. "When Support and Confidence are at Odds: The Public's Understandig of the Social Security Program." Paper prepared for the National Academy of Social Insurance, May.

Office of the Actuary. Social Security Administration 1992. "Memorandum on Long-Range OASDI Financial Effects for Alternative Proposals to Increase the Normal Retirement Age." December 23.

Quinn, J.F., R.V. Burkhauser, and D.A. Myers. 1990. *Passing the Torch: The Influence of Economic Incentives on Work and Retirement.* Kalamazoo, MI: W.E. Upjohn Institute for Employment Research.

Steuerle, E. and J.M. Bakija. 1994. *Retooling Social Security for the 21st Century: Right and Wrong Approaches to Reform.* Washington, DC: The Urban Institute Press.

Weaver, C.L. 1993a. "Social Security's Infirmity." *The American Enterprise* 4(2): 30-41.

________. 1993b. "Baby-Boom Retirees, Destined To Go Bust." *The Wall Street Journal* (August 26).

________ (ed.). 1990. *Social Security's Looming Surpluses: Prospects and Implications.* Washington, DC: The American Enterprise Institute.

________. 1994. "Social Security Reform After the 1983 Amendments: What Remains to be Done?" Paper presented at the Annual Meetings of the Eastern Economics Association, May.

________. 1995. "Social Security Investment Policy: What Is it and How Can It Be Improved?" In K. Stephenson (ed.), *Social Security: A Time for Change,* Vol. 79 in *Contemporary Studies in Economic and Financial Analysis,* pp. 155-172. Greenwich, CT: JAI Press.

SOCIAL SECURITY: IF IT AIN'T BROKEN, DON'T FIX IT

Robert Myers

Does the social security system need repair? While small adjustments are needed to the system and will always be needed as demographic, economic, and political conditions change, the basic answer to this question is "No."

I believe that social security operates reasonably well. Every month, about 43 million checks are sent out on time, reasonably accurately, and get to people when they are supposed to. Also, every January, 1099 forms are sent out to about 45 million beneficiaries or former beneficiaries, recording the benefits which they received during the previous year, the Medicare premiums paid, and so forth. That is quite an accomplishment.

Another demonstration that it is operating well is that administrative expenses are quite low. The administrative expenses of OASDI are about 0.75% of contribution income. Of course, the system is not without some minor flaws. First, the administrative procedures of the Social Security Administration are not what they ought to be. This is largely because of general budget considerations. Some politicians have the misconception that, if you cut down social security administrative expenses, this helps balance the general budget of the United States. I believe the administrative expenses should be somewhat higher, closer to one percent of contribution income. The staff could then be larger and better trained so that disability claims could be administered promptly and anyone could walk into a social security office and see someone quickly, instead of getting an appointment for two months later.

Another problem is the long-range actuarial lack of balance. According to the intermediate estimate, the fund will go bankrupt in 2030. The long-range actuarial imbalance is percent of payroll or, if you look at it on a pay-as-you-go basis, roughly 5½ of payroll will be needed ultimately in addition to the present tax rate. I believe that adjustments can readily be made, and they should be made immediately. The contribution schedule should be revised, and we should not have this roller-coaster method of financing that was envisioned in 1983, where the fund would build up to a maximum and, at the end of the 75-year valuation period, would be down to zero.

There are essentially only two choices. We could go to a pay-as-you-go basis, which is what I prefer—having a small contingency fund to handle temporary economic fluctuations. Alternatively, we could build up the fund and maintain its level over the long-run future, by the appropriate financing method. This second option is going full circle; that was the intent of the 1935 Act.

One change that should be implemented, even if we did not have financing problems, is to increase the normal retirement age. That is the age at which so-called unreduced benefits are first payable. Under present law, this age has been 65 ever since the start but it will begin to rise in the year 2003 and, by the year 2027, it will reach age 67. I think that we should also change the definition of what we mean by "elderly" or "aged." This is a dynamic concept. It did not come down from heaven on a tablet that said age 65 is it. Hence, we should change the normal retirement age. I suggest that the present law be changed to raise the ultimate age from 67 to 70; this should be done in about the same length of time as the present law raises it to 67.

At the same time, we should schedule the tax rates as pay-as-you-go financing mechanisms. Tax rates could be lowered a little now, so as not to have annual excesses of income over outgo, which create problems when you try to deal with budget deficits. However, we should have higher ultimate rates—perhaps 1%-1.5% higher on both the employer and the employee; this, when combined with a normal retirement age of 70, would restore the system to long-range balance.

Under either of these two methods of financing—pay-as-you-go or building up a large permanent fund—any fluctuations and changes in the actuarial assumptions will not show the sensitivity that the present financing procedure system does, which just creates public alarm and lack of confidence in the system.

Regarding major changes to the system, there are really two schools, and they are at opposite ends of the pole. One holds that, because of the budget deficit, we should cut entitlements because they are ever-increasing, distort incentives, and so forth. This is not the right way to balance the budget. The social security program is not responsible for the budget deficit; it has always been self-supporting and has had, over the years, some $450 billion more of income than outgo. The people who advocate this say, "Let's means-test the benefits." As Barry Bosworth of the Brookings Institution attests (Bosworth 1995), this is just a bad idea all around and will discourage savings, not encourage them.

The other suggestion that people make is to privatize the system so that there is complete individual equity—everyone gets benefits that are exactly equal in value to his or her contributions. Such criticisms remind me of Winston Churchill's statement, "Democracy is a bad form of government, but it is the best we've seen so far." There is a mixture in the social security system such that the end result is about as good as we can get. If there were complete individual equity, people at the lower end of the economic scale would not receive large enough benefits to get by, and then we would have to supplement the benefit with Supplemental Security Income (SSI). That sounds good in theory but, as everyone familiar with SSI knows, it is a terrible mess. It is inefficient; it is costly; it is subject to abuse and fraud; and it sometimes penalizes people with very high degrees of self-pride, who will not accept any sort of public assistance. We need SSI, but we should have a social insurance system that provides benefits that are large enough so that only a tiny minority of people need this very inefficient and costly program.

In summarizing my views, I would like to say that, on my tombstone, I expect to have inscribed "social security will outlive us all."

REFERENCE

Bosworth, B. 1995. "The Policy Response to an Aging Population." In K. Stephenson (ed.), *Social Security: A Time for Change,* Vol. 79 in *Contemporary Studies in Economic and Financial Analysis,* pp. 25-50. Greenwich, CT: JAI Press.

PART II

FOREIGN RETIREMENT SYSTEMS

"PAY OR PLAY" PENSIONS IN JAPAN AND THE UNITED KINGDOM

John Turner and David M. Rajnes

INTRODUCTION

"Pay or play" refers to a government benefits policy for workers that has two options. Under "pay," the firm contributes to a mandatory government-sponsored program. Under "play," the firm provides a benefits plan that substitutes for the government program and, in exchange, the firm pays a reduced mandatory contribution.

"Pay or play" permits firms to voluntarily privatize government benefits programs. The extent to which privatization occurs depends on whether complete or partial privatization is allowed. It also depends on the voluntary choices made by firms, and in some variants by workers. Firms presumably pick the private-sector option if it minimizes their long-run costs for providing a desired level of benefits.

"Pay or play" has been used to refer to policy options for health care reform. The term has not been used to refer to similar pension policy options, but it applies equally well for pension policy.

To understand how a pay or play policy could privatize social security and how, once started, such a policy might evolve, we can look to experience outside the United States. The pay or play option for pensions originated in the United Kingdom in 1961, but it was discontinued for a period. It has operated there continuously since 1978. Such a system has operated in Japan since 1966.[1] Firms that meet certain criteria can withdraw, or "contract out," from part of the Japanese and British social security systems. The term "contract out" means that a qualifying firm can pay a reduced social security tax rate but, in exchange, must provide a pension benefit that replaces the social security benefits eliminated.[2]

This option would allow firms to voluntarily privatize part of the social security system by paying a reduced contribution to social security as long as they provided a replacement private pension plan of sufficient generosity.[3] This option is attractive because it expands the range of choice open to the private sector while assuring adequate retirement income.

The current forms of contracting out in Japan and the United Kingdom have evolved from simpler programs. The initial programs may provide insight into how such a program could be started, while the historical development in those countries suggests possible refinements to a system after the initial framework has been established.

The Japanese and British defined-benefit pay or play systems compete with the mandatory Chilean defined-contribution system as an alternative model for pension reform.[4] The patterns of risk bearing are much different in the Chilean defined-contribution option than they are in the Japanese and British defined-benefit systems. Although pension experts have debated the relative merits of defined-benefit and defined-contribution plans, defined-benefit plans have traditionally been preferred by most workers and employers.

JAPAN

Pay or play pensions in Japan can only be understood in relationship to the Japanese social security system. The Japanese social security system has a program called the National Pension, where benefits are based on years of flat amount monthly contributions. It also has an earnings-related part called Employees' Pension Insurance. Benefits from Employees' Pension Insurance are based on a flat rate times average earnings times years of service. Employers can contract out of the earnings-related part of the Employees' Pension Insurance and establish plans called Employees' Pension Funds. Unlike the U.S. social security system, the Japanese social security system earnings-related benefit formula is not progressive in that it does not provide higher benefits relative to covered earnings for low-wage workers.

There are three ways that an employer can qualify to contract out of the social security Employees' Pension Insurance. First, large employers may contract out. When this option was first available, the size requirement for a firm to be eligible was 1,000 full-time employees, but it has been reduced so that a firm with 500 full-time employees can contract out. Second, a controlled group of employers can contract out. A controlled group is a group of allied employers having substantially the same ownership. Initially, 5,000 employees were required, but this has been reduced to 800. Third, a group of smaller employers in the same industry can form a multiemployer group in order to contract out. Initially, 5,000 employees were required but that number has been reduced to 3,000. A liberalization of the rules also allows firms to form groups composed of employers in different industries within the same region. The minimum size for such a regional group is also 3,000 employees.

In 1992, data on contracted-out plans indicated that there were 547 single-company plans, 612 allied company plans, and 566 multiemployer plans (Pension Fund Association, 1993).

The Japanese government requires a minimum number of employees in a contracted-out pension plan because of concern for the financial stability of the plan. The volatility of plan finances is larger for plans composed of smaller employers because smaller employers have a greater risk of bankruptcy than do larger employers. For that reason, contracted-out plans composed of small employers have a higher minimum number of employees than do plans where only large employers participate.

Besides the minimum plan size requirement, four other requirements must be met for establishing a contracted-out plan. First, the firm must have made a profit for each of the preceding three years. Second, at least half the full-time employees of the firm must vote in favor of establishing a plan. Third, if the firm has a union representing at least a third of the employees, the union must approve the plan by a majority vote. Fourth, the firm must

Table 1. Reduction in the Social Security Tax Rate Due to Contracting Out in Japan

	Reduction	
Year in Which Rate Began	*Male (%)*	*Female (%)*
1966	2.4	2.0
1971	2.6	2.2
1980	3.2	2.9
1988	3.2	3.0
1994	3.2	3.2

have had a stable or growing labor force for the preceding three years. Once a firm has established a contracted-out plan, it can continue such a plan even if it later fails to meet the initial size and profitability requirements.

By setting up such a plan, contributions to Employees' Pension Insurance were reduced in 1994 by 3.2 percentage points, from 14.5% to 11.3% (see Table 1). The payment of contributions and the reduction in rates is shared equally by the employer and the employee.

These pay or play plans must participate in a national association called the Pension Fund Association. This association is a nonprofit private sector organization heavily influenced by the government through the Ministry of Health and Welfare. The Association provides several services. First, it insures the benefits in the plans. If an employer were to go bankrupt, the Pension Fund Association guarantees the benefits provided by the plan and pays beneficiaries.[5] Second, the association assures that there is no loss of benefits for employees changing jobs. The amount that has been accumulated for a job-changing employee is transferred to the Pension Fund Association. Third, for smaller employers, the Association, for a fee, provides administrative and record-keeping services. In this way, smaller employers can gain economies of scale in plan administration. The association also consults with plans at no charge concerning administrative problems. Fourth, the association researches issues concerning the administration and structure of plans.

The Japanese government has encouraged contracting out without subsidizing it. The government has the goal of having 50% of the full-time labor force participating in a contracted-out pension plan. The percentage has been growing over time; in 1993,

36% of the full-time labor force was in such a plan. That percentage has grown due to the reduction in the minimum-size requirement for employers to contract out and to regional groups of small employers having been allowed.

THE UNITED KINGDOM

While virtually every developed country has a social security system, the United Kingdom is unique in giving every employer and employee the option of contracting out of part of social security. Like Japan, the United Kingdom has a two-tier social security system supplemented by a voluntary private pension system. The British social security system consists of a flat benefit, called the National Insurance benefit, and an earnings-related benefit, called the State Earnings-Related Pension Scheme (SERPS), where benefits are financed by a tax levied within an earnings band. The flat rate benefit in the United Kingdom is related to years of service but not to earnings. Like in Japan, it is not possible to contract out of the British flat rate benefit, although such a policy has been discussed.

The British system differs considerably from the Japanese in the conditions under which contracting out can occur. While the Japanese restrict contracting out to certain firms or groups of firms, in the United Kingdom all firms can contract out of the earnings-related part of social security as long as they provide a benefit at least as generous. Most contracted-out defined-benefit plans provide benefits considerably greater than the minimum required. Contracted-out defined-benefit plans must base benefits on years of service and final earnings.

While the British place no restrictions on the types of firms contracting out, they attempt to assure that firms fully fund their contracted-out plans. The Occupational Pensions Board, an agency of the national government, has a statutory responsibility to ensure that employers fully fund the accrued liabilities for Guaranteed Minimum Pension (GMP) benefits. The plan's actuary must provide a regular certificate to this effect, and the Occupational Pensions Board relies heavily on this oversight provided by actuaries.

In addition, the British social security program guarantees that the Guaranteed Minimum Pension will be provided. This benefit equals the benefit that would have been provided had the social security benefit not been contracted-out. If a firm becomes bankrupt, the state assumes responsibility for paying the Guaranteed Minimum Pension. Contracted-out salary-related defined-benefit plans must pay at least the Guaranteed Minimum Pension. The Guaranteed Minimum Pension is approximately 25% of the worker's average indexed salary up to the ceiling salary, but the percentage will gradually fall to 20% in the early part of the next century.

In the United Kingdom, firms may unilaterally decide to contract out. They are required to consult with the relevant unions, if their workforce is unionized, but the decision is the employer's. About 50% of workers in the private and public sectors combined are covered by an employer-provided pension. Virtually 100% of public-sector employees covered by a pension are contracted out. In the private sector, 78% of members of occupational pension plans are contracted-out (Daykin, 1995).

When an employee joins a pension plan and becomes contracted out, the administration is simple. All that is required is for the employer's payroll department to deduct contributions for social security at the lower rate. When year-end filings are made to the Department of Social Security, the worker's change from contracted-in to contracted-out status will be recorded.

However, when an employee ends a job that is contracted out and moves to a job that is not contracted out, the administration is more complicated. Whenever an employee leaves a contracted-out plan, the government needs to know: (1) if contracted-out benefits are being preserved in the plan, (2) if contracted-out benefits are being transferred to another plan and who will be liable for paying them after the transfer, and (3) if the worker will be contracted-out in the new job.

If the job-leaver has less than two years of work in a contracted-out defined-benefit plan, the leaver may pay a premium to the government to restore the social security earnings-related benefits as if they had not been contracted-out.

Contracting Out With Defined-Contribution Plans

As in Japan, in the United Kingdom the contracting-out option has been expanded over time to make it available to more workers. Before the Social Security Act of 1986, the only way a firm or worker could contract out was by the firm providing a replacement defined-benefit plan. Since 1988, firms can also contract out using a money purchase defined-contribution plan. Unlike a salary-related plan, in a contracted-out money purchase plan there is no Guaranteed Minimum Pension. The employer and employee simply contribute to the contracted-out plan the amount they would have contributed to the State Earnings-Related Pension Scheme. Employers may offer workers a choice of a contracted-out money purchase plan or a contracted-out defined-benefit plan.

The participant in a contracted-out money purchase plan has "protected rights." These are the benefits secured by the value of the assets based on the social security contributions that are returned to the worker. Benefits based on protected rights can only be taken as an annuity at retirement age and then no earlier than age 60. The conversion to an annuity must be at a unisex rate. The pension must provide survivor's benefits to a widow or widower who has dependent children or is age 45 or older.

As well as allowing firms to contract out, British workers are permitted to contract out individually. Workers can opt out of the employer's contracted-out plan, providing instead a personal defined-contribution plan called an Appropriate Personal Pension. For personal pension plans, contracting out means authorizing the government to pay a rebate of social security contributions into a personal plan. This option represents a fundamental change from compulsory to voluntary membership in employer-provided plans.

Appropriate Personal Pensions purchased with contracting-out rebates must be taken as an annuity, with 3% a year pension increases and a benefit to a surviving spouse of half the member's pension. Additional contributions can be applied for other forms of benefits.

Appropriate Personal Pensions can be used by all employees regardless of whether or not their employer offers a plan. However, Appropriate Personal Pensions are not financially sensible for low-income workers because there are fixed costs for establishing and maintaining such plans. Because the contributions of low-income workers into these plans are necessarily low, the fixed costs are too high a percentage of the contributions to make these plans feasible.

Like any personal pension, an Appropriate Personal Pension can be arranged directly with the provider with no involvement from the employer. Providers include insurance companies, banks, building societies, unit trusts, and friendly societies.[6] Since the employer will often be unaware that the worker has an Appropriate Personal Pension, the existence of such a pension plan has no effect on the worker's social security contributions, which continue to be paid in full. The rebate is achieved by a payment, after the end of each tax year, from the Department of Health and Social Security directly to the provider. In addition, a rebate is made of the personal income tax paid on the employee's share of the social security contribution. The rebate does not include interest on the social security contributions or income tax payments, which could have been paid in part more than 12 months earlier.[7] Under this method, as late as the end of the tax year, contracting out can be backdated to the beginning of the tax year. An employee may opt out of his company's contributory pension plan, where he may be paying as much as 5% or 6%, in favor of a contracted-out personal pension plan where he would only be required to contribute 2%. His retirement income would be reduced, however.

Using an Appropriate Personal Pension, employees can opt out from a contracted-out employer-provided pension plan. This option complicates the financial calculus for the employer attempting to decide whether to provide a contracted-out plan. If all young employees opt out, it may not be financially beneficial for the employer to provide a contracted-out plan because the employer is left with the responsibility of paying for the older, high-cost employees. Whether or not it is financially advantageous to a firm to contract out will depend on the age-sex composition of the plan after individuals elect to opt out.

Between 1988 and 1992, it has been estimated that the British government paid £10.5 billion to people taking out personal pensions, in the form of rebates on social security contributions. But not all these rebates end up as assets in pension plans. Insurance industry experts estimate that companies selling personal pensions typically take between 4% and 13% in commissions and charges for sales agents and management fees (Cohen, 1994).

As of April 1992, more than 300,000 men and women who contracted out of the social security State Earnings-Related Pension Scheme through a personal pension were going to receive lower benefits on retirement than if they had remained contracted-in. That is because the rebate system gives more than a young person needs to buy pension benefits equivalent to the social security State Earnings-Related Pension Scheme benefits, but far less than an older person would need (Cohen, 1994).

Contracting out through use of a personal pension plan is a reversible decision. Workers can later change their minds and rejoin the government program, but that option is available only once. For workers who opt out of their employer's contracted-out pension plan, the employer need not give the option to rejoin. Employers allowing workers to rejoin may require evidence of good health so that the employer's death benefits are not exploited.

Inflation Protection

For early job-leavers, the contracted-out plan is required to provide cost-of-living adjustments to the value of accrued benefits between the point of job leaving and retirement in the United Kingdom.[8] In Japan, by contrast, social security is responsible for such adjustments for the basic contracted-out benefit.

Both the Japanese and British governments have been reluctant to impose the full cost of postretirement inflation indexing on firms with contracted-out plans. In the United Kingdom, the government pays much of the cost of indexation for the Guaranteed Minimum Pension after the worker retires. For benefits accruing after 1988, the firm is obligated to pay the cost of indexation up to 3% a year. For workers contracted out using a defined-contribution plan, the annuity benefits from such a plan must be indexed for inflation up to 3% a year. Since inflation generally is higher than 3%, the annuity benefits provided by the employer effectively become an increasing annuity with a 3% annual increase. For inflation higher than 3%, the government provides full indexing. In the Japanese pension system, the government pays all the cost of postretirement inflation indexing of contracted-out benefits.

The Contracted-out Rebate

The reduction in social security contributions when contracted out is based on the estimated cost to plans of providing the Guaranteed Minimum Pension. With these three methods of contracting out—defined-benefit plans, employer-provided money purchase plans, and personal pension plans—social security benefits are reduced for someone who has been contracted out by an amount based on the worker's earnings while contracted out. This reduction is the same for each method. The amount of the reduction is intended to be sufficient to provide the worker with the same level of benefits as would have been provided through social security alone.

The contracted-out rebate has been independent of both the age and sex of the worker. The cost of an employee's contracted-out benefit, however, rises with age. At age 25, it is between 2% and 3% of earnings. At age 55, it may be 9% or more. Because of the constancy of the rebate across ages, the likelihood of having a better financial deal through a personal pension than through the government program declines as workers age. Different investment advisers suggest different ages for contracting back into the government program. For example, Prudential advises men age 49 and older and women age 42 and older to rejoin. The age is lower for women because they can currently receive social security benefits at younger ages than men. The calculations underlying these figures depend on assumptions about annuity rates at retirement and investment returns before then.

The British have provided stronger incentives for contracting out than the Japanese. Between April 6, 1988 and April 5, 1993, in addition to the regular rebate, incentive payments of 2% of covered earnings were made to workers in newly contracted-out plans. Incentive payments of 2% were also made to workers in Appropriate Personal Pensions. In this way, the British government has favored contracting out through personal plans, an option unavailable in Japan. Also, workers who had been in contracted-out employer-provided plans for less than two years could receive the 2% incentive payment if they started an Appropriate Personal Pension. About two-thirds of contracted-out workers are in employer-sponsored plans; the other third is in personal pension plans.

The contracting-out incentives continue to change over time in the United Kingdom. A 1% incentive for Appropriate Pension Plan holders over the age of 30 began in April of 1993. The British government has announced its intention to consider a more finely tuned age-related rebate structure starting in 1996.

Other incentives encourage contracting out. First, pension contributions of workers are tax deductible, while their social security contributions are not. Second, social security benefits are only payable at age 65 for men and 60 for women, while contracted-out benefits can be provided earlier.

Over time, the contracting-out rebate has fallen in the United Kingdom, while it has risen in Japan (Table 1). Table 2 shows the decline in the contracting-out rebate over time in the United Kingdom. This decline has occurred in part due to the decline in the generosity of the state earnings-related pension. The rebates are periodically reviewed and have been reduced after considering the underlying economic and demographic assumptions. The rebate is calculated based on assumptions about the age/sex/earnings profile of the contracted-out population and assumptions about future investment returns and earnings growth, as well as other actuarial assumptions.

The economic assumptions used in calculating the 1988-1989 rebate were a 8.5% investment return and a 7% annual growth in earnings. The assumptions provide a generous rebate. The reduction in the rebate made in 1988 was due in part to the reduction that year in the accrual rate for future social security State Earnings-Related Pension Scheme (SERPS) benefits. The terms for contracting out became less favorable starting in 1993. This may result in many workers in contracted-out plans rejoining the State Earnings-Related Pension Scheme program. The 1% incentive for workers over 30 is designed to counteract that.

Table 2. Contracting-out Rebate in the United Kingdom

Starting in Tax Year	*Employer (%)*	*Employee (%)*	*Total (%)*
1978/79	4.50	2.50	7.00
1983/84	4.10	2.15	6.25
1988/89	3.80	2.00	5.80
1993/94	3.00	1.80	4.80

Note: The tax year runs from April 6 through April 5 of the following year.

Contracting out can be thought of as a means of borrowing from the state. The firm or worker receives contribution rebates now but will have to meet future pension obligations. Moreover, in the United Kingdom it is a form of indexed borrowing because of the requirements for indexation of benefits. It follows that the attractiveness of contracting out will depend on the rate of return that can be earned on pension plan assets versus the implicit rate of return earned on contributions to social security.

Administrative Considerations

For every person in paid employment, the government keeps a record of social security contributions, the earnings on which those have been paid, and the rate at which the contributions have been deducted. It uses this information to calculate the worker's social security earnings-related benefits, the worker's contracted-out Guaranteed Minimum Pension benefits, and which employer is liable to pay the contracted-out benefits. At retirement, an earnings-related social security benefit is calculated as if the employee had been earning benefits in the government program for the whole period of employment. The Guaranteed Minimum Pension relating to contracted-out service is deducted from this amount and the balance is paid by the government. Each year, the state increases the earnings-related pension benefits of retirees in line with the Retail Price Index and deducts the Guaranteed Minimum Pension plus any post-1988 increases that are paid by the employer-provided plan.

The process is similar for employees who have participated in contracted-out defined-contribution (money purchase) plans. On reaching retirement age, the government calculates the Guaranteed Minimum Pension that would have accrued if the employee had been in a contracted-out defined-benefit plan. This is deducted from the earnings-related benefit based on having not contracted out, and the difference is paid by the government.

Risk Bearing

In contracted-out defined-contribution plans, the worker bears the investment risk. If the actual benefit based on the assets in the defined-contribution plan is lower than it would have been had the worker contracted out into a defined-benefit plan, the government does not make up the difference. Similarly, if the actual benefit is higher, the government does not reduce the social security benefit it provides. Thus, while contracting out through a defined-benefit plan does not affect a worker's entitlement or risk, contracting out through a defined-contribution plan alters the worker's risk because the government defined-benefit plan is replaced by a private-sector defined-contribution plan.

CRITIQUE

Attractive features of contracting out include reduced reliance on the government and greater reliance on the private sector, greater incentives for private savings and investment, and more flexibility in shaping pension plans.

With contracting out, a public pension program that is largely underfunded is replaced by a private pension program designed to be fully funded and invested in the private sector. Thus, an advantage of contracting out is that it may increase savings and the national capital stock.

Contracting out expands the range of options open to firms and workers for providing for retirement income. The expanded range of choice provides greater flexibility and may allow individuals to better provide for their retirement in the manner they wish to.

In both Japan and the United Kingdom, when the social security earnings-related benefit program was started, there were already well-developed private pension plans. Contracting out was a way to protect the interests of the middle class who had substantial pension rights.[9] Thus, contracting out can be thought of as a way of providing an option for higher-income workers who are covered by a private pension to not fully participate in social security.

Financing the Transition

One of the issues in privatizing social security is how to pay for the existing social security liabilities during the transition period from a fully state-run program to a privatized program. When employers in Japan establish Employees' Pension Funds, the size of the government social security program is reduced.

The size of contributions are reduced immediately, and the level of benefit payments are reduced in the future. If the Japanese social security system had operated on a pay-as-you-go basis, it would have been necessary to raise the social security payroll tax rate when contracting out was started in order to make up the lost revenue needed for current benefit payments. The Japanese social security program is not operated on a pay-as-you-go basis, however, but rather is partially funded. For that reason, an increase in tax rates was not required when the Japanese contracting-out option was begun.

With a redistributive social security system, where it is possible to contract out fully from the redistributive portion, such a system would not be viable because all the high earners would contract out, leaving nothing to be redistributed to the low earners. In the United Kingdom, the higher-earnings contracted-out employees pay considerably more in social security taxes than do lower-earnings employees, but both receive the same flat benefit. Thus, the redistributive aspect of the system is maintained.

Some Problems with Contracting Out

In the United Kingdom, contracted-out defined-benefit plans only need replace the level of benefits that would have been provided by social security, while in Japan the contracted-out benefits must be at least 30% higher than the social security benefits. Many employer-provided contracted-out plans in the United Kingdom provide higher benefits than the minimum required, but that is not the case for the personal contracted-out plans (Appropriate Personal Pensions). There is concern that people relying on those plans will end up with low retirement income.

State-run social security systems presumably have an advantage over private systems in cost. Because participation in state-run systems is mandatory, those systems incur no advertising costs. They also may be more efficient due to economies of scale. However, because they do not run under a profit motive, their incentives for efficiency are less.

When contracting out is an individual decision, a greater burden of responsibility is placed on the individual for becoming informed and making prudent decisions concerning his or her retirement financing. There is also the possibility of abuse, due to workers' lack of knowledge, by pension service providers with a financial interest in workers contracting out. There is considerable concern in Britain that more than two million people who have contracted-out may have been wrongly advised by insurance companies to leave the social security earnings-related program or employer-provided plans and take out personal pensions.

A criticism of the British contracting-out system is that it is too complicated. While complexity has the advantage that it may create a range of choices, it also increases costs because it creates a demand for the services of actuaries and other highly paid benefits consultants.

Adverse Selection

Critics of contracting out often cite adverse selection as a problem for the financing of such plans. With adverse selection, the firms with employees for whom benefits can be provided inexpensively leave the government program, as they can provide benefits more cheaply on their own. This exodus of low-cost firms raises the average cost of providing benefits for firms remaining in the government program, which causes a further exodus of firms that have relatively low costs.

A requirement that only large firms can contract out limits adverse selection to the extent that large firms have workforces with age distributions similar to that of the national workforce. The Government Actuary's office in the United Kingdom has argued that the age structure of the British workforce does not differ greatly across firms. However, in Japan, as in the United States, some large computer software companies have young workforces, while some steel producing companies have older workforces. Benefits are generally less expensive to provide for younger workforces through contracting out than through the government program.

Adverse selection is also limited by not allowing firms to freely withdraw from contracting out once they have established a contracted-out plan. If firms can withdraw when it is favorable to do so, adverse selection is increased. In Japan, a firm must have the approval of its employees to end an Employees' Pension Fund plan.

Adverse selection is also limited in Japan because the earnings-related part of the Japanese social security system is not redistributive from high-to low-income workers. The redistributive aspect of the U.S. social security system makes contracting out more difficult to establish because high-income workers and firms would tend to favor contracting out while low-income workers and firms would tend to favor remaining fully in the system. That problem has been solved in the United Kingdom, however, where redistribution occurs through the higher social security tax rates paid by higher-income contracted-out employees.

In spite of the incentive for adverse selection in the Japanese system and the possibility of adverse selection by small firms joining regional or industry groups, according to government actuaries the average age in contracted-out plans is similar to the average age in the workforce in Japan.

To limit adverse selection in Japan, one proposal being considered would vary the terms of contracting out based on the average age of the employees in the firm. Firms with an older average age would be allowed more favorable terms for contracting out because it is more expensive for those firms to provide the required benefits. A similar proposal on an individual basis is being considered in the United Kingdom.

CONCLUSIONS

The British and Japanese systems provide a program for voluntarily privatizing government benefits. The British and Japanese together have had more than 50 years of experience with their programs. Both programs have been modified several times, consistent with the desire to encourage firms and workers to contract out.

Compared to the Chilean approach of privatizing social security through a mandatory defined-contribution plan, the British and Japanese approaches have more options and allow firms to select the form in which retirement income is provided. British and Japanese workers in defined-benefit plans do not bear the risks of pension asset value fluctuations, while those risks are borne by Chilean workers and British workers in contracted-out defined-contribution plans. Both defined-benefit and defined-contribution approaches offer funded alternatives to unfunded social security systems.

ACKNOWLEDGMENT

The material in this chapter the responsibility of the authors and does not represent the position of the Institut de Recherches Economiques et Sociales or any other institution with which the authors are affiliated.

NOTES

1. See Clark (1991) for a description of the Japanese pension system and Turner and Dailey (1991) for a description of the British and Japanese systems.
2. The term "contract out" is synonymous with "pay or play;" it is the term that has been used in describing such an option for pensions.
3. In the United States, state governments that have historically not participated in social security are allowed to opt out of social security, but there are no requirements concerning alternative retirement plans they might provide. The option is not available to firms.
4. In addition, pay or play pensions in Japan provide a possible model for privatizing U.S. unemployment insurance, where large firms could privately contract for such insurance.
5. The insurance program has operated since 1989. As of 1993, no plans had terminated with insufficient assets.
6. A friendly society is a type of small financial institution in the United Kingdom, owned by its members, that offers sickness, retirement, unemployment, and death benefits, as well as savings plans, to its members.
7. An advantage of a contracted-out money purchase plan is that the rebate is paid directly into the plan with no delay.
8. The contracted-out plan can choose between three methods for revaluing benefits: (1) complete indexation, (2) a fixed 7% per year, and (3) 5% per year or full indexation if lower.
9. That situation was similar to the situation in the United States, where workers in the railroad industry and state, local, government, and federal workers were not required to participate in social security when it was started.

REFERENCES

Clark, R.L. 1991. *Retirement Systems in Japan.* Philadelphia, PA: The Pension Research Council of the Wharton School, University of Pennsylvania.

Cohen, N. 1994. "Pensions Switch May Have Cost Taxpayers 1.2 Billion Pounds." *Financial Times* (February 28): 1.

Daykin, C. 1995. "Occupational Pension Provision in the United Kingdom." In Z. Bodie, O. Mitchell and J. Turner (eds.), *Securing Employer-Provided Pensions: An International Perspective.* Philadelphia: University of Pennsylvania Press, forthcoming.

Pension Fund Association. 1993. *Pension Fund Association.* Tokyo.

Turner, J.A. and L.M. Dailey (eds.). 1991. *Pension Policy: An International Perspective.* Washington, DC: U.S. Government Printing Office.

FINANCING OLD-AGE PENSIONS: THE CHALLENGE TO PUBLIC PROVISION IN CENTRAL AND EASTERN EUROPE

David M. Rajnes

INTRODUCTION

Old-age pension systems in central and eastern Europe (CEE) share a common predicament experienced by many systems worldwide. Such public systems provide inadequate protection while imposing a heavy fiscal burden. This is nowhere more apparent than in countries of the CEE region, who are attempting a radical economic transformation from a planned economy to a market economy. Public provision of state pensions that rely on largely unfunded mechanisms to see them through is becoming increasingly difficult for such countries in transition. Forced to deal with systemic flaws built into a public pay-as-you-go (PAYG) framework, policymakers watch as pension transfers consume an ever-increasing share of state budgets. Given their unsustainability under current circumstances, pension reform is demanded.

This paper sets out to accomplish two goals. First, an overview of CEE regional pension systems is outlined. A general picture is formulated of these systems as they emerged from nearly five decades of Soviet influence. This is followed by brief descriptions of individual country situations and their respective reform agendas since the collapse of the Iron Curtain in 1989. CEE regional countries analyzed in this paper include: the Czech and Slovak Republics, Poland, Hungary, Bulgaria, and Romania. A second objective of this paper is to describe the Hungarian experience with old-age pension reform. That country poses an interesting case study for several reasons. First, Hungary's future demographic pressures are among the most severe in the region. The country's reputation as a trendsetter in a number of reform areas, including pension reform, is a second aspect that attracts our attention. Finally, the current gridlock in Hungarian pension reform efforts reflects the institutional, political, and economic constraints in which such a reform process must operate.

THE PUBLIC PENSION PROBLEM

Countries in the CEE region share a common social security heritage that includes similar public provision for old-age pensions. Virtually all public pension systems in CEE countries find themselves in severe financial difficulties. Their situations are not linked to past or current demographic developments. Current problems tend to be more systemic. The main features of CEE retirement income programs in the early postsocialist era have included: rather nonintegrated pension programs across professions favoring certain work categories; low standard retirement ages (60 for men, 55 for women), generally, with even lower standards for special categories; extremely progressive benefit formulas containing very small annual accrual factors and virtually no actuarial decrements (increments) for early (late) retirement; absence of retirement tests for beneficiaries receiving untaxed (but unindexed) benefits; and benefit financing exacted through social security contributions covering all main social programs (pension, sickness, and family benefits)—that is, no earmarking for pensions (Holzmann, 1992; Atkins, 1991).

Table 1. Financial Characteristics of Central and East European Retirement Systems, 1993

Country	*Normal Retirement Age Men (M), Women (W)*	*Average Replacement Rate*[1] *(%) [Pension as Percent of Average Wage]*	*Automatic Inflation Index*	*Employer Payroll Tax Rate*[2]	*Employee Payroll Tax Rate*[2]
Czechoslovakia	M: 60	55	No	20.4	6.8
	W: 53-7	[49]		20.6	5.9
Hungary	M: 60	70	Yes	24.5	6.0
	W: 55	[49]			
Poland	M: 65	80	Yes	32.0	0.0
	W: 60	[74]			
Bulgaria	M: 60	80	No	35.0	0.0
	W: 55	[34]			
Romania	M: 60	54-85	No	25.5	0.0
	W: 55	[43]			
United States	65	41	Yes	6.2	6.2

Notes: [1] The "average replacement rate" represents the percentage of previous earnings accounted for by retirement income received across all age groups.
[2] Self-employed tax rates often approach or equal that of the combined payroll tax rate.

Sources: Pension as percentage of average wage in column three taken from *The Economist*; average replacement rates in column three taken from Hambor (1992), Hambor and Ross (1992), and Romania (1993); indexation listing from country source materials; all remaining information from U.S. Social Security Administration (1994).

The benefit structures themselves, as expected in formerly centrally planned systems, have had great redistributive features. As a consequence, expenditure levels are high, requiring firms—both public and private—to contribute extensive portions of their payrolls and to demand supplemental financing from the state budget. Table 1 shows the generosity characteristic of CEE retirement schemes—relatively young retirement ages and high replacement rates—as well as the high payroll tax. Although several countries now require employee contributions, employers (consistent with the Soviet-era practice) assume most of this burden. The United States is included for comparison.

Looking to the future, a key problem area will lie with the demographic profile of these countries. Projected reductions in fertility along with increasing life expectancy rates will translate into relatively fewer and fewer workers to support a rising retiree population. Table 2 provides ample evidence that CEE country financial difficulties are not only immediate but long term. The "aged" dependency ratio, defined as the population 65 years or older per 100 persons considered potentially active in the labor force (ages 15-64 years), is a reasonable indicator of future

Table 2. Aged and System Dependency Rations in Selected Central and East European Countries, 1990-2025

		Projections	
Country	*Age [System] Dependency Ratios 1990*[1]	*2010*	*2025*
Poland	18 [49]	21	36
Czechoslovakia	21 [—]	24	35
Hungary	23 [59]	28	40
Bulgaria	23 [87]	30	39
Romania	18 [62]	26	34
United States	19.1	19.1	29.0

Note: [1] "Aged" dependency ratios are defined here as the number of elderly (age 65 or older) per 100 labor force participants (aged 15-64). These figures will tend to understate CEE experience to the extent that actual retirement ages are in the 55-60 year range. A more appropriate figure is the "system" dependency ratio of pensioners to labor force contributors noted in brackets.

Sources: 1990 figures for system dependency ratio come from Fox (1993); the U.S. data was taken from United Nations (1992, Table A.17); remaining information from Velkoff and Kinsella.

developments. Any movement upwards in that statistic suggests that the workforce will have to support an increasing number of retired persons—an expectation for each CEE country listed here by the year 2025.[1] More realistic is the "system" dependency ratio relating the actual pensioners to covered workers. Figures for 1990 indicate that most CEE countries are experiencing levels in excess of 50—that is, two workers per retiree or worse.

Data on ratios for potential workers-per-retiree are available for a select group of countries to the year 2025 (shown in Table 3).[2] That statistic, given some modification for "normal" retirement age, is the reciprocal of the system dependency ratio. The decline in this ratio over time clearly shows a narrowing of the revenue base per retiree, a development expected well into the 21st century due to the mortality and fertility rate developments discussed previously. We can use this data to gauge the future claim of pensions, measured as a percentage of payroll, for the same group of PAYG systems listed in Table 3.

Drawing on demographic patterns and benefit levels in each country (circa 1992), "simplified PAYG cost rates" may be constructed. This is done by multiplying the reciprocal of the worker-retiree ratio introduced in Table 3 by the average "replacement rate"—that is, the percentage of preretirement income that pension beneficiaries receive, as shown in Table 1. These figures are entered in Table 4 for three CEE countries and the United States. Several simplifying assumptions are built into these projections, for example, 1990 wage indexation of benefits and estimated average replacement rates continued throughout the projection period.[3] Thus, the figures entered are not exact products

Table 3. Potential Workers Per Retiree for Selected Central and East European Countries and the United States, 1950-2025

Country	*1950*	*1990*	*2025*
Czechoslovakia	3.7	2.6	2.0
Hungary	3.8	2.1	1.5
Poland	4.9	2.9	2.0
United States	7.1	4.7	2.9

Note: Information is based on *normal* retirement ages for each country.

Sources: Calculated from United Nations (1988) and Hambor (1992, table 4).

Table 4. Simplified Pay Cost Rates for Selected East European Countries and the United States, 1990-2025

Country	*1990*	*2025*	*Percentage Increase*
Czechoslovakia	21.3	28.2	32.4
Hungary	34.0	45.3	33.2
Poland	28.0	40.7	45.4
United States	8.7	14.3	64.4

Note: Rates represent the percent of payroll claimed by social security system and are constructed by multiplying the reciprocal of worker-retiree ratios by replacement ratios with some modifying assumptions.

Source: Hambor (1992, table 5).

of corresponding entries from Table 1 and Table 3. The data show these cost rates rising with the projected increase expressed as a percentage. That information suggests that Czechoslovak (combined Czech and Slovak) and Hungarian cost rates would increase by approximately one-third by the year 2025, while the future cost of pensions in Poland should rise by over 45%. Equally sobering are the financial implications that the absolute cost rate amounts entail—reaching above 28% for the Czechoslovak area and approximately 45% and 41% for Hungary and Poland, respectively, in the next century. Table 5 shows the 1992 situation for pensions both as a percentage of national GDP (ranging from 6.7% to 11.4%) and within CEE government expenditure patterns (accounting from 16.8% to 24.8%). An Organization for Economic Cooperation and Development (OECD) (lower) average is listed for comparison.

REVIEW OF INDIVIDUAL COUNTRY SITUATIONS

Poland

Broad agreement exists that the system[4] is experiencing a crisis. A separate social insurance trust fund for workers has existed since 1987. Rising social security taxes on employers (currently 45% of the wage bill) and a steady increase in subsidies from the central budget have not been sufficient to stem a growing gap between revenues and expenditures since 1989. The three primary factors contributing to the situation include an aging population, several years of economic slowdown eroding the tax base, and an overly

Table 5. Selected Fiscal Pension Indicators, 1992

Country	*Pension Expenditure as Percent of GDP*	*Pensions as Percent of Government Expenditure*
Poland	11.4	24.8
Hungary	10.6	18.6
Czechoslovakia	9.5	16.8
Bulgaria	8.4	21.5
Romania	6.7	16.8
OECD[1]	6.1	—

Note: [1] OECD is an average of the seven largest economies.

Sources: OECD information from OECD (1988); remaining data taken from World Bank figures as given in "Old and Unaffordable" (1994).

generous benefit system favoring certain occupations, the unemployed, and the disabled. These factors have contributed to a declining worker-retiree ratio. Economic restructuring in the 1990s has brought with it tax evasion and nonpayment of payroll taxes by enterprises.

Since 1989, the government has been politically pressed to make the benefit system fairly inflation-resistant but at considerable cost, through revaluation in 1991 of virtually all pensions and the quarterly indexation of pension benefits. The 1991 legislation established a new benefit formula and gradually increased the number of working years used to calculate the earnings base, placed a ceiling on pension benefits equal to 250% of the average wage, and eliminated certain sector-specific occupational benefits. Despite its reform efforts, the government was unable to reach a political consensus to continue in this direction; instead, some of its previous achievements were soon repealed—for example, sector-specific benefits were reintroduced in 1993. Capping a growing state budget subsidy remains a prime concern. That subsidy is forecast to equal $6 billion in 1994—a 34% rise over 1993—or about 18% of GDP. Successive Polish governments have answered the crisis by focusing on a number of proposals: creation of a new agency to oversee the collection of social insurance premiums, introduction of individual social security accounts, elimination of excessive or unjustified benefits, raising the retirement age for both men and women (and their eventual equalization), and changes in the tax code to allow for premium deductions from income tax for both firms and employees. The government is considering a two-tier framework that calls for a basic grant to be financed by shared (employer-employee) contributions guaranteed by the government and supplemented by a funded scheme.[5] The latter funding mechanism will require some oversight. No change is expected in the near future, given the current political climate.

Czech Republic and Slovakia

Demographic developments threaten the future finance picture of both republics.[6] The Czech Republic, unlike Slovakia and other CEE countries, possesses a state pension system that operates in surplus—representing 6% of total social expenditure in 1993 (Czech Statistical Office)—so much so that the government has resisted delinking the social security system from the central budget. No doubt, shrewd fiscal management and a low unemployment rate have helped keep Czech pension revenues relatively high. Before the partition in 1993, both Slovakia and the Czech Republic had laid the groundwork for future legislation that included a shared (employer-employee) PAYG funding structure, an autonomous budget, the elimination of privileged treatment for certain occupations, and unification of the retirement age between sexes and its gradual rise to age 62 (from 57) after the year 2005.

Several proposals that are to be acted on by the Czech government in 1995 include: extending the base period on which to calculate benefits, taxation of those benefits, reducing noncontributory periods of credit, automatic indexation of the earning, base used to compute pensions, and tightening eligibility requirements for invalidity conditions. A private pension law was implemented in the Czech Republic in 1994; it relies on a government subsidy rather than tax exemptions. Legislation to both reform the public provision and provide for some manner of private scheme in Slovakia is expected in the near future.

Hungary

The country's public pension system[7] is fiscally unsustainable. Many analyses note its many adverse incentives. Reform efforts have been driven by the need to restrain rising costs. Several factors account for these high expenditures: demographics, a low retirement age, certain features of the benefit formula, and the ease of obtaining disability and early retirement pensions. Keeping pace with much higher rates of inflation has been difficult for pensioners despite a twice-yearly, ad hoc indexation of pensions, since these increases have been at amounts less than the level of inflation. High payroll taxes have encouraged tax evasion. A 1993 government report stated that approximately one-fifth of expected Social Security Administration contributions were in arrears. This situation will continue to threaten the solvency of the Pension Insurance Fund.

A separate trust fund for social insurance was established by 1990 and superseded by a pension-specific trust fund two years later. During that time, the parliament made a number of modifications to the pension law: the minimum service period required for eligibility was raised from 10 to 20 years; the insurance period limitation was lifted to encourage longer working lives; the base period for averaging earnings was extended to the five years preceding retirement; taxable remuneration provided by employers was broadened to include insurance and in-kind employee benefits; an income ceiling was set for employee (not employer) contributions; and postretirement income for retirees was made taxable at the employee rate. More recently, institutional modifications and a new law on private pensions have taken effect.

Bulgaria

Affordability is a major problem for public pension provision in Bulgaria,[8] as pension expenditures rose above 8% of GDP in 1992. Fed by low retirement ages, unfavorable demographic patterns, emigration of young people, and the rapid rise in retirements since the late 1980s (a generous early retirement policy), the pension system dependency ratio rose from 0.56 in 1989 to 0.87 in the early 1990s. Pensioners, currently around 40% of the population, pose a potent political force. For example, when hyperinflation devalued the average pension benefit by 40% over 1991-1992, pensioners successfully pressured the government to offer partial compensation during 1992.

Government concern over these problem areas and the rising system deficits they cause led to adoption of the Pension Reform Act in 1992. Beginning in January of 1993, the early retirement age was raised by two years; a simpler benefit formula was invoked to encourage those above the retirement age to keep working, and a ceiling was placed on the benefit amount. To address the erosion of benefits from high inflation, the government is considering a costly wage-based indexation of benefits. Since the pension fund along with other social funds was separated from the state budget in 1990, a draft law has called for an independent social security agency and the delinking of trust funds from the central budget.

Romania

Pension expenditure is a significant and growing share of Romania's[9] GDP and the country's largest public expenditure item, rising above 7% in 1990. Retirement ages, while quite low, differ among designated work categories and, within them, by sex and profession. Until 1992, six different pension systems coexisted. All of this diversity tends toward unequal treatment. Areas of concern include: the loss of purchasing power due to inflation (given ad hoc indexation), the absence of a ceiling on employer contributions (a potential distortion for the labor market), decreasing accrual rates that discourage workers from continuing beyond the standard retirement age, the presence of noncontributory periods in the base on which the benefits are calculated, and the exemption of pensions from tax liability. In addition, the nation's demographics weigh heavily on future system liabilities. Tax evasion is a growing problem, owing to voluntary compliance, weak penalties, and inefficient tax collection.

Since 1991, the social security budget, including the state social security fund and a supplemental pension fund, have been managed apart from the state budget. System unification has been pursued since 1992, when several of the smaller pension schemes were integrated into the primary system. Amendments to the social security law in 1992 specified higher contribution rates, particularly for those employed in occupations subject to early retirement programs. The 1993 government White Paper proposed a number of changes: complete integration of all independent pension systems, a new semiautonomous agency, a simpler benefit formula to improve the link between contributions and benefits, raising the retirement age, lowering the employer tax rate by employing a shared contribution format, and lengthening the earnings period. A private pension scheme is anticipated.

Analysis

Evidence since 1989 would seem to indicate that all CEE countries are making efforts to change much of the state pension systems they have inherited from the Soviet era. There have been similar attempts to tighten eligibility, establish separate trust funds, mandate shared (employer-employee) payroll taxes earmarked for these funds, raise retirement ages, initiate indexing of pensions, and deal with pension formulas in ways to encourage longer working lives. Cost containment is paramount behind all of this activity.

It should be obvious, though, that the PAYG model is here to stay, as no movement to transform existing systems is expected, save in the Czech Republic. Yet, even the Czech move to a two-tier scheme still retains a PAYG format in the earnings-related portion, and the overall retention of the system within the central budget places pension flow-of-funds on a nontransparent basis. Other countries—for example, Poland and Bulgaria—have been constrained by politics in a time of severe structural adjustment. Private sector initiatives for pensions are scarce, though they can be found in the Czech Republic and Hungary. In summary, transitional countries of the CEE region have not escaped (with one exception) the financial woes attending public pension provision. The question to be asked is: Can they do so? Hungary offers some lessons.

HUNGARIAN PENSION PROVISION: A CASE STUDY

Pension Reform in Postsocialist Hungary

During the late 1980s, intense discussion centered on pension reform, leading to the creation of a Social Insurance Fund (SIF) in 1990 responsible for financing all pensions as well as other social security programs, including health care. By 1992, the Pension Insurance Fund (old age, disability, and survivors) and the Health Insurance Fund were formally separated from the SIF. Earlier analyses drafted by the government in 1991 that focused on changing the system of publicly provided pensions were submitted to parliament for study.[10] Three proposals stood out: a two-tier system combining a redistributive basic grant along with an earnings-related scheme; provision for voluntary forms of insurance that would replace much of the PAYG structure by establishing a network of nonprofit pension funds (related to regions or professions) based on institutional or personal contract; and the encouragement of defined-contribution pension plans through tax incentives.

In late 1991, Parliament passed the Law on the Management of Social Insurance at the Local Self-Government Level that would establish the future governance structure for public pensions. By 1993, a self-governing "board" began to oversee the independent Pension Insurance Fund (PIF).[11] Its role is to represent participating employers and employees in the pension system (World Bank 1993b). Employees directly elect their board representatives for four-year terms (board elections are held jointly with those for trade unions), while employers delegate their representatives through employer organizations (Buttrick, 1991). The board contains a general assembly, presidium, and a supervisory board. Power rests with the general assembly.[12] More than half (36) of its 60 members are elected by employee delegates. The board's general assembly sets pension policy, including control of the property owned by the public insurance system. A two-thirds vote of delegates is required to: modify the board's constitution, alter the development of pension policy, approve the budget, or elect (appoint) respective officers (managers). Daily business is conducted by an 11-member presidium with the aid of an employer-dominated supervisory board that monitors the management and financial matters of the insurance self-government body.

In addition to important institutional changes in pension fund administration, the legislature also prescribed a separation of the pension benefit into flat-rate and earnings-related components in 1992.[13] Private pensions in the form of voluntary mutual benefit funds (VMBFs), based on the principle of mutual insurance, were also established on a defined contribution basis in late 1993. VMBFs possess a number of favorable tax consequences, particularly the exemption of employer contributions from social security charges (IBIS, 1993-1994; Batty et al., 1994). Under the legislation, funds may be established for a particular employer as well as on a regional, occupational, or trade basis.

Future Pension Reform Prospects

The future path of pension reform is unclear, as change in the public system ground to a halt in 1994. An examination of three dimensions contributing to the present situation—institutions, politics, and economics—helps to explain the current impasse.

Institutional Setting

The Hungarian pension fund board is entitled to consult with and advise parliament. The Hungarian parliament, for its part, must confer with the board prior to voting on legislation affecting pensions. However, if the board disagrees with a particular piece of legislation, it may exercise veto power over the law—something no other European country with a similar system has granted its board (Pataki, 1993). Ownership rights to pension fund assets mean that the board wields considerable economic power and political influence—another more unusual aspect of the Hungarian situation.

Political Environment

Following national elections in 1990, the then-victorious Hungarian Democratic Forum (HDF) formed a three-party coalition. Over the next four years, party fragmentation hampered the coalition's ability to move forward on its stated goal to privatize and let markets reverse state dominance of the economy (Okolicsanyi, 1994). Elections in April and May of 1994 restored the former communists, reborn as the Hungarian Socialist Party (HSP), to power in the country. Their pledge to forge ahead on reforms remains to be tested. The strong HSP showing in the general elections might encourage the National Federation of Hungarian Trade Unions (MSZOSZ) or other HSP factions to exert pressures to slow reforms, to ease the pain of economic transformation, or to demand higher social spending (Oltay, 1994).

Economic Constraints

Hungary's 1990-1994 reform experience reflected a tradeoff between a fledgling multiparty parliamentary system of government and the speed of fiscal reform. The magnitude of the reform agenda burdened an inexperienced legislature. Over time, it became increasingly difficult to enact reform proposals as scheduled without amendments that diluted key program issues. As the process slowed down, powerful interest groups strove to prevent a relatively weak legislative body from enacting reform measures calculated to close preferential loopholes, for example, entitlement for early retirement as advocated by employee groups (Kopits, 1993). Further (nonpension) reforms lie ahead, for example, transformation of the banks and the financial system. Complicating the calculus is a limited or no-growth prospect for the economy.

Analysis of Hungary's Situation

On balance, the confluence of this trio of forces—institutions, politics, and economics—strengthens the public pension system's resistance to change in the near term. Since parliament's 1991 review of proposed solutions to the pension problem, no one strategy has attracted a sufficient following.[14] What Hungary can expect in the short run is further tinkering with the PAYG framework. As the VMBF system expands, higher wage earners will be drawn to these defined contribution plans to supplement their retirement, opening the door to the privatization of old-age pensions. A VMBF evolution into defined-benefit plans has been discussed. It would allow for explicit replacement of some or all of the social security benefit promise under the concept of so-called "recognized pension funds" (Daykin and Skrabski, 1993).

The strategy most likely to be put forward by either the government or the PIF board will entail some manner of multi-tier framework, especially given the existence of a statute allowing a de facto separation between a basic (flat-rate) pension and an earnings-related component. Government management of the earnings-related scheme may be sought. A less likely option would be a radical scrapping of the entire PAYG structure in favor of a regulated private system of competing investment or mutual funds along the lines of the system operating in Chile. Such funds invest on behalf of individual-specific client accounts (Santamaria, 1995). Instead, pension reform might proceed by allowing individuals an opportunity to opt out of participation from the earnings-related tier and into a private pension plan.

Firms, or perhaps individuals, could contract to provide a benefits plan that would substitute for the government program. This "contracting out" mechanism could be thought of as a means of borrowing from the state: the firm or worker receives contribution rebates—that is, a reduction in payroll tax—up front but has to satisfy future pension obligations. A receptive government would view this strategy as a method of reducing its long-term pension financing obligations.

CONCLUDING REMARKS

The former Soviet satellites share a tradition of old-age pension provision based on a pay-as-you-go (PAYG) approach to public pension finance. Financing these pension schemes has been difficult in the transition to a market economy. Public pension system insolvency may be inevitable for a transitional economy operating a PAYG model, as fast-paced political and institutional changes complicate the steps necessary to correct system deficiencies. However, many of the basic issues appear to be quite similar to those found in more economically advanced countries grappling with public PAYG pension system unsustainability.[15] Generally, PAYG systems inside and outside the CEE region promise more than they can deliver. Political factors then proceed to overtake economic fundamentals in the policymaking that follows.

Hungary's public pension problems pose a complex puzzle. An inefficient PAYG system seems impervious to the kind of radical change demanded. In that sense, the country exemplifies the forces at play that have prevented change from taking place in the CEE region. Squeezed on all sides by institutional, political, and economic constraints, a good deal of systemic inertia is present. Minor modifications will not sufficiently address systemic problems. Clearly, a major institutional shake-up is called for. Movement away from a one-dimensional PAYG framework toward a hybrid (public-private) approach appears likely within a few years.

What does the Hungarian experience suggest about future CEE regional developments? It displays a number of salient features. First, Hungarian political instability speaks to other CEE countries (except the Czechs). Only in a stable political environment (and one accompanied by economic growth) can we expect to witness substantive change. Such change should then be evaluated on its merits to effect long-lasting fiscal solvency. Second, private pension activity is indeed possible prior to alteration of the public system—for example, Hungary and the Czech Republic. A CEE reform sequence need not entail a wholesale focus upon the public scheme to the exclusion of private pensions—the mainstream view to date (Kopits et al., 1990; World Bank, 1993a). A different viewpoint would admit of a coincidental or even preliminary role for private pensions prior to overhauling a CEE state system. This development would not only involve stimulating capital markets but also provide an avenue by which to encourage individual pension provision to take place in anticipation of the downsizing, or perhaps elimination, of PAYG-style public provision altogether. Third, a number of new twists to more traditional private pension vehicles can be suggested for countries in the CEE region. Hungarian VMBFs in addition to the Czech subsidy alternative are just two possibilities.[16] Such options may be utilized by governments seeking ways to shift the burden of provision but in a responsible manner. The basic point is that CEE governments may not be able to await political conditions favorable to change but can create such conditions.

NOTES

1. Descriptions in the literature for the recently separated nations of Slovakia and the Czech Republic still refer to the former Czechoslovakia. This approach is preserved in the current discussion and data presentation.
2. The countries shown in this table are also those CEE nations that have taken pension reform discussions the furthest.
3. An explanation of these assumptions is given in Hambor (1992).
4. Poland's country description draws on Vinton (1993), Fox (1993), Fougerolles (1994), FBIS (1994), Poland (1993), and the U.S. Department of State (1994).
5. The 1994 "Strategy for Poland," a government document, develops much of the thinking present in a 1993 White Paper issued by the Polish Ministry of Labor and Social Policy, taking the two-tier framework as a long-term goal and laying out what measures might be taken over the 1994-1997 period.
6. Separate data and analyses of the two countries is still in its early stages since the 1993 partition. Information for this description comes from Hambor and Ross (1992), Tomes (1994a, 1994b), and Romania (1993).

7. The country description draws on Atkins (1991), IMF (1990), World Bank (1992), Hambor and Ross (1992), and IBIS (1993).

8. Bulgarian information comes from Hambor and Ross (1992), Gotovska-Popova (1993), Engelbrekt (1992), Fox (1993), and the World Bank (1994).

9. Information on Romania comes primarily from the Romanian government's White Paper (1993) but also draws on Fox (1993) and the U.S. Social Security Administration (1994).

10. See annexes in Buttrick (1991) for details on these issues.

11. An identical arrangement oversees the health care system as a result of the 1991 legislation.

12. This paragraph and the next are an amalgam of Buttrick (1991) and Pataki (1993).

13. Until there is subsequent legislation as to the financing arrangements of the two components, the statute remains a moot point (World Bank undated).

14. A November, 1993, seminar in Matrahaza (Hungary), sponsored by the World Bank and the Hungarian Academy of Sciences, could not provide a conclusive statement as to the likely framework of a future public pension system. Discussant answers to such questions as the direction and speed of reform, for example, were often mutually exclusive. This left little room for compromise among competing strategies (World Bank undated).

15. Most OECD member countries, for example, are reevaluating the burden placed upon their national budgets by over-extended PAYG state pension systems.

16. For other alternatives, see Turner and Rajnes (1994).

REFERENCES

Atkins, G.L. 1991. "Social Security and Pension Reform in Central Europe." Paper prepared for Meetings of the Institut fur die Wissenschaften vom Menschen inVienna, Austria, on Social Costs of the Political and Economic Transformation of the CSFR, Hungary and Poland.

Batty, I., R. Stumpa, and I. Kovari. 1994. "Pension Reform in Eastern Europe." *Benefits & Compensation International* (May): 8-14.

Buttrick, S.M. 1991. "Social Security in Hungary." Report submitted to the International Affairs Office of the U.S. Department of Labor, July.

Daykin, C. and A. Skrabski. 1993. "Mutual Fund Proposals in Hungary." *Benefits and Compensation International* (March): 14-16.

Engelbrekt, K. 1992. "Growing Poverty among Bulgaria's Pensioners." *RFE/RL Research Report* (February): 64-66.

Foreign Broadcast Information Service (FBIS). 1994. "The Strategy for Poland." In Daily Report Supplement: East Europe, June 15.

Fougerolles, J. de. 1994. *The Need for Pension Reform in Transitional Economies: The Case of Poland.* Institute for EastWest Studies, September.

Fox, L. 1993 (December 6). "Old Age Security in Transition Economies." Paper prepared as part of the World Bank Old-Age Security Research Project.

Gotovska-Popova, T. 1993. "Bulgaria's Troubled Social Security System." *RFE/RL Research Report* (June 25): 43-47.

Hambor, J.C. 1992 (June). "Issues in Eastern European Social Security Reform." U.S. Treasury Department, Office of Policy Analysis. Research Paper No. 9201.

Hambor, J.C. and S.G. Ross. 1992. "Social Security Reform in Eastern Europe." *Social Insurance Update* 22 (March): 10-17.

Holzmann, R. 1992 (May). *Reforming Old-Age Pension Systems in Central and Eastern European Countries in Transition: Necessity and Change.* Vienna: Boltzmann Institute for Economic Analysis.

IBIS. 1993-1994 (various issues). *Briefing Service*

Kopits, G. 1993. "Hungary: A Case of Gradual Fiscal Reform." In V. Tanzi (ed.), *Transition to Market: Studies in Fiscal Reform.* Washington, DC: International Monetary Fund.

Kopits, G., et al. 1990. International Monetary Fund (IMF). "Social Security Reform in Hungary." Unpublished manuscript, Fiscal Affairs Department, International Monetary Fund, October 12.

Okolicsanyi, K. 1994. "Hungary's Budget Deficit Worsens." *RFE/RL Research Report* 3(January 14): 36-38.

"Old and Unaffordable." 1994. *The Economist* (April 30): 55.

Oltay, E. 1994. "The Former Communist Election Victory in Hungary." *RFE/RL Research Report* 3(June 24): 1-6.

Pataki, J. 1993. "A New Era in Hungary's Social Security Administration." *RFE/RL Research Report* 2(July 2): 57-60.

Poland, Ministry of Labor and Social Policy. 1993 (May). *Pensions and Disability Pensions: The Creation of the System: Chances and Risks.* Warsaw.

Romania, Ministry of Labor and Social Protection. 1993. *The White Paper on Social Insurances and Pension Reform.* Bucharest.

Santamaria, M. 1995. "What Can the United States Learn from Chile?" In K. Stephenson (ed.), *Social Security: A Time for Change,* Vol. in *Contemporary Studies in Economic and Financial Analysis,* pp. 123-148. Greenwich, CT: JAI Press.

Tomes, I. 1994a (June). "Supplementary Pension Insurance with State Allowance in the Czech Republic." Ministry of Labor and Social Policy of the Czech Republic.

________. 1994b "The Czech Social Security Reform." Paper prepared for the World Bank Conference on Averting the Old-Age Crisis, October 12.

Turner, J.A. and D.M. Rajnes. 1994. "The Development of Private Pension Systems: Central and Eastern Europe." Working Paper No. 94-17, Wharton School Pension Research Council, University of Pennsylvania.

United Nations. 1988. *World Population Prospects: The 1988 Revision.* New York: United Nations.

United Nations. 1992. *World Population Prospects: The 1992 Revision.* New York: United Nations.

U.S. Department of State. 1994. Selected unclassified cables.

U.S. Social Security Administration. 1994. *Social Security Programs Throughout the World—1993.* Washington, DC: U.S. Government Printing Office.

Vinton, L. 1993. "Poland's Social Safety Net: An Overview." *RFE/RL Research Report* (April 23): 3-11.

World Bank. 1992. *Hungary: Reform of Social Policy and Expenditures.* Washington, DC: World Bank.

World Bank. 1993a. *Poland: Income Support and the Social Safety Net during the Transition.* Washington, DC: World Bank.

World Bank. 1993b. "Staff Appraisal Report: Republic of Hungary Pensions Administration and Health Insurance Project." Human Resources Sector, Operations Division of the Central and Southern Europe Departments, Europe and Central Asia Region. Report No. 11291-HU (March 5).

World Bank. 1994. "Bulgaria: Public Finance Reforms in the Transition." Report No. 12273-BUL (unpublished), Country Operations Division, February 23.

World Bank. (undated). "Memorandum: Pension Seminar in Matrahaza, November 16-18, 1993."

WHAT CAN THE UNITED STATES LEARN FROM CHILE?

Marco Santamaria

INTRODUCTION

Over the last decade, it has become increasingly apparent that providing retirement income through publicly run defined-benefit systems will become a difficult task for governments, not least for the U.S. government. In broad terms, the difficulty arises from OECD-wide demographic trends that indicate that by the year 2040, the number of retired persons will rise significantly in proportion to the labor force.[1] Given these trends, logic suggests that governments that operate public defined-benefit social security systems will face unpleasant options in the administration of their retirement programs. Specifically, they will have to: (1) raise social security taxes on the relatively smaller number of economically active persons to retain current real levels of retirement income, or (2) cut retirement benefits on the growing population of elderly to minimize tax increases on the labor force, or (3) run ever larger budget deficits to avoid either of the first two options. None of these options seems politically—or even economically—appealing. Not surprisingly, the search for alternative ways of providing retirement income has gained increasing prominence.

Unfortunately for those looking for a painless solution to the problem, there is an inescapable fact that *someone* has to bear the increasing costs of supporting a rapidly aging population. The appropriate question to ask oneself, therefore, is not whether it is possible to avoid these costs but whether there are benefits to be gained from having the private sector, rather than the public sector, bear them. In this context, it is instructive to evaluate the experiences of Chile when it dealt with a similar set of issues in 1981. Faced with a public pay-as-you-go social security system well on its way to bankruptcy, the Chilean government enacted possibly the most radical social security reform ever attempted at that time; it phased out its public *defined-benefit* system and replaced it with an individually funded and privately administered mandatory *defined-contribution* system. The reform seems to have eased a longer-term fiscal quagmire (at a short-term fiscal cost) without compromising employee disposable income levels, increasing firms' labor costs, or diminishing the adequacy and equitability of retirement income. At the same time, although the reform's impact on total domestic saving is unclear due to its depressing effect on public sector saving, the reform seems to have provided strong impetus to private sector saving. Higher private sector saving is likely to have financed investments more productive than those previously financed by public sector savings, and has catalyzed a significant deepening of local capital markets. The favorable results of the Chilean social security system have encouraged other developing countries—notably Mexico, Argentina, Peru, and Colombia—to adopt variants of the Chilean model.

This paper discusses the implementation of the Chilean private pension system and examines the economic, financial, and institutional consequences of the social security reform. Those consequences suggest that the United States and other OECD countries could benefit from the implementation of a similar system in terms of higher private savings (and, thus, increased productivity of capital investments), increased individual and intergenerational equity, a greater degree of retirement income insulation from political considerations, and stronger political incentives for prudent macroeconomic management.

THE NATURE OF THE CHILEAN SOCIAL SECURITY PROBLEM

The Chilean social security system faced severe financing difficulties by the end of the 1970s.[2] In much the same way as the industrialized countries do now, Chile faced a secular deterioration in its "support ratio"—the ratio of social security contributors to social security beneficiaries. Between 1960 and 1980, that ratio fell dramatically from 10.8:1 to 2.2:1, due to demographic factors as well as to widespread contribution evasion and ever-laxer benefits qualification criteria. To compound the problem, the real value of the country's public pension trust fund—accumulated during the system's early years of collecting contributions but not yet providing benefits, and invested primarily in unindexed debt obligations—had been essentially erased by Chile's high rates of inflation, particularly in the mid-1970s.

These problems were further aggravated by other features of the public pension scheme, including its high administrative costs, inequitability of benefits, and pervasive fraud. Established in 1924, Chile's social security system was the first in the Western hemisphere (the U.S. system was set up in 1935, Canada's in 1927). Over time, Chile's pension system developed into over 30 separate subsystems, with participation determined by workers' occupations. Beyond contributing to elevated administrative costs, the fragmented nature of the system gave rise to highly disparate qualification criteria and benefits, in many instances a function of the political and economic influences of each occupational group (see Table 1). Thus, white-collar workers tended to obtain pensions equal to 100% of final pay, with final pay defined as an average of the last five years' earnings partially indexed to inflation. Manual laborers, on the other hand, tended to obtain pensions equal to 70% of final pay, with final pay defined as an average of the last five years' earnings adjusted to an index that ran well below inflation. Moreover, manual laborers had to work more years than white-collar workers to qualify for their benefits. Beyond the inequitability of the system, the minimal protection from inflation in the determination of final pay (particularly for manual laborers) created incentives to underreport wages—and, thus, contributions—because pensions would tend to equal the minimum benefit regardless of reported income.

Table 1. Pension Eligibility Requirements Under the Old System

Employee Category	*Requirement*
Manual Laborers	65 Years of Age
Private Sector White Collar	35 Years of Employment
Public Sector White Collar	30 Years of Employment
Banking Sector Employees	24 Years of Employment
Parliamentarians	15 Years of Employment

The various problems in the system began to have negative repercussions on fiscal management. By the time social security reform was enacted in 1981, the government was providing significant subsidies to the social security system from its general revenue account. In 1978, for example, central government expenditures on the social security system constituted 32% of total central government expenditures, and by 1980, government transfers from general revenues made up nearly a third of benefits paid by the social security system. Projections indicated that government transfers from general revenues would increase tenfold in real terms over the following 20 years if substantial revisions to the system were not made (Kritzer 1981).

THE SOLUTION TO THE PROBLEM

The government viewed the long-term difficulties of the system as so severe that in 1981, it opted for a radical reform rather than a modification of the existing structure. The new system eliminated social security taxes for both employees and employers and required employees to contribute to individually funded and privately administered pension funds. Although employers were no longer asked to pay social security taxes, they were required at the time the program was instituted to grant a one-time 17% wage increase to their employees. The size of this wage increase was intended to offset the new employee contributions for their pensions (10% of earnings), survivors and disability insurance (3%), and health insurance (4%).[3]

Under the current system, each employee is required to continue contributing until retirement (age 65 for men, 60 for women) or until the payable annual pension reaches 70% of his or her average indexed wage during the last 10 years of employment. The new system is completely indexed in that all monetary values are expressed in a currency unit called Unidad de Fomento (UF). The peso value of the UF is adjusted monthly in accordance with changes in the consumer price index.

Employee contributions are made to newly formed private institutions called Administradoras de Fondos de Pensiones (AFPs), whose task is to invest the contributed funds. Employees can choose which AFP they want to contribute to and can move their funds among AFPs with relative ease. The pension fund business is highly competitive, with 20 funds vying for the workforce's retirement contributions. Information on the performance of AFPs is readily available from newspapers, the Superintendency of AFPs, and the central bank's monthly statistical bulletin.

The switch to the private pension plan was effected gradually. Employees covered by the old system were given until May 1986 to decide whether to join the new private pension plan or to remain in the old system. Approximately 85% to 90% of workers covered under the old system switched to the new system. Since January 1, 1983, workers entering the labor market for the first time have been required to join the private pension system.

It is important to note that the Chilean government did not completely divest itself of responsibility for providing social insurance. Under the 1981 program, the government committed itself to supplementing retirement income for those pensioners whose individual pension trusts do not provide them with an income equal to a defined minimum level—generally about 85% of the minimum wage. The minimum pension guarantee applies only to those pensioners who have contributed to their AFP accounts for at least 20 years and have reached the legal retirement age. In addition to the minimum pension guarantee, the government offers a means-tested public assistance pension for the indigent which is very small (about U.S.$40 per month) and which is statutorily limited to 300,000 persons.

THE ECONOMIC AND FINANCIAL EFFECTS OF THE REFORM

The defined-contribution pension system launched in 1981 has had far-reaching economic and financial consequences. It has eased long-term budgetary pressures without diminishing benefits to contributors, reducing take-home pay for employees, or raising labor costs for firms. More importantly from a long-term perspective, the reform has significantly boosted private sector savings, although its effect on total domestic saving is uncertain. Higher private saving (at the expense of lower public savings) may well have contributed to the elevated rate of growth experienced by Chile since the mid-1980s, by financing investments whose economic and financial return can be expected to have exceeded that of public sector investments. Finally, the system is credited with having spurred a rapid deepening of Chile's financial markets, both by channeling large sums of money into them and by promoting an increased awareness of the market's risks and regulatory needs.

Fiscal Effects

The elimination of social security taxes in 1981 was not offset by the immediate elimination of the government's responsibility for providing retirement income to those already in retirement. Additionally, older members of the workforce who for most of their working lives had contributed to the old system would not have enough time to capitalize a large individual account; the government recognized that those workers would need government assistance in securing adequate retirement income.[4] The result was that—for the short to medium term—continuing but gradually declining social security expenditures had to be financed from the central government's general revenues, thereby significantly worsening fiscal balances. Having foreseen this short-term fiscal effect, the Chilean government had endeavored to bring central government accounts into a significant surplus (equal to over 5% of GDP in 1980) prior to the enactment of the reform.[5] Nevertheless, by 1984 the enlarged social security deficit (equal to over 7% of GDP) contributed to a central government deficit equal to 3% of GDP.

Over the longer term, however, as the number of pensioners covered by the old defined-benefit system dwindles, the government will continue to face an ever-decreasing fiscal burden in providing retirement income. Consequently, the large initial deficits of the social security system will continue to fall gradually;

Table 2. AFP Annual Rates of Return on Assets

AFP Name	*1982*	*1983*	*1984*	*1985*	*1986*	*1987*	*1988*	*1989*	*1990*	*1991*	*1992*
Alameda	29.7	21.4	4.4	—	—	—	—	—	—	—	—
Concordia	30.1	24.7	2.2	13.0	12.7	4.8	7.3	7.9	16.2	28.7	2.8
Cuprum	25.5	18.5	3.2	13.7	15.5	8.5	7.8	9.5	18.2	30.4	3.6
El Libertador	23.2	20.2	3.3	13.2	13.5	5.8	6.9	8.2	16.6	30.8	3.4
Futuro	—	—	—	—	—	—	—	4.0	17.0	31.2	4.1
Habitat	25.7	24.3	3.7	13.3	12.5	5.5	6.4	6.8	15.9	30.4	2.8
Invierta	25.1	20.7	3.4	13.4	11.8	5.5	8.7	9.1	19.4	27.9	0.9
Magister	27.6	20.5	5.1	13.5	12.3	4.5	7.1	6.9	15.8	34.3	3.0
Planvital	24.4	22.2	3.5	13.0	11.5	5.2	7.2	8.9	18.7	32.0	3.6
Proteccion	—	—	—	—	10.6	7.0	7.7	8.2	17.7	32.7	4.2
Provida	29.5	20.3	4.0	13.5	11.8	5.1	6.3	5.9	13.3	25.8	3.1
San Cristobal	27.6	20.7	3.9	—	—	—	—	—	—	—	—
Santa Maria	30.2	20.0	3.0	13.0	11.8	5.1	5.9	6.5	14.6	30.1	2.9
Summa	28.1	22.5	2.8	14.3	12.4	5.2	6.4	7.3	18.1	33.1	3.0
Union	—	—	—	13.6	13.3	6.3	7.1	8.7	17.2	30.9	2.8
System	28.5	21.1	3.6	13.4	12.3	5.4	6.5	6.9	15.6	29.7	3.0

Note: The central bank reports only the historical performance of the 15 largest AFPs.

already, the public social security system's deficit has declined from a high of 7.4% of GDP in 1984 to about 4% in 1993. In theory, the deficits could disappear entirely in the long term, but the government has committed itself to guaranteeing a minimum retirement benefit. Therefore, if the individually funded pension system fails to provide retirees with a pension equal to at least 85% of the minimum wage, the government stands to make up the difference from the budget's general revenues. However, current rules make it difficult to qualify for a minimum pension benefit; a worker must have contributed to his AFP account for at least 20 years and must meet the minimum retirement age. Furthermore, on present trends it seems unlikely that the government will need to make significant expenditures for this purpose given that average annual returns for AFP investments (over 13% in real terms since inception; see Table 2) have far exceeded the return required to provide a retirement benefit larger than the government-guaranteed minimum benefit (Gillion and Bonilla, 1992).[6]

Equitability and Adequacy of Benefits

The fact that the reform has averted long-term fiscal pressures—at a short-term fiscal cost—is not in itself a noteworthy accomplishment if retirement benefits have been diminished or if the new system engenders widespread distributional inequities. In fact, neither seems to be the case. Under the new system, the state guarantees a minimum benefit equal to about 85% of the minimum wage—no better and no worse than under the old system. Furthermore, returns on pension investments to date have been (and are likely to remain) high enough that the chances of obtaining only a minimum pension benefit are small (unlike the old system, where a majority of workers obtained the minimum pension). Equitability has not suffered either under the new system. All participants in the system can retire at any time they please, provided their pension trust can provide retirement income equal to 70% of final pay. Unlike the old system, final pay for *all* occupational categories is determined by the average indexed earnings in the last 10 years of employment, and eligibility for the government's minimum pension guarantee is based on a uniform retirement age regardless of occupation.

One criticism sometimes leveled against the new system is that it does not adequately cover seasonal workers who may have a hard time both capitalizing their individual pension fund and fulfilling the state's requirement for the minimum pension guarantee. These types of workers do, in fact, fall through the pension cracks. However, available data show that pension coverage as a percentage of the entire economically active population (EAP) has improved significantly under the new system. It is estimated that 61.2% of the EAP was covered for pensions and sickness under the defined-benefit system in 1980; in 1985, after the introduction of the new system, it is estimated that 79.2% of the EAP was covered for pension and sickness. More recent estimates suggest that coverage under the new pension system alone is 80% of the labor force, with a portion of the remaining labor force—including military personnel—covered by the old system.[7]

Disposable Income Effects

Because workers initially were permitted to choose between the private defined-contribution pension system and the existing

Table 3. Employer and Employee Contribution Rates

	Old System		*New System*	
	Employee (%) of earnings)	*Employer (% of payroll)*	*Employee (% of earning)*	*Employer (% of payroll)*
Before March 1981				
Blue Collar	8	34	—	—
White Collar	18	29	—	—
After March 1981				
Blue Collar	17	4	17	4
White Collar	17	4	17	4

public system, the government wanted to create incentives for workers to opt for the new system. A strong incentive came in the form of the positive disposable income effects of choosing the new private system. Under the public system, a worker whose monthly gross pay equaled 100 pesos would take home P92 after the deduction of an 8% social security tax (see Table 3). The same worker opting for the new system obtained a government-mandated 17% increase in gross pay to P117 per month, and would then contribute 17% to a private social security account. Therefore, take-home pay would rise to P117 − (117 * 0.17), or P97.1, an increase of 5.5% over the previous take-home pay. A white-collar worker who had contributed as much as 18% of salary to social security under the old system, would see take-home pay rise by up to 18.4%.

It is possible that the take-home pay effect is overstated to the extent that employees evaded contributions under the old system. It is also possible that employers reduced the pace of wage increases in subsequent years to offset the immediate 17% wage hike and that new entrants into the labor market after 1982 were not paid 17% more than they otherwise would have been. However, because labor costs are likely to have fallen—even taking into account the mandated wage increase—it is not evident that firms had strong incentives to behave in this manner.

Labor Cost Effects

Firms whose workers switched to the new system experienced a decline in labor costs despite the mandated wage increase because employer-paid social security contributions were greatly reduced.

Under the old system, a white-collar worker earning P100 a month cost the firm P129 once social security contributions of 29% of wages were added (see Table 3). Under the new system, the same worker costs P117 in wages plus only a maximum of 4% (a work injury insurance that ranges from 1% to 4% of wages), for a total of P121.7—a reduction in labor costs of at least 5.7%. A shift to the new system for blue-collar workers provided an even greater reduction in labor costs (at least 12.7%) because of the greater portion of employer-paid social security contributions for this type of worker under the old system. Of course, the labor cost effects as described would hold only to the extent that firms did not evade contributions under the old system.

Saving Effects

One of the more debated aspects of the reform is its impact on domestic savings. If the domestic investment rate is determined by the sum of domestic and foreign savings rates ($I = S_{dom} + S_{for}$), changes in a country's domestic savings patterns will necessarily affect either its investment rate or its demand for foreign financing (or a combination of the two). Assuming that domestic savings is positively correlated with domestic investment,[8] the impact of social security reform on domestic savings rates has implications for the long-term growth prospects of the economy through its effect on domestic capital formation. However, in order to assess the reform's impact on domestic savings (and implicitly on capital formation, given our assumptions), it is necessary to look at the behavior of the two components of aggregate savings: public and private savings.

The reform's fiscal effects as described above can be expected to have had a negative effect on public savings rates; the government relinquished a source of revenue without abandoning the related expenditure responsibility. The facts bear out the expectation; the public sector savings rate fell from a high of 10.2% of GDP in 1980 to −3.1% of GDP in 1985 (Table 4). A simple estimation of the reform's impact on public savings, netting out the influences of copper prices, real interest rates on external (dollar) liabilities, and real GDP growth, suggests a statistically significant downward shift in the public savings function (Santamaria, 1992).

On the other hand, private sector savings rates can be expected to have increased as a result of the reform. The most obvious reason

Table 4. Saving and Investment (percent of GDP)

	1976	*1977*	*1978*	*1979*	*1980*	*1981*	*1982*	*1983*	*1984*	*1985*	*1986*	*1987*	*1988*	*1989*	*1990*	*1991*	*1992*
Gross National Saving	13.8	10.0	11.7	11.8	13.4	7.9	1.7	3.9	2.4	8.1	11.3	16.9	21.8	23.1	22.1	21.5	21.2
Of which private	6.0	2.1	3.8	4.5	3.2	-0.1	1.2	4.5	3.7	11.2	12.4	14.0	17.8	15.8	16.9	16.9	14.6
Of which private	7.8	7.9	7.9	7.3	10.2	8.0	0.5	0.6	-1.3	-3.1	-1.1	2.9	4.0	7.3	5.2	5.2	6.6
Foreign Saving	1.0	-4.4	-6.1	-6.0	-7.5	-14.8	-9.6	-5.9	-11.2	-9.1	-7.6	-5.3	-1.0	-2.4	-2.7	-0.7	-2.5
Investment	12.8	14.4	17.8	17.8	21.0	22.7	11.3	9.8	13.6	17.2	18.9	22.2	22.8	25.5	24.7	22.2	23.7

for this expectation is the fact that households were able to convert what was once a tax on income into a contribution to a private savings account. Therefore, the switch in accounting for social security contributions alone can be expected to have boosted private sector savings. Furthermore, even after the accounting of social security contributions, there may well have been an income effect for both households and firms, as described above. A higher disposable income may have to led to higher savings rates; as income rises, the marginal propensity to save can be expected to increase. The available data, in fact, shows a significant rise in private savings rates from −0.1% of GDP in 1981 to 14.6% of GDP in 1992.

It is difficult to show empirically that, because of the income effect generated by the reform, the increase in private savings rates more than offset the decline in public sector savings rates. Even over the long term, as social-security-related public sector expenditures diminish, aggregate savings rates are not certain to rise as a result of the reform. This is because as the government reduces its social security expenditures on retirees covered under the public system (increased public saving), retirees covered under the new system will begin to draw down from their own accumulated funds (decreased private saving). Therefore, the behavior of public and private savings rates tend to offset each other even in the long term. It is, therefore, not necessarily accurate to state that the reform has increased the rate of domestic savings or the *amount* of capital formation financed domestically.

However, one may plausibly argue that the reform increased the *efficiency* of capital formation in the country. A greater pool of private savings to fund private domestic investment implies a greater availability of funds for those investments whose financial return is highest and, presumably, whose economic rationale is strongest. The public sector, unlike the private sector, does not necessarily seek high financial or economic returns for its investments; it may, for example, be equally or more concerned with investing to protect employment, regardless of the economic rationality of such an investment. This being the case, one could expect that in an economy where the private sector generates the bulk of domestic investment, the contribution to GDP growth associated with an increase in the domestic investment rate would be higher than in an economy where the public sector generates the bulk of domestic investment. Indeed, Chile's national accounts suggest that the responsiveness of GDP growth to changes in the investment to GDP ratio did, in fact, increase after the implementation of the social security reform. In the 1976-1982 period, a one percentage point increase in the investment to GDP ratio was associated with an increase in the real GDP growth rate of 0.246 percentage points. In the 1983-1992 period, however, a one percentage point increase in the investment to GDP ratio was associated with an increase in the real GDP growth rate of 0.276 percentage points.[9] To the extent that this change is due to the higher productivity associated with the increased share of private sector investment in total domestic investment, it can be argued that Chile's reform of the pension system contributed to the country's positive long-term economic prospects.

Financial Market Effects

The creation of a substantial pool of private saving has had far-reaching consequences on the development of local capital markets. As of December 1993, 21 AFPs managed a total of $15.9 billion in assets, equal to about 40% of Chile's gross domestic product. The growth in AFP assets contributed to a rather pronounced growth in the broadest measure of money supply (row *M7* in Table 5), which includes all domestic private sector financial assets. Table 5 shows that financial assets in the Chilean economy grew from 39% of GDP in 1982 to over 67% of GDP in 1993, an increase of 28% of GDP. Even taking into account Chile's prospects for strong economic growth, AFPs could manage funds in an amount equal to well over 60% of Chile's GDP by the year 2000. This rapid growth of assets managed by AFPs, coupled with the AFPs' fiduciary role as protectors of the nation's retirement income, has instilled great—in some cases perhaps excessive—caution in setting up a regulatory framework.

The AFPs are regulated by the Superintendency of Pension Fund Administrators (SAFP, to use the Spanish acronym). The creation in 1981 of a separate regulatory body in itself signaled the financial authorities' desire to instill confidence in the system. The Chilean banking system required extensive government intervention in the late 1970s, and the authorities hoped that by separating the banking and pension fund regulators, there would be fewer doubts as to the ability of a regulatory entity to prevent a mishap with

Table 5. Monetary Aggregates (percent of GDP)

	1979	*1980*	*1981*	*1982*	*1983*	*1984*	*1985*	*1986*	*1987*	*1988*	*1989*	*1990*	*1991*	*1992*
M2	17.4	19.3	23.7	25.9	18.6	20.1	20.4	20.6	22.8	22.9	26.9	27.7	27.1	28.5
M7	—	—	—	39.2	37.0	39.9	44.2	47.6	52.0	51.9	60.0	68.2	65.7	67.4

Notes: M2 = Cash + Demand Deposits + Time Deposits.
M7 = Total Private Financial Saving.

the AFPs. Barriers to entry in the pension fund business are not prohibitive: the SAFP requires investment funds to maintain capital in fixed proportion to the number of their affiliated investors and to maintain a cash reserve equal to at least 1% of assets. However, each fund must meet strict investment performance criteria.[10] Failure to meet these performance criteria gives the SAFP the authority to shut down an offending AFP and redistribute its assets to other AFPs. The SAFP requires investment funds to disclose their investments and performance to the public on a monthly basis.

Regulatory caution is also evident in the authorities' reluctance to phase out indexed long-term debt instruments, the use of which is designed to protect investors from inflation. This regulatory stance results from the unfortunate history of the pension trust of the old defined-benefit pension system, the real value of which was eroded by the high inflation rates of the 1970s. At present, because there are no unindexed long-term government debt instruments setting benchmarks, the Chilean private sector has steered clear of issuing unindexed obligations. Although not an optimal condition from the perspective of gauging inflationary expectations, financial indexation has permitted the development of a long-term local currency debt market (nonexistent in many other Latin American markets) with guaranteed real rates of return for AFPs. The authorities are likely to be extremely careful in introducing unindexed instruments to minimize the potential negative impact on AFP returns.

Investor protection is also offered via investment guidelines the SAFP has drawn up for the fund administrators. Guidelines have been quite detailed, restricting AFP investments by type of instrument, by obligor, and by credit quality. Over time, the guidelines have slowly been liberalized, but in general the

Table 6. AFP Investment Guidelines

Asset Class	*Limits by Individual Issuer*	*Limits by Instrument (percent of fund assets)*
Government Entities	45% of fund assets	45
Mortgage Bonds	Not Applicable	80
Fixed Income Instruments Issued by Banks	The lesser of: • 15% of fund assests • 3 × fund capital × (*Fa*/*Ft*) • 2.5 × (*Kb*/*Kt*) × risk factor × *Fa*	50 (30 for maturities < 1 year)
Corporate Bonds	The lesser of: • 20% of a particular issue • (8.8 × net capital of issuer × Fa/Ft × risk factor) −	
Stocks	The lesser of	
• Ownership Widely Distributed.	• 7% of fund assets × concentration factor	30
	• 7% of issuance × concentration factor	30
• Concentrated Ownership	• 1% of fund assets • 1% of company issuance	10
• Real Estate Companies	• 7% of fund assets × concentration factor • 20% of issuance × concentration factor	10
Participation in Other Pension Funds	5% of fund assets	20
Participation in Other Investment Funds	The lesser of: • 5% of fund assets • 10% of investment fund participation	10
Trade Credits	The lesser of: • 20% of a particular issue • (0.2 × net capital of issuer × *Fa*/*Ft* × risk factor)-fund investments in issuer bonds	10

Notes: *Fa*/*Ft* = fund assets divided by AFP system assets.
Kb/*Kt* = individual bank capital divided by banking system capital.
Concentration Factor = a measure of the dispension of stock holdings.
Risk Factor = a credit rating assigned by an independent government credit risk rating agency.

liberalizing trend has not kept pace with the growth of the funds. Table 6 gives an idea of the extent of the restrictions to which the funds adhered until recently. Although wide-ranging regulations were initially warranted by the important public policy role of the AFPs and the undeveloped nature of local capital markets, past investment regulations have resulted in a rather severe portfolio concentration problem for the AFPs: (1) an almost complete exposure to Chilean country risk, (2) the bunching of AFP equity holdings in a very limited number of companies, and (3) large AFP positions in government obligations. However, a landmark piece of legislation approved in January 1994—the Capital Markets Law—will significantly increase AFP asset diversification by allowing expanded foreign investment, permitting greater AFP participation in the stock market, and broadening the types of financial instruments in which the AFPs can invest.

Restrictions on AFP stock market participation have meant that the funds have had an unnaturally small equity component in their portfolios. As of December 1993, the AFPs owned slightly more than 9% percent of all traded stocks, representing only 31.9% percent of total AFP assets.[11] By comparison, U.S. investment funds invest about 50% of their assets in equities. As a measure of the portfolio concentration created by the SAFP regulations, there have been times when roughly 75% of all pension fund money invested in the stock market was invested in just five companies. Yet, despite their highly regulated stock market participation, the AFPs have played a crucial role in the development of Chile's equity markets. AFPs were heavy investors in the seven utilities that began Chile's privatization drive in 1985. The AFPs' very presence may also have helped to encourage foreign investment; the AFPs—captive to the local market and likely to increase their participation as regulations ease—constitute a stabilizing influence in the Chilean stock market. Since 1989, foreign funds have poured over $1 billion into Chilean investments, nearly 80% of which has been in the stock market. For a $40 billion dollar economy in which foreign funds must overcome administrative barriers to be able to invest in the local markets, the $1 billion figure is quite substantial.

Because of the heavy restrictions on stock market participation, the pension funds have been very active in domestic debt markets. AFPs have increased their holdings of corporate bonds of both public and private enterprises from 1.9% of the amount outstanding in 1981 to about 70% in December 1993, equal to 7.3% of total AFP assets. This tremendous growth in holdings of corporate debt occurred even as the stock of corporate bonds grew by a factor of 15 from 1981 to 1993. The supply of pension money available to finance corporate debt has lowered financing costs and reduced dependence on foreign financing. In fact, despite the attractive terms some of the more visible Chilean companies could command abroad, Chilean entities have been conspicuously absent from the large group of Latin American borrowers returning to the Euromarkets.

AFPs have also been consistent heavy buyers of Chilean Treasury and central bank bills. There is no minimum investment requirement for government obligations, but the investment funds have grown so large and other investment options have been so limited that AFPs have tended to hold as much government paper as SAFP regulations permit (up to 45% of assets). As of December 1993, AFPs had invested 39.3% of their assets in government obligations. On the simplest level, the large purchases of government paper can be viewed as a slightly different form of conventional taxation: The AFPs take money from contributors and use the funds to finance public sector expenditures. A more careful examination reveals that the AFPs' role in the domestic government paper market has had more far-reaching implications. Since 1985, the Chilean Treasury has been retiring its domestic debt, thus decreasing the stock of debt available to AFPs and others, while the central bank has steadily increased the domestic stock of its debt. The growth of central bank debt throughout the late 1980s is in part attributable to Chile's now-defunct debt-equity swap program, through which foreign investors swapped Chile's foreign debt for peso- or dollar-denominated central bank bills. The foreign investors then sold their central bank bills in the local secondary market to obtain cash for equity investments. The primary purchasers of the central bank bills from foreign investors were the AFPs. Thus, AFPs were not simply covering a general shortfall in government revenues but were indirectly reducing the country's external debt and facilitating foreign investment by foreigners. As much as $11 billion dollars of foreign debt was exchanged for equity with the indirect participation of the AFPs.

Despite the beneficial effects of the investment funds on the local capital markets, the AFPs' portfolio concentration problems demanded a significant change in the regulatory environment. The Capital Markets Law approved by the Chilean congress in January 1994 eases investment limits while increasing regulatory oversight of market practices. The law permits AFPs to invest in both highly rated foreign debt instruments and blue chip equities up to 12% of AFP assets and actually sets a foreign investment floor of 6% of AFP assets. The funds will also be permitted to invest in a broader range of Chilean companies listed on the stock market;[12] over 250 companies can become eligible for AFP investment under the new law. Furthermore, AFPs will be permitted to increase their participation in venture capital funds, revenue bonds, convertible debentures, and derivatives (for hedging purposes only). At the same time, the Capital Markets Law increases sanctions on insider trading and further restricts ties between fund directors and the companies in which the funds invest.

Beyond their direct role in the development of the domestic capital markets, it should also be noted that the AFPs have stimulated the growth of other institutional investors, particularly life insurance companies. The individual pension trusts have been used by workers to purchase annuities at retirement. Moreover, as part of the social insurance reform, AFPs are required to purchase disability, survivors, and health insurance from private insurance companies for their contributors. The insurance companies, like the AFPs, have become important participants in the domestic financial markets and have also contributed to their development.

A VIABLE ALTERNATIVE FOR THE UNITED STATES

The far-reaching and generally positive economic and financial consequences of the Chilean social security reform offer strong incentives for other countries to adopt similar reforms. Indeed, several other countries in Latin America—including Mexico, Argentina, Colombia, and Peru—have very recently approved the implementation of variants of the Chilean private social security system. In none of these countries, however, was the adopted reform as radical as in Chile; in most cases, a limited public social security system will continue to coexist alongside the private system. One reason why most of these countries did not adopt exact replicas of the Chilean system is that the Chilean reform is politically difficult to sell in democratic systems with traditions of government-run social insurance schemes, particularly where powerful trade unions have historically enjoyed close relationships with the public social security system.[13] In 1981, Chile was not a democracy, nor did it have powerful trade unions; as a consequence, any political resistance to the measure was easily stifled. Nevertheless, Colombia, Argentina, Mexico, and Peru overcame the political resistance to reform and each stands to reap—in varying degrees—the same benefits as Chile.

Given that the privatization of social security seems to be attractive to countries other than Chile, it is appropriate to ask whether such a measure would be desirable in the United States. Although there is no great need to promote the further development of U.S. capital markets, the prospect of stimulating the comparatively low U.S. private savings rate without compromising employee disposable income, increasing labor costs, or reducing benefits is appealing. But beyond the private savings effects discussed above (which of themselves seem to be a significant macroeconomic benefit), there are other considerations that make a Chilean-style reform attractive. Among these are a higher degree of individual and intergenerational equity, as well as the stronger political incentives for long-term macroeconomic discipline.

Increased Individual and Intergenerational Equity

Some analysts have claimed that a radical reform of Old Age, Survivors', and Disability Insurance (OASDI) is unnecessary because the system has been placed on firmer financial footing. It is true that the health of the U.S. social security system is better now than it was in the late 1970s and early 1980s. At that time, the Old Age and Survivor's Insurance trust fund had been virtually depleted and urgently needed recapitalization if it was to pay benefits on time (or avoid transfers from the government's general revenues). A schedule of tax increases was approved in 1977 to rectify the situation. By 1983, further measures had become necessary, including: (1) accelerating the schedule of tax increases legislated in 1977, (2) increasing taxes on the self-employed, (3) imposing income taxes on social security benefits for those beneficiaries with incomes over a certain level, (4) raising the retirement age in the 21st century, and (5) delaying annual cost of living adjustments for six months.

Although these measures have improved the medium-term financial health of the system, they have not resolved longer-term financing issues. The Social Security Trustee's Report of 1983 projected that the measures enacted that year would keep the social security system solvent through the year 2060. True to expectations, the social security system has been posting surpluses since 1984, permitting the social security trust fund to grow in 1993 to an amount equal to the annual outlays of the system. However, by 1991 the Trustees were already projecting that the system would remain solvent only through 2041. Further downward revisions to the projections have since occurred, with the most recent prediction of insolvency at 2029. Although there may be no immediate crisis in the system, further tax increases and/or benefit cuts are going to be necessary in coming years if OASDI is to remain self-sustaining.

Since continued adjustments to taxation and/or benefits in the public social security system are going to be required, radical reform of the system may be a preferable course of action from the perspective of individual and intergenerational fairness. Continued marginal adjustments to the current defined-benefit program imply that younger workers will have to make ever-larger social security contributions only to face the likelihood of smaller benefits when they retire. A defined-*contribution* system avoids the "political risk" of retirement benefits provision—that is, the exposure to political decisions regarding contribution rates and retirement benefits—by ensuring that each worker will obtain at least as much as was contributed during working years. A worker can make a retirement choice based on a personal evaluation of the adequacy of expected retirement income from a personal investment account, removing the increasing burden of providing retirement income from the shoulders of the younger generation of workers. A worker can, therefore, choose to retire earlier with less retirement income, or later with more retirement income, with no individual or intergenerational equity consequences.

Increased Discipline in Macroeconomic Management

As discussed above, phasing out a publicly run defined-contribution system involves significant short-run general revenue fiscal costs. This creates the danger that if OASDI is indeed phased out, short-term fiscal adjustments in non-OASDI revenues and/or expenditures will not be made, resulting in significant budget deficits, a run-up in the national debt, and increased long-term debt-servicing costs. However, with political tolerance for large budget deficits and a growing national debt on the wane in Washington—see the recent Perot phenomenon and the rather close Balanced Budget Amendment vote—it could be argued that the prospect of privatizing the social security system would provide additional impetus to budgetary discipline prior to the enactment of the reform. In a sense, the United States is more fortunate than Chile was in 1981 because the fiscal adjustment could be softened by gradual draw-downs on the existing social security trust fund. In addition, the political pain of cutting expenditures could be mitigated by targeting those types of capital expenditures that the private sector would be willing to carry out—with financing provided by the emergence of the new pool of investment capital looking for investment projects.

However, in the event that the necessary short-term fiscal adjustment was not made, the larger pool of private savings could be used to finance those deficits. As long as such financing remains market-based—that is, not coerced by investment regulations—there need not be negative implications on the resulting adequacy of retirement income provided by the defined-contribution system. Of course, the use of the rapidly growing private funds to finance larger fiscal deficits would crowd out the expected increase in private investment that the reform would otherwise generate, thereby undermining a major—but by no means the only—benefit of the reform.

But there is a more direct political incentive to macroeconomic discipline under a private defined-contribution pension plan. In a public defined-*benefit* plan, workers have a comparatively stronger incentive to vote for politicians who pledge to protect retirement benefits and minimize social security taxes for as long as possible, potentially at the expense of fiscal management. Under a defined-*contribution* system, instead, as individual wealth and the adequacy of retirement income become increasingly linked to the performance of domestic stock and bond prices, workers will have a comparatively stronger incentive to vote for politicians who endorse economic policies that will be beneficial to stock and bond markets (Hale, 1993). That is to say, they will tend to vote for politicians who support sound fiscal policies, low inflation, and increased international competitiveness.

It can further be argued that in an economy where a greater portion of the population becomes owners of and creditors to firms, the interests of labor and management become increasingly similar (i.e., both are interested in the health and profitability of companies).[14] Thus, the historically antagonistic relationship between labor and management can slowly diminish. Certainly that has been the case in Chile, where a remarkable degree of economic policy consensus across economic classes has emerged. Interestingly, in Chile that consensus has centered not around unfettered capitalism but on market liberalism combined with a sensitivity to the country's social needs. The policy consensus has created an environment of political stability that has contributed to high rates of economic growth, strong export performance, and a gradual reduction in inflation.

CONCLUSION

Although the U.S. OASDI system is not facing a crisis of the severity faced by the Chilean social security system prior to 1981, the system's as-yet unresolved long-term financing issues suggest that a Chilean-style social security reform is an attractive option for U.S. policy makers. The Chilean experience provides evidence that a switch from a public defined-benefit to a private defined-contribution pension system can simplify long-term fiscal management, stimulate private savings, and provide a significant boost to local capital markets. The benefits need not be achieved at the expense of reducing workers' disposable income or increasing firms' labor costs. In addition, a switch to a defined-contribution system eliminates the intergenerational and individual inequities and the long-term income uncertainties that can arise from repeated changes in OASDI's taxation rates and benefits. Although the short-term fiscal effects of a switch to a defined-contribution system could give rise to wider fiscal deficits, political incentives are likely to work against this. With political tolerance for fiscal deficits already on the wane in Washington, politicians may well face even greater pressure to maintain a prudent fiscal stance: As voters' wealth becomes increasingly linked to stock and bond market performance, politicians will seek to win votes by supporting economic policies beneficial to those markets. Last, it can be argued that as employees become ever more important owners of and creditors to corporations, the traditional labor-versus-management psychology can slowly fade, as the interests of the two groups become increasingly similar.

ACKNOWLEDGMENT

The views represented in this paper are those of the author and do not reflect the views of the author's current or past employers.

NOTES

1. In the United States, for example, it is estimated that the ratio of people ages 15-64 to people over age 65—the so-called "support ratio"—will drop from just under 6:1 in 1980 to about 3:1 in 2040. An even more pronounced decline in the support ratio is expected in Japan, France, and Germany (John Hills, London School of Economics, as quoted in Balls, 1993).

2. For further discussion of the difficulties of the system, see Myers (1985) and Iglesias and Acuna 1991.

3. Beyond privatizing the pension system, the social security reform also privatized survivors, disability, and health insurance. This paper focuses primarily on the pension system reform.

4. The government dealt with the issue of older workers by refunding worker contributions to the old system via *bonos de reconocimiento* (recognition bonds) at retirement. The value of the bond was equal to 80% of the employee's average salary in the 12 months leading to mid-1979 (indexed), times the number of years the employee contributed to the system (up to 35 years), divided by 35, times an annuity factor (10.35 for men, 11.36 for women).

5. Some analysts argue that this fiscal surplus was achieved at a substantial social cost. Although this may well have been the case, the achievement of the fiscal surplus to implement the new social security system avoided arguably even more costly future tax increases or benefit cuts necessary to shore up the old system.

6. Gillion and Bonilla (1992) estimate that a worker who contributes 10% of his or her salary for 45 years and lives 14 additional years, would obtain a benefit equal to 44% of final insured wages assuming a 3% real rate of return on AFP investments (a number of other relatively conservative assumptions are also made). It should be noted that final insured wages are generally considerably higher than the minimum wage. Furthermore, AFP annual real returns since inception have averaged over 13%, so the benefit is likely to be considerably higher than their estimate. Iglesias and Acuna 1991, p. 53) estimate that a 5% real rate of return on investments will provide men with a pension income equal to 79%

of final salary and women with a pension income equal to 56% of final salary. The difference in retirement income between men and women is due to women's earlier retirement age (60 versus 65 for men) and longer life expectancy.

7. For the 1985 coverage estimate, see Mesa-Lago 1991, p. 150). For the more recent estimate, see Myers (1992). Not everyone in Chile is covered by the new system; older workers may have opted to remain in the public defined-benefit plan.

8. That is, we assume that the supply of foreign financing is fixed or nearly fixed. This assumption is the subject of heated debate, as it goes to the heart of the question of whether there is perfect global capital mobility. If capital is not perfectly mobile, then domestic investment rates and domestic savings rates will be positively correlated. In the case of Chile, capital controls have historically restricted capital flows and the assumptions made here may not be far from reality. Historical data on Chilean domestic savings and investment from 1976 to 1992 show a positive correlation coefficient of 0.7.

9. In the 1986-1992 period, when the shift from public to private sector savings became even more pronounced, the addition to the GDP growth rate associated with a one-point change in the investment-to-GDP ratio rose even further, to 0.296.

10. Each AFP must, on a monthly basis, post 12-month real investment returns at least equal to either (1) the average real return of the entire AFP system minus two percentage points, or (2) 50% of the return posted by the AFP system if the system's real return is less than 2%. AFPs can build up reserves during times of overperformance to meet the requirement during times of underperformance. AFPs can also use the 1% cash reserve requirement to meet the performance criteria. If these are not sufficient, then AFP capital can be drawn down. Only after all these sources of funding are employed will the SAFP intervene.

11. The equity exposure limit is set at 30% of AFP assets over the course of the year. However, AFP exposure to equities at any given point in time can exceed 30% of assets as long as the average limit is not exceeded.

12. The new regulations will ease ownership concentration limits and will allow AFP investment in companies that have posted profits in the last two years. Specific rules will be worked out in the next several months by the SAFP and the Chilean equivalent of the Securities and Exchange Commission.

13. In the United States as well, the idea of eliminating Old Age Survivors' and Disability Insurance (OASDI) entirely is not likely to be popular. An AP-NBC News poll taken in 1982 during the height of the system's crisis revealed that 78% of respondents opposed the idea of phasing out OASDI and relying on private pension income (Meyers, 1992). However, this is not to say that U.S. social security reform would be unpopular after its implementation. The reform was certainly disliked in Chile at first, but now that the benefits of the reform have become clear, the new system enjoys overwhelming public support.

14. For a far more detailed exposition of this idea, see Drucker (1976).

REFERENCES

Balls, E. 1993. "Delayed Effects of Japan's Demographic Time-Bomb." *The Financial Times* (December 5).

Drucker, P. 1976. *The Unseen Revolution.* New York: Harper and Row.

Gillion, C., and A. Bonilla. 1992. "Analysis of a National Private Pension Scheme: The Case of Chile." *International Labor Review* 131(2): pp. 171-195.

Hale, D. 1993. "Experiment in Democracy." Paper presented at the 1993 Davos World Economic Forum.

Iglesias, A. and R. Acuna. 1991. *Chile: Experiencia con un Regimen de Capitalizacion 1981-1991.* Santiago, Chile Comision Economica para America Latina y el Caribe (CEPAL) and Programa de las Naciones Unidas para el Desarrollo (PNUD).

Kritzer, B.E. 1981. "Chile Changes Social Security." *Social Security Bulletin* 44(5, May): pp. 33-37.

Mesa-Lago, C. 1991. "Social Security and Prospects for Equity in Latin America." World Bank Discussion Paper No. 140. Washington, DC: World Bank.

Myers, R.J. 1985. "Privatization of Chile's Social Security Program." *Benefits Quarterly* 1(3): 26-35.

_______ 1992. "Chile's Social Security Reform, After Ten Years." *Benefits Quarterly* Vol. 8 (3): pp. 41-55.

Santamaria, M. 1992. "Privatizing Social Security: The Chilean Case." *Columbia Journal of World Business* XXVII(1, Spring): pp. 41-55.

THE CHILEAN SYSTEM: A MODEL FOR OTHERS?

Robert Myers

After studying the Chilean system for a decade, I believe that it is a very good thing for Chile to have done. It was not necessarily the only solution, but they have gone down this road quite successfully and should not return to the traditional social insurance system.

However, this solution is not necessarily a good one for any other country, especially the United States. The social insurance system in Chile in the late 1970s was very bad. The assets had been depleted by inflation; there was very poor administration; there was a wide diversity of systems; the benefit structure was unsound—the benefits were very high and the retirement ages were very low, particularly for economically favored groups; and everything was really in chaos. As a result of this, the government had to inject massive amounts of general revenue into the system, and had been doing so for some years.

However, there are several concerns, not so much for Chile as for any other nation that might attempt a similar plan. There are huge government subsidies involved. Chile had the money available to make some of these subsidies. They had been doing it all along, so they were not going from having no general revenues to suddenly high general revenues, as the United States would have to do if it went to a privatized system.

Of course, some of the money from general revenues that is going into the system is like recycling: the government getting the money from the pension funds and giving them government bonds, because almost half the assets of the pension funds are indexed government bonds at a relatively high rate of interest. That is one way to earn a high rate of return. So, it is a little hard to say where the money is coming from.

These huge government subsidies are necessary for two reasons. First, they are for prior-service credits, since people are given credit for prior service under the old system, not paid when the person starts in the new system but rather when the person retires, so that for quite a number of years as people retire, the government will be transferring huge sums of money to the pension companies and, in turn, the pension companies will buy more government bonds. At any rate, there is an obligation for the government to pay this money and incur more debt.

The prior-service obligations will disappear over time. Of long-run concern are the relatively large minimum pensions. If the accumulation does not provide enough to reach the minimum, currently the government makes up the difference, and this can happen either for people who retire and buy an annuity that is insufficient to meet the minimum or for people who take the option of systematic withdrawal and later, if they live too long, their account is exhausted and then they switch over to the minimum pension.

The minimum pension is 85% of the minimum wage for people ages 65 to 70, and 90% for people age 70 and over. Furthermore, the minimum pension is, in a way, indexed to the cost of living—not automatically, but on a de facto basis, because each year the Chilean legislature must reexamine the situation, and the general practice in recent years has been to give an increase in the minimum wage corresponding to the increase in the cost of living. If inflation is greater than 15% in any period less than a year, then the legislature has always considered the matter sooner. The legislature is not forced to do it, but politically there are great pressures to increase the minimum pension. So, there is this long-range cost to the general revenues, and the finances of the country have to take this into account.

Another problem that this system has is that there is not universal coverage compliance. Not only is there a situation like

"Nannygate" in this country of not covering low-paid employees because of ignorance or laziness. There is also the planned underreporting of wages for low-paid workers because to be eligible for a pension, all that is required is 20 years of contributions, and there is no use reporting wages higher than what is necessary. Even if wages are underreported, a year of coverage is obtained. The contributions that would have been paid computed on the worker's real, higher wage would just have been wasted, because the minimum pension will apply to them anyhow. So, there is that problem of benefit design.

There is also the problem of high administrative expenses. The administrative expenses, other than the investment expenses, run roughly 12% or 13% of contribution income, which is quite high relative to other systems.

An additional concern of the Chilean system is that the people who operate it say that, in the long run, the real interest rate that they expect to achieve on average is not the current 12% or 13%, but rather 7% or 8%; with that and a 10% contribution rate, they believe that adequate pensions will be provided. Over the long run, when an economy develops well, it would be very difficult to average a 7% or 8% real annual interest rate.

Another element, too, is that the life expectancy in Chile will improve in the future. With an increase in general education and prosperity in the country, people will live longer in the future, so that even though a worker accumulates a lump sum at the time of retirement that seems adequate to provide a reasonable pension, with a longer life expectancy, it will not be sufficient.

One final question that needs to be raised, not only for Chile but also probably for some of the emerging countries, is: what are they going to do with all of this money? Are there viable investments, or will there be so much money that there will be great sums chasing a relatively small number of reasonable investments? Will this lead to all sorts of waste and fraud? Whenever large "pots of money" accumulate, swindlers quickly follow, and the money may be wasted.

One of the investment vehicles that Chile can get into, in a small way, is investing abroad. That can be very unpopular politically because people will say, "Hey! You are sending our money out of the country. We need the money in this country to improve our conditions."

To summarize, while the Chilean system is certainly superior to its predecessor, it has some problems and it arose from circumstances unique to Chile. Therefore, it is not necessarily an ideal system for others to emulate.

PART III

THE SOCIAL SECURITY TRUST FUND INVESTMENT POLICY

SOCIAL SECURITY INVESTMENT POLICY: WHAT IS IT AND HOW CAN IT BE IMPROVED?

Carolyn L. Weaver

INTRODUCTION

The assets of the social security trust funds are enormous. At the end of fiscal year 1994, they stood at $422 billion (or a whopping $549 billion, including the Medicare trust fund),[1] dwarfing the assets of the nation's largest corporate and public employee pension funds. For comparitive purposes, the assets of the largest corporate pension plans in the United States—General Motors, AT&T, GE, or IBM, for example—are on the order of $30-$50 billion, and the assets of the largest public employee pension funds—the California or the New York City retirement systems, for example—are on the order of $50-$70 billion.[2] At $422 billion, the social security reserve fund amounts to more than one-tenth of corporate equities outstanding and over one-fifth of corporate and foreign bonds outstanding.[3] According to the government's own projections, the social security reserve will double within a decade and peak at $1.3 trillion (in constant 1994 dollars) in 2015.[4] The much-discussed social security surplus now tops $50 billion annually, the equivalent of about $1 billion a week.

Despite the accumulation of these vast sums of private resources through the social security payroll tax, the federal government has yet to set in place policies to ensure that surplus tax receipts are productively saved and invested for the future. Ironically, it was not until Senator Daniel Patrick Moynihan proposed cutting the payroll tax and substantially reducing the size of future trust fund accumulations that attention really focused on the government's "investment policy" for social security.[5] Under present law and procedure, virtually all monies not needed to pay benefits are held in special issue U.S. government bonds, which are, quite literally, IOUs from one part of the government to another. Thanks to Senator Moynihan, a lively debate has ensued as to whether this policy makes any economic or fiscal sense.[6]

In this paper, I describe, and then discuss the shortcomings of, present funding and investment policies. I then evaluate a number of alternative investment strategies, ranging from expanding the powers of the federal government to investing in a broad array of public and private obligations to granting individuals the right to invest their own tax contributions. Each of these strategies is evaluated in terms of its ability to deal with the central flaw in present law: the absence of any requirement that, on a sustained, long-term basis, surplus monies are productively saved and invested for the future.

FUNDING AND INVESTMENT POLICY

Over the course of the next 75 years—the social security actuaries' official long-range measuring period—social security is slated to spend $21 trillion in present-value terms. (Counting Medicare, the projected liability is closer to $35 trillion.)[7] Under the 1983 Social Security Amendments, this liability is scheduled to be met through partial advance funding. The payroll tax is projected to generate more revenues than necessary to meet benefits for the next 20 years or so. During this period, the trust funds will amass a large, interest-bearing reserve of U.S. government bonds. Interest earnings, together with tax income, are projected to keep social security in surplus for another five or six years. Beginning around 2020, when expenditures begin to outstrip tax and interest income, benefits are to be met by rapidly redeeming the trust funds' bond holdings. Within a decade, in 2029, the social security reserve is projected to be exhausted and the system insolvent. Medicare is financed in basically the same way, only the projected surpluses are smaller, the deficits are larger, and reserves are depleted much more rapidly.[8]

The term "partial advance funding" refers to the fact that social security's assets are not, and never will be, large enough to fund accrued liabilities, as would be implied by the term "full funding." Even when reserves are at their peak, they amount to only about two years' worth of benefit payments—a tiny fraction of the liabilities that would have accrued by then. Nevertheless, over the next two to three decades, reserves are projected to surpass the needs of a system financed on a current cost, or pay-as-you-go, basis.[9]

As spelled out in the law, all monies not needed to meet current benefit payments must be invested in interest-bearing obligations of the U.S. government guaranteed as to both principal and interest (see Section 201(c) of the Social Security Act; Kollmann 1991; U.S. Senate 1982).[10] The managing trustee of the trust funds, the Secretary of Treasury, is required to invest in "special issue" government bonds unless he determines that the purchase of ordinary marketable government bonds is "in the public interest." The special issue bonds held by the social security trust funds earn interest at a rate equal to the average market yield on long-term U.S. government bonds; they are redeemable at par, meaning that there is no risk of capital loss for redemption before maturity (which is of value to the trust funds if early redemption is necessary and interest rates are rising), and maturities are set "with due regard" to the needs of the trust funds. Special issue bonds are not available to the general public.

Under operating procedures established by the Secretary of Treasury, maturities on new special issues range from one to 15 years and are set so that roughly one-fifteenth of the portfolio comes due in each of the next 15 years.[11] When securities must be redeemed to meet benefits, those with the shortest durations until maturity are sold first. In the event that there are several securities with the same duration until maturity, those with the lowest interest rate are redeemed first.

Under these guidelines, all of the assets of the old-age and survivors insurance trust fund and virtually all (over 95%) of the assets of the disability insurance trust fund are held in special issue bonds. (DI holds a small amount of marketable long-term government bonds.) The interest rate on new special issues as of June 1993 was 6.25%; the average effective yield on trust fund assets in 1993 was 8.3%.[12]

The Forest for the Trees

When evaluating present policies with regard to funding and investments, it is easy to become distracted by the details of the special issue bonds—rates paid, maturity distributions, redemptions schedules, and the like—and, in so doing, lose sight of the forest for the trees. Certainly this appears to be what happened to Congress in 1983. When attention might have focused on how large a reserve fund to accumulate and how quickly, or how best to invest and manage those reserves, policymakers considered just one small side issue: the formula used for setting the interest rate on special issue bonds. But the rate paid on special issues simply determines the direction and extent of cross-subsidies between the trust funds and the general fund of the Treasury. It is of no practical import to the quality of the investment (the burden of future benefits, for example) independent of the stance of overall fiscal policy—as the debate triggered by the Moynihan proposal has helped illuminate. Likewise, the rate paid on special issues, or on any other investment for that matter, is of limited import when the initial investment and accrued interest can be appropriated for other uses.

Practical Problems

There are two practical problems with the way the government advance funds social security's long-term liability and invests the system's assets. First, there is no mechanism in the law to ensure that the surpluses are, in fact, saved—meaning that real resources are transferred from present to future generations. When surplus monies are "invested" in new, special-issue government bonds, the trust funds are credited with a bond—an IOU from one part of the government to another—and the Treasury gets the cash. From the standpoint of the Treasury, these monies are indistinguishable from any other monies and are available to finance the general operations of the government. Only if Congress forgoes the opportunity to use the excess social security revenues to cut income or other federal taxes, or to expand spending on other programs, can the surpluses amount to government saving.[13]

As explained by Harvard University economist Martin Feldstein, a strong proponent of advance funding, social security surpluses *can* add to the nation's real capital investment, albeit indirectly, provided they are used to buy outstanding government debt from private investors (Feldstein 1976). As private investors substitute new private securities for the government debt they relinquish, funds are made available for increased private investment. This, in turn, allows for increased capital formation and, ultimately, higher future real incomes with which to meet the cost of retirement benefits in the coming decades. Payroll taxes can be lower than otherwise because of the substantial interest accruing to the trust funds. Meanwhile, the income tax necessary to finance the interest payments need not be any higher. Since there is no change in the government's overall indebtedness, only a change in ownership—from the public to the trust funds—monies that would have been paid to private investors would be paid to the trust funds instead. The overall tax burden thereby can be lowered by advance-funding social security.

But, as the debate kicked off by the Moynihan proposal has revealed, there are a number of important "ifs" in this positive scenario.[14] If the availability of surplus social security revenues relaxes fiscal restraint in the rest of the budget, there is no meaningful advance funding or investment policy. There is simply a hidden reallocation of taxes—toward payroll tax financing of the general operations of the government today and toward general fund financing of social security tomorrow. The $1.3 trillion reserve projected for the next century then represents nothing more than social security's claim on the general fund of the Treasury at that time—its accumulated spending authority—with no real capital backing up that claim. And those interest payments, scheduled to amount to almost one-seventh of trust fund income in 2015 ($77 billion in constant 1994 dollars), would amount to a new liability incurred on account of the trust fund build-up! National saving and economic growth would be undermined by advance funding, as would the fiscal integrity of social security and the federal budget.

The concern here is not with the use of the social security surpluses to "fund the deficit," about which there has been so much discussion. Presumably, funding the deficit means reducing the amount of new borrowing the federal government must do, which is as intended. The concern is that the surpluses allow for an *increase* in the deficit in the rest of the budget, in which case, they have little or no beneficial impact on the overall federal deficit or the amount of public debt outstanding.[15]

The second practical problem with current policy is that nothing ensures that the surpluses, if saved, will be saved on a sustained, long-term basis. Throughout history, Congress has increased benefits and met part of the cost by depleting reserves rather than by raising taxes (or cutting other benefits) to replenish reserves. As reserves accumulate, the political pressures will be strong to pay larger benefits to groups deemed "particularly deserving"—whether aged widows, two-earner families, "notch babies," the incapacitated near-elderly, nonworking spouses, or any other group. And there is always Medicare, ever in need of a helping hand. The long-range Medicare deficit is so large that it alone could consume all of social security's available reserves and surplus monies, rendering the entire system insolvent by 2020. Increasing benefits or bailing out Medicare through interfund borrowing would undermine saving just as surely as any mishandling of the federal budget today.

Importantly, there are no minimum funding rules with which social security must comply, such as those imposed on private pension plans through the provisions of ERISA (the Employee Retirement Income Security Act). There is no requirement in the law, for example, that a certain level of reserves must be maintained against a portion of accruing liabilities, or even that annual balance between spending and revenues must be maintained. Without rules that define, for the general public and members of Congress, what can and cannot be afforded with current resources, or what must or must not be saved, there is every reason to believe that benefits will be increased or monies will be diverted to the Medicare trust fund, and a portion of the reserves will be spent rather than saved.

SOME ALTERNATIVE INVESTMENT POLICIES

Social security is obviously in need of a meaningful "investment policy" since, as noted above, the surpluses are not automatically or even necessarily saved and invested on an ongoing basis. Trust fund assets can be dissipated by program expansions or undermined by a loosening of control in the rest of the budget.

Alternative investment policies must be evaluated in terms of their ability to deal with these central problems.

Government-Controlled Portfolio of Government Bonds Coupled with Fiscal Rules

At present, the trust funds can be thought of as government-controlled portfolios of government bonds that are "passively" rather than "actively" managed. Except in the most unusual circumstances (such as in 1985, when the public debt limit was about to be reached) everything is on automatic pilot.[16]

A policy such as this—or more generally, a policy of advance funding with investments limited to government bonds—can only make sense if Congress adopts, and lives by, rules that ensure long-term government saving. In particular, to ensure that trust fund surpluses actually increase government savings (or reduce the public debt outstanding), the federal budget *excluding* social security must be balanced.[17] The overall federal budget would then run a *surplus* equal to the social security surplus.

Second, to ensure that trust fund surpluses reduce social security's unfunded liability, reserves must be maintained at a specified level relative to accruing liabilities. The "funding ratio" in the law may vary over time—a period of accumulation and partial depletion may well be deemed appropriate—but the chosen path must be retained.

Together, these rules would ensure that the social security surpluses were used exclusively to retire outstanding publicly held debt for the purpose of lightening the burden of retirement benefits, and government spending generally, in the next century. Although it is unlikely that retaining the current policy of investing in special issue government bonds, with these constraints in place, would produce the best possible return on investments (the portfolio would remain passively managed with limited investment options), it would expose the trust funds to minimal risk of capital loss and allow for an increase in capital investment without involving the federal government in direct management and control of private resources.

But alas, the feasibility (or unfeasibility) of this option is determined entirely by the government's willingness to impose on itself, and abide by, fiscal rules it has been quite unwillingly to impose or abide by to date. Absent enforceable rules, this option relies on a degree of fiscal discipline unseen during the better part of this century. The efficacy of this approach, moreover, would depend crucially on the mix of policies used to balance the non-social-security budget. Adherence to rules per se does not create capital. Tax increases on investment, for example, could undermine private saving and offset the gains to be achieved by increasing government saving.

Individually-Controlled Investments in a Broad Portfolio of Financial Instruments

An altogether different approach, which recognizes the considerable reluctance of Congress to live with binding constraints, is to give individuals covered by social security the right to control the investment of surplus taxes in a broad portfolio of financial instruments. The principal of advance funding would be retained, but the role of the government in managing surplus funds would be eliminated. This is what Representative John E. Porter has in mind with his proposed legislation.[18]

Unfortunately, it is not possible to analyze this approach assuming it were superimposed on the present system. Given the redistributive nature of social security, only a small portion of the typical individual's taxes is potentially available to finance his or her benefits; most will be used to finance someone else's benefits—someone older or someone poorer, for example. If individuals are to gain ownership and control over their share of surplus taxes, some restructuring of benefits in relation to taxes is unavoidable.

Consider, for example, a possible two-tiered system.[19] One tier would offer a flat or means-tested payment to retirees, financed on a pay-as-you-go basis. The other tier would offer an earnings-related payment, financed on a fully funded basis. Under the second tier, which would amount to a defined contribution pension plan, taxes could be channeled directly into individualized private savings accounts, possibly along the lines of Individual Retirement Accounts (IRAs); benefits would be paid directly out of the proceeds of these accounts, based on contributions plus interest. By design, there would be no surplus tax receipts to be managed by the federal government and, thus, no funds available to underwrite an expansion in the rest of the budget. The second-tier benefits would place no demands on the federal budget.

This option would allow for real saving and real capital investment in the private sector, and it would do so without involving the federal government in direct management and control of vast sums of private resources. Investment decisions would be fully decentralized and competitively determined. At the same time, individuals would be directly involved in their retirement-savings decisions, accumulating legally enforceable claims to future benefits.

This option, it should be stressed, is *not* equivalent to empowering the government to engage in direct investment of trust fund assets in the private sector, as has been suggested by some. Were the power to control a portfolio of several hundred billion dollars—potentially, several trillion dollars—delegated to a government entity, it is inconceivable that investment decisions would be made "as if" by individuals or private portfolio managers in a competitive market place. The problem is political and informational. In the political market place, where individuals bear only a small share of the costs they impose on others (and reap only a small share of the benefits they produce), incentives are weak to make well-informed, efficient decisions. Critical decisions regarding how to allocate trust fund monies to various securities, and when and how quickly to change such allocations, would be monopolized and, inevitably, politicized. This would be true whether the investment board were, say, the Social Security Board of Trustees (which comprises the Secretaries of Treasury, Health and Human Services, and Labor; the Commissioner of Social Security; and two members of the public, all appointed by the President and confirmed by the Senate) or a politically appointed board (which might comprise people appointed by the legislative and executive branches to reflect various political interests or people elected by social security workers and retirees). Investment decisions would be politically determined and resources would flow toward politically favored projects. One can easily imagine the list of disallowed investments, right alongside the list of preferred investments. It would be a fine line indeed between "investments" and public spending by another name.[20]

Two recent studies of the influence of political factors on the performance of state and local pension funds are illuminating in this regard. Yale University Law Professor Roberta Romano, for example, reports that "public pension funds are subject to political pressures to tailor their investments to local needs, such as increasing state employment, and to engage in other socially desirable investing." She notes that "numerous states mandate or encourage local investment by funds ... often termed social investments, or economically targeted investments, and the return is typically not commensurate with the risk" (see Romano 1993a, pp. 44-45; see also Romano, 1993b). In a separate study of over 200 state and local pension plans, University of Pennsylvania economist Olivia Mitchell reports that social investing in in-state projects has a significant negative impact on investment returns (Mitchell 1993).

What would be gained by direct private investment—whether by government or by individuals? Monies that now go toward the purchase of special-issue U.S. government bonds would go instead toward the purchase of private securities. This *could* improve returns on trust fund assets, but what would it do to create capital? It all depends on how the government responds to the loss of surplus tax revenues. While there is no direct empirical evidence to draw on one way or the other, I believe (as many analysts do) that the government is spending the social security surpluses on current consumption—by relaxing fiscal restraint in the rest of the budget—rather than saving them, and that the government's fiscal decisions would be more prudent were these surpluses to vanish. In this case, a shift toward direct private investment would result in less debt accumulation and, thus (potentially), in the purchase of more private securities, not just in a swap of government securities for private securities. With government-directed investments, however, the problems surrounding politically controlled investment decisions would remain.

If the goal of reform is to short-circuit the direct and indirect spending of reserves, to bolster rates of return, and to achieve the full benefits of capital accumulation, a policy of government-directed investments is unlikely to be successful. Such a policy would put taxpayers' monies at risk and likely distort the allocation of capital in the economy. Managers of a large public portfolio would have the capacity to make or break individual firms and to concentrate the ownership and control of U.S. corporations to an unprecedented degree. Already there is concern, whether warranted or not, about the concentration of resources in corporate pension funds, the largest of which hold assets a fraction of the size of social security's current reserve. Romano's conclusion, shared by me, is that protecting public pension assets requires *insulating* investment decisions from politics.

Having said that, I wholeheartedly support proposals to shift toward private investment of social security monies—provided that the government is kept at bay and not left in a position to "play the market" or to influence others to do so. This is the appeal of the two-tiered proposal described above, which allows for direct investment through a highly decentralized, market-based mechanism.

Subcontract with Professional Money Managers

Proponents of an expanded role for the private sector argue for yet another option, which is to allow for direct private investment by professional money managers operating on behalf of the federal government. This option offers a number of advantages over the present system; it carries risks, however, that are not unlike those associated with direct government investment. In particular, given the size of the social security "portfolio" and the inherently political nature of the system, Congress would certainly place restrictions on allowable investments and investment strategies. The net effect of these restrictions would be determined by whether they were designed to control risk or to politically influence the allocation of capital in the economy.

To avoid certain obvious control problems, one of two requirements (possibly both) would be desirable in subcontracting with private money managers: first, require that assets be managed by a group of competing money managers, preventing any single manager from controlling more than a portion of investments;[21] second, require that assets be passively managed. For example, one could envision the Trustees subcontracting for the management of, say, a fixed-income securities fund and a stock index fund. This is basically the way the federal government operates its supplemental retirement fund for civil service employees, known as the Thrift Savings Plan.[22] The Thrift Investment Board competitively contracts with Wells Fargo Institutional Trust Company to manage two separate funds, a common stock index fund and a bond index fund. With index funds such as these, money managers do not actively "play the market;" assets are carefully allocated to securities so as to track closely the performance of some segment of the market—the S&P 500 index, in the case of the common stock index fund, and the SLBA (Shearson Lehman Brothers Aggregate) bond index, in the case of the bond index fund.[23]

This option offers some clear advantages over the present arrangement. Most importantly, monies flowing into the index funds are not comingled with other federal monies. If social security is to remain advance funded, this option provides more certainty that trust fund surpluses would increase government saving. Likewise, this option affords the opportunity to take at least partial advantage of known or anticipated tradeoffs between risk and return that might result in a higher average return (or more favorable risk-adjusted return) on trust fund assets. Compared to direct private investment by the government, this option is attractive because it depoliticizes investment decisions to a significant degree.

This option does not, however, foreclose the possibility that Congress will use its command over trust fund assets to politically influence the allocation of capital—and, thus, the distribution of wealth and income—in the economy. For example, Congress might insist that a certain fraction of assets be invested in a fund comprising only securities of "socially responsible" companies or of U.S.-owned companies. While some might argue that the risk of this is minimal and point to the Thrift Savings Plan as evidence, social security is an altogether different animal than the Thrift Savings Plan. Under the Thrift Savings Plan, individual contributions are entirely voluntary.[24] If displeased with restrictions imposed on a particular fund, or its performance, individuals can shift their contributions and interest earnings to another fund, stop making contributions, or, in certain circumstances, withdraw their contributions and earnings altogether.[25] In a very real sense, the various funds compete head-to-head with private funds and other private investments, not just with one another. The competition fostered by individual choice and the mobility of resources places real limits on the inefficiencies that can be imposed by the Congress.

Also, this option does not preclude trust fund reserves from being spent—by Congress, not by the money managers—on unfunded increases in social security benefits. The Thrift Savings Plan avoids this problem because it is a defined-contribution plan. Defined-contribution plans, unlike social security which is a defined-benefit plan, are fully funded and workers own the proceeds of their pension accounts; monies invested cannot (absent fraud) be diverted for other uses.

The beauty of the two-tiered system described above is that it moves further in the direction of the Thrift Savings Plan and, in so doing, gives individual workers, not a government board or government-influenced money manager, the right to control the investment of their social security taxes.

SUMMING UP

When all is said and done, an effective—and effectively controlled—investment policy requires that competition be fostered wherever possible. The inefficiencies of the present arrangement derive in no small measure from the government's monopoly control over trust fund investments coupled with its inherent monopoly over fiscal policy. Competition provides the information needed by individual policymakers and citizens generally to evaluate alternative investments; it enables resources to flow to their highest valued uses.

With that said, expanding the powers or discretion of the federal government to manage trust fund investments cannot, in my view, be justified. The economic consequences would be either negligible (in the event that the Trustees began investing in the obligations of government-sponsored agencies, for example) or potentially quite adverse (in the event that the Trustees began spending surplus monies on "public investments" or in other ways diverting resources to lower-valued uses).

A continuation of the status quo can not be justified either. For most American taxpayers, social security is a heavier tax burden than the federal income tax. Using this high and regressive tax to generate surplus revenues that are diverted to fund current government consumption makes no sense on economic or social grounds. Cutting taxes and moving back to pay-as-you-go financing would clearly be preferable.[26]

Proposals to increase the role of the private sector in the investment of trust fund assets are, it seems to me, very attractive—

provided they involve meaningful competition. Subcontracting the management of trust fund assets to competing money managers (who presumably would invest in a mix of private and government obligations) would offer real advantages over the present system. Allowing individuals covered by social security a measure of control over investment decisions would offer even greater advantages, expanding their role as private investors and as stakeholders in the capital that will form the basis of their retirement incomes. The latter option, however, would necessitate a restructuring of benefits in relation to taxes and, thus, must be seen as a long-term reform involving issues other than just saving and investment.

ACKNOWLEDGMENTS

The author wishes to acknowledge the helpful comments of David Koitz and Robert Mackay on an earlier version of this paper.

NOTES

1. Social Security refers to the old-age and survivors insurance program and the disability insurance program, each of which has its own trust fund. The actuarial data on these two funds are typically merged in discussions of the financial condition of social security, although the operations of the programs are entirely separate. There is also a trust fund for hospital insurance, or Medicare part A. Data on trust funds is contained in Dickstein (1994).
2. Data is contained in The Money Market (1993).
3. As of year-end 1990 (see Federal Reserve 1994, p. 67).
4. For this data and other projections, see, Board of Trustees OASDI (1994) and Board of Trustees FHITF (1994) intermediate assumption.
5. Senator Daniel Patrick Moynihan introduced legislation in 1990, S.2016, to cut payroll tax in the near term and raise the tax in the longer term to restore pay-as-you-go financing. His proposal, which was revised over time, was finally defeated on the Senate floor when offered as an amendment to the FY1992 budget resolution. Senator Moynihan argued that current policy amounted to "thievery" of workers' tax payments (Moynihan, 1990).
6. For two books that deal directly with these issues and provide a range of opinions, see Weaver (1990a) and Aaron et al. (1989).
7. Data supplied by Office of the Actuary, SSA, April 25, 1994.
8. Based on the Trustees' intermediate II-B assumptions, the Medicare trust fund will be insolvent in 2001; the disability trust fund is slated for insolvency

in 1995. Under less optimistic assumptions, the financial condition of each of the trust funds is much more adverse.

9. Social security also differs from a fully funded system (or a sensible advance funded system) in that reserves are not maintained or replenished to ensure a stream of interest income that would help meet swelling expenditures; instead, as expenditures mount, reserves are drawn down rapidly and finally depleted altogether, almost as if the program would cease to exist or, at least, that expenditures swollen by the retirement of the baby boom would drop back to pre-baby boom levels. Such is not the case. Low fertility and increasing longevity conspire to produce a cost rate that drifts up for at least 50 years after the last of the baby-boom retirees reaches 65.

As one social security official has described the long-term financing picture, "It's more like a python swallowing a telephone pole than a python swallowing an elephant."

10. According to a 1982 study by the Congressional Budget Office, the vast majority of federal trust funds hold special issue government bonds; however, policies with regard to interest rates, redemption schedules and maturity dates vary widely (see Rivlin 1982). According to a 1988 study by General Accounting Office (cited in Koitz 1990), there were 167 federal trust funds.

11. Actually, excess monies are invested immediately in short-term certificates of indebtedness, which mature the following June 30. Each June 30, all of the certificates issued in the preceding year are rolled over into new (longer term) special issue bonds.

In 1993, the usual procedure of spreading the maturity distribution of special issues was not followed for investments in the disability insurance trust fund because its financial condition was deteriorating so rapidly. The number of bonds purchased was very small (less than one month's benefit payments) and the fund was expected to be drawn down during the balance of the year. Only one-year bonds were purchased and they were all redeemed by August 1993 Board of Trustees, OASDI, 1994, p. 44).

12. This is the average effective yield for the OASI trust fund; for DI, it is 8.6% (see Board of Trustees, OASDI, 1994, pp. 40-44).

13. For a fuller discussion of these issues, see Weaver Board of Trustees, OASDI, (1990, pp. 167-178).

14. Apart from those mentioned here, there is the over-arching issue of whether increased government saving actually increases national saving, as assumed by Feldstein, which is part of a broader debate over whether or to what extent government policies tend to be neutralized by the offsetting behavior of private individuals. My assumption is that government saving does influence national saving, even if not to the extent assumed by Feldstein.

15. At the present time, it is impossible to observe the size and composition of the budget to determine whether the social security surpluses are being spent in this way. Either we would have to know what the size and composition of the budget would have been in the absence of the trust fund buildup, or the budget excluding social security would have to be in balance. However, if the long-term target is budget balance for the overall budget, the surpluses would obviously be spent rather than saved.

As noted below, even though there is no direct empirical evidence on the issue, many analysts, myself included, believe that the surpluses are not being saved, certainly not on a dollar-for-dollar basis. For more on this, see essays in Weaver (1990).

16. On three occasions in 1985, the Secretary of the Treasury did not immediately invest monies credited to the trust funds (transfers from the general fund reflecting payroll tax income anticipated during the month) because total Treasury borrowing was already at or about to reach the statutory limit. The monies remained temporarily in non-interest-bearing accounts. In addition, one month when (as is typical) Treasury needed to borrow from the public in order to redeem the special issue bonds and pay benefits, it could not do so without first reducing borrowing below the statutory limit. To reduce total borrowing, it redeemed some long-term securities held by the trust funds (see U.S. Comptroller General 1985).

17. Alternatively, the surplus or deficit in the rest of the budget could bear some fixed relation to, say, GNP. The key is that the rest of the budget be unaffected by changes in social security reserves.

18. Representative John E. Porter has proposed refunding surplus monies for deposit in individualized retirement accounts; future social security benefits would be reduced accordingly. To retain the progressivity of the social security benefit structure, the reduction in future benefits would be relatively greater for high-income workers. See Porter (1990) and U.S. General Accounting Office (1990) for more details.

19. For more on this, see Weaver (1993, 1994). It should be noted that this option does not preclude subsidies to low-paid workers. These subsidies would be simple, explicit, and general-revenue financed, however, unlike under the present system where subsidies are complex, hidden, multi-directional, and payroll tax financed (see Weaver 1989).

Michael Boskin has proposed a two-tiered system that is similar in terms of the structure of benefits but different in terms of financing. Under his proposal, the earnings-related payments would be made by the federal treasury, as is presently the case, and financed on a pay-as-you-go basis. There would be no private sector accounts (Boskin 1986).

20. Quoting Rudolph Penner: "spending on physical investments has traditionally constituted a large share of the contents of the government's pork barrel. There has been enormous waste as the Federal government has squandered resources on low yielding investments, especially in the area of water projects" (Penner 1990, p. 26).

21. It is interesting to note that the largest money manager in the United States, Wells Fargo Investment Advisors, has assets of $139 billion, just one-third of the assets of the OASDI trust funds and one-quarter of the assets of the OASDI and HI trust funds combined ("1994 Directory of Money Managers." 1994, p. 20).

22. The Thrift Savings Plan was created in the 1986 legislation reforming the Civil Service Retirement System, the Federal Employees' Retirement System Act of 1986, P.L. 99-335.

23. Wells Fargo Institutional Trust Company is the largest and oldest investment manager of index funds in the United States, managing roughly

$117 billion in assets (Federal Retirement Thrift 1992, p. 8). The stock index fund, referred to as the C (for common stock) Fund, is invested in virtually all the 500 stocks included in the S&P 500. While the bond index fund, referred to as the F (for fixed-income) fund, does not invest in each security in the SLBA index, it is diversified and consists of a large number of government, corporate, and mortgage-backed securities. There is a third fund in the Thrift Savings Plan, the G Fund, comprised of short-term special issue government bonds. It is managed by the staff of the Thrift Investment Board (see Federal Retirement Thrift 1990, pp. 1-2).

24. Under the law, individuals covered by the Federal Employees' Retirement System (generally people hired after January 1, 1984, who are not covered by the Civil Service Retirement System) can contribute up to 10% of salary on a tax-deferred basis. The government (i.e., the employing agency) makes an automatic contribution of 1% of base salary then matches the first 5% (on a dollar-for-dollar basis up to 3% and fifty cents on the dollar thereafter) of employee contributions. Individuals can direct their contributions to any one of the three funds.

Employees covered by the CSRS can contribute up to 5% of salary and there is no government contribution or matching of contributions (see Federal Retirement Thrift 1990, pp. 3-18).

25. An individual who leaves government employment can, for example, transfer his or her vested account balance to an IRA or other eligible retirement plan. Experience with the Thrift Savings Plan is still quite limited and, thus, provides relatively little comparative information on this point. During a start-up period, a fixed (and declining) proportion of individuals' contributions had to be made to the G Fund of special issue government bonds, and all of the government's matching contributions had to be made to this fund, as did all of the contributions of employees covered by the old CSRS. It was not until 1990 that individuals were able to freely allocate their contributions (and accumulations) among the three funds. As recently as February 1990, for example, total assets were $5.3 billion, 98% of which were in the G Fund of special issue government bonds; as of year-end 1993, assets were $20.8 billion, 72% of which were in the G fund (see Federal Retirement Thrift 1990).

26. Returning to pay-as-you-go financing does not "solve" the saving and investment problems posed under present financing arrangements; it just makes those problems smaller. Even under the Moynihan proposal, the system would amass and maintain a reserve of hundreds of billions of dollars. In my view, a return to pay-as-you-go financing should be coupled with restraints on long-range benefits that bring spending back into line with available resources. For more on this, see Weaver (1990b).

REFERENCES

Aaron, H.J., B. Bosworth, and G. Burtless. 1989. *Can America Afford to Grow Old?* Washington, DC: The Brookings Institution.

Board of Trustees of the Federal Hospital Insurance Trust Fund (FHITF). 1994. *Annual Report.* Washington, DC: U.S. Government Printing Office.

Board of Trustees Federal Old-Age and Survivors Insurance and Federal Disability Insurance Trust Funds (OASDI). 1994. *Annual Report.* Washington, DC: U.S. Government Printing Office.

Boskin, M.J. 1986. *Too Many Promises: The Uncertain Future of Social Security.* Homewood, IL: Dow Jones-Irwin.

Dickstein, J. 1994. Memorandum, Office of the Actuary, Social Security Administration, dated July 25.

Federal Reserve System, Board of Governors. 1994 (March 9). *Flow of Funds Accounts: Flows and Outstandings, Fourth Quarter 1993.* Washington, DC: U.S. Government Printing Office.

Federal Retirement Thrift Savings Investment Board. 1990. *Summary of the Thrift Savings Plan for Federal Employees.* Washington, DC: Federal Thrift Savings Investment Board.

________. 1992. *Trift Savings Plan Investments: Options and Operations.* Washington, DC: Federal Thrift Savings Investment Board, August.

Feldstein, M. 1976. "The Social Security Fund and National Capital Accumulation." In *Funding Pensions: Issues and Implications for Financial Markets,* Conference Series No. 16. Boston, MA: Federal Reserve Bank of Boston, pp. 32-64.

Koitz, D. 1990. "Trust Funds and the Federal Deficit." In *CRS Report for Congress.* Washington DC: Congressional Research Service (February 26).

Kollmann, G. 1991. "Social Security: Investing the Surplus." In *CRS Report for Congress.* Washington DC: Congressional Research Service (January 27).

Mitchell, O.S. 1993. "Public Pension Fund Governance and Performance: Lessons for Developing Countries." Working Paper No. 9, Institute for Labor Market Policies, Cornell University, May.

The Money Market. 1993. *Directory of Pension Funds and Their Investment Managers, 1993.* Charlottesville, VA: Money Market Directories, Inc./ McGraw Hill.

Moynihan, D.P. 1990. "It's a Matter of Trust, Rosty." *The Washington Post* (March 22): A23.

"1994 Directory of Money Mangers." 1994. *Pensions and Investments* (Special Issue, March 16): 20.

Penner, R.G. 1990. "Federal Spending Issues of the 1990s." Paper presented to the American Enterprise Institute, January 26.

Porter, Representative J.E. 1990. Testimony before the Committee on Finance, U.S. Senate, Hearing on Social Security Tax Cut, February 8.

Rivlin, A.M. 1982. Memo to Senator William L. Armstrong, June 25.

Romano, R. 1993a. "Getting Politics Out of Public Pension Funds." *The American Enterprise* (November/December): 42-49.

________. 1993b. "Public Pension Fund Activism in Corporate Governance Reconsidered." *Columbia Law Review* 93(4, May): 795-853.

U.S. Comptroller General. 1985. Memo to Representative James R. Jones, Chairman, Subcommittee on Social Security, Committee on Ways and Means, U.S. House of Representatives, December 5.

U.S. General Accounting Office. 1990 (December). *Social Security: Analysis of a Proposal to Privatize the Trust Fund Reserves.* Washington, DC: U.S. Government Printing Office.

U.S. Senate. 1982. "Social Security Trust Fund Investment Policy." Hearing Before the Subcommittee on Social Security and Income Maintenance Programs of the Committee on Finance, 97th Congress, 2nd Session, June 8. Washington, DC: U.S. Government Printing Office.

Weaver, C.L. 1989. "The Social Security Surpluses: Changes are Needed to Ensure They are Saved," Testimony before the Committee on the Budget Task Force on Economic Policy, U.S. House of Representatives, Hearings on the Social Security Surpluses, May 18.

________. 1990a. Editor. *Social Security's Looming Surpluses: Prospects and Implications.* Washington, DC: The American Enterprise Institute.

________. 1990b. Testimony before the Committee on Finance, U.S. Senate, Hearing on Social Security Tax Cut, February 8.

________. 1993. "Social Security's Infirmities." *The American Enterprise* (March/April): 30-41.

________. 1994. "Social Security Reform After the 1983 Amendments: What Remains to be Done?" Paper presented at the Annual Meetings of the Eastern Economic Association, May.

NO WAY TO RUN A RAILROAD: SOCIAL SECURITY FUNDS SHOULD INVEST IN COMMON STOCKS!

Robert C. Perez

INTRODUCTION

Can we maintain a self-supporting national retirement system and if so, at what cost? This question has been raised repeatedly since the establishment of the social security system in the mid-1930s. American workers were promised in 1935 that if they worked hard, social security would afford them a safety net in retirement in the form of a guaranteed minimum pension. That promise is in jeopardy because the investment performance of the social security fund is inadequate to maintain the benefits.

In its present form, social security is a ticking timebomb. Although the program was initially designed to invest some contributions to build up funds for retirement, it was changed over the years to a pay-as-you-go system. It resembles a giant Ponzi or pyramid scheme—a system that pays off early investors with the money of later investors but generates little real growth. Ironically, even though workers pay as much as 15% of their incomes into the system (counting the employer's matching contribution), they have no legal claim to their social security. In 1960, the Supreme Court (in *Flemming v. Nestor*) ruled that workers do not have any accrued property rights associated with social security. When beneficiaries learn that the government does not invest their retirement money and that they have no legal claim to their benefits, they react with shock and disbelief (Genetski 1993).

Through the efforts of Senator Daniel Patrick Moynihan and others, the public is becoming more and more aware that social security contributions are not "invested" to finance future retirement benefits. As the General Accounting Office has stated: "The present situation means that the payroll tax is being used, not to make provision for future retirement benefits, but to pay for today's general operations of government" (Whalen, 1991, p. 10).

RETIREMENT GOALS AND BENEFITS

Most studies show that retirement security ranks as the highest priority in worker's goals. But the government-sponsored social security, which was designed to provide a retirement security blanket for all working Americans, has failed to provide workers with adequate supplementary retirement income; the average annual social security payment in 1993 was $7,600, close to the poverty level. Even for the highest earning individuals, the benefit schedules called for an annual payment of only $15,326 a year.

By comparison, if social security contributions had been invested in private annuities, a retiree would receive a guaranteed lifetime income of up to $49,509 per year. Even in a savings plan earning only a very conservative 5.5% per year, the retirement nest egg would grow to $450,000 over the average working lifetime of about 40 years. An average worker with a nonworking spouse could save enough to receive a yearly retirement income of $21,351 and leave $388,000 to their children (Boaz 1990). More venturesome savers willing to take higher risks in pursuit of higher returns would be able to triple this retirement fund, according to figures prepared by Ibbotson Associates.

Given the nature of the problem, there are only three possible ways to maintain an adequate self-supporting system in the future: increase taxes, cut benefits, or improve the investment performance of the trust funds. The public wants to avoid the first two of these options; thus, the third deserves further consideration.

THE 1983 SOCIAL SECURITY STUDY

When social security faced bankruptcy in the early 1980s, Perez and Malley (1983) found that the major reason underlying the precarious condition of the system was the historical reliance on a "Treasuries-only" investment policy. They reconstructed the social security accounts using nine alternative asset allocations, including one which replicated the actual asset mixes of the private pension funds of corporations over the 50-year life of the social security system.

The study showed that had social security followed the stock-bond investment approach of private corporate pension plans, assets at the end of 1981 would have been an estimated $94 billion, almost four times the actual $25 billion in assets in the system at that time. Had the social security funds been invested entirely in equities, their value would have been an estimated $637 billion. All of the models that included some equities outperformed allocation models based on an all-government-securities or fixed-income-securities allocation strategy

Moreover, if the social security funds had used the flexible asset allocation strategies employed by private pension funds during the balance of the 1980s, the trust funds would have reached $343.4 billion in assets by the end of 1991—22% greater than the actual assets listed in the Social Security Trustees 1992 Annual Report. This record was achieved by the private funds despite the October 1987 stock market crash.

The Perez-Malley paper demonstrated that strategies which included equities generally surpassed all-debt strategies substantially during social security's first 50 years, in spite of periodic negative equity returns such as the debilitating two-year bear market that eroded stock prices by close to 50% in 1973 and 1974. However, Congress decided in 1983 to leave the investment method unchanged and opted instead to raise additional funding of about $165 billion by the end of the decade through a combination of increased taxes and reduced benefits. Since that time, the social security current account has swung from deficit to surplus.

Hammerbacher and Perez (1993) have utilized computer simulations of flexible investment strategies to project future results 78 years into the future. The simulations took into account the effects of three different economic scenarios and assumed annual returns ranging from 6% to 10%. These projections are compared with the future returns projected by the social security trustees in their 1992 annual report. The study shows that a stock-bond portfolio mix could enhance future performance of the funds by an amount approaching 100 times greater than those projected by the social security trustees utilizing the Treasuries-only approach. Obviously, modern asset allocation—for example, investing across a cross-section of stocks and bonds—is a viable alternative to a Treasuries-only system.

If nothing is done, the trust funds will become exhausted again by the early part of the next century, when the "baby boomers" begin to retire en masse, necessitating another wrenching round of tax increases and/or benefit cutbacks to bail out the system. Of course, making economic or other predictions is always precarious, but one sure fact is that the closer the baby boom generation comes to retiring, given their sheer numbers, the harder it will be for politicians to make the critical changes needed to prevent enormous deficits or huge tax increases after the turn of the century.

Our grandchildren may pay as much as 40% of their incomes in taxes (including their employers' shares and the separate costs of Medicare) to pay for their parents' retirement (the social security trustees' own "best" estimate is a 26% tax rate). Either tax rate is high enough to impede the growth of the economy and possibly cause intergenerational hostility. As it is, the social security system now costs far too much, accounting for almost half of all federal spending aside from the military and interest on the national debt. In fact, 74% of all taxpayers now pay more in social security taxes (including their employers' shares) than in personal income taxes.

NEED FOR REFORM

Carolyn Weaver, the director of the Social Security and Pension Project at the American Enterprise Institute, notes that:

> In a world with international capital markets and a wide array of investment opportunities—a world vastly different from that of the Depression 1930s when social security was enacted—it should come as no surprise that the system needs revamping for the 21st century. It is a costly and poorly targeted system of income transfers that fails to reflect the advances in economic and financial institutions that have widened and improved opportunities for ordinary citizens to save for their own retirement (Weaver, 1993, p. 10).

Significantly, the states and municipalities have increasingly adopted flexible investment strategies for their employee plans similar to those employed over the years by private corporate pension plans and have achieved excellent results. Moreover, a study of foreign retirement systems by Leif Haanes-Olsen (1990) found that the state-run pension plans in Sweden, the Canadian Province of Quebec, and Japan now utilize flexible asset allocation strategies, including common stocks along with corporate bonds, to fund their public retirement plans.

Probably the most successful foreign program was the move by the Chilean government to privatize their social security program in the early 1980s (see Santamaria 1995, this volume). Others have followed Chile's lead, including Mexico, and several other Latin American countries are on the verge of adopting modern investment strategies and/or privatizing their plans. Even Eastern European countries such as Poland have become interested in these reforms for their own systems.

Chile provides a case study of how a truly free-market economy can organize a social security program. Chile's program, actually the first such plan in the Americas when originally adopted in 1924, became a financial and social disaster decades later when the government embraced radical programs, but all of that was changed in the 1980s. Today, Chileans contribute 10% of their wages and salaries into privately administered, individual accounts. A state-sponsored "safety net" assures that poor citizens or workers with low lifetime salaries are guaranteed a minimum pension. After one decade, Chile's public-private pension funds had gained $12.5 billion in assets—becoming the backbone of that country's capital markets and a major factor in the nation's remarkable economic success (Whalen 1991).

PAY-AS-YOU-GO ADVOCATES

There are many who believe the present social security system should be maintained, with the trust funds invested solely in U.S. government debt instruments and with social security deficits made up from general revenues. For example, Robert Myers, former chief actuary for the social security system, believes the retirement system should be based on current-cost financing (i.e., a "pay-as-you-go" plan), with a current fund balance equal to no more than one year's outgo to provide stability. He believes that investment in other than U.S. government securities is most undesirable—from a political, economic, and philosophical standpoint.

Actually, the original 1935 Social Security Act was funded on a partial-reserve basis—not on a fully funded basis. The 1939 Act, which expanded the program to include auxiliary and survivor benefits, was also funded on a partial-reserve basis. During the 1960s and 1970s, social security funding was more or less on a current-cost basis although the estimated future experience was still predicated on a "partial-reserve" basis. The 1972 Act introduced the concept of current-cost funding over the long range, but the 1977 Act (and the 1983 Act as well) did not follow this principle. The present funding is designed to build up a mammoth fund to begin meeting the benefits of the baby boom generation starting in 2010, becoming steadily depleted thereafter (Myers 1991).

USING SOCIAL SECURITY SURPLUSES TO FINANCE THE FEDERAL DEFICIT

Others note that if the trust funds were allowed to invest in stocks, the government would be faced with a major problem in financing its recurring deficits. The government would have to either raise taxes or cut spending to close the deficit shortfall, or the Treasury would have to compete for funds in the private market, driving up interest rates on long-term government securities.

But this view overlooks the global financial market. If long-term bond interest rates rise in the United States, investors around the world will react quickly and buy U.S. treasuries to benefit from the higher rates, driving rates down to those prevailing in the overall marketplace. Besides, as Senator Moynihan points out, the government's use of social security to finance its growing deficit is hardly a justifiable use of public retirement funds.

To view the government's deficit problems in isolation also overlooks the fact that the great bulk of the state and local government pension funds have shifted their asset allocation from primarily debt to an equities-debt mix over the past quarter-century and the financial markets have adjusted to this shift in asset mix efficiently and with little damage to our economic system or to the government bond market. In other words, our private economic and market systems are self-correcting. Hardly impeded by the shift of states and localities to a debt-stock mix, the Treasury's outstanding debt has increased three-fold to over $4 trillion over the past decade. Equities, valued at about $4.8 trillion, have increased nearly four-fold in the same period.

The social security trust funds currently own $331 billion (at book value) of Treasuries, or less than 10% of the outstanding total. This is not a large enough holding to cause any major turmoil in the government securities markets if the trust funds were to sell a portion of their holdings. In an expanded portfolio, as contemplated in this paper, it is likely that the social security funds would hold a significant amount of Treasuries, approaching or even exceeding the current holding.[1] Besides, including equities in the trust funds should reduce the overall volatility of the stock market, providing a more reliable source of equity financing for the expansion of new as well as older businesses.

THE 1993 SOCIAL SECURITY STUDY

As stated earlier, Perez and Hammerbacher (1993) conducted computer simulations projecting the present assets of the combined social security funds into the future to see how well modern investment techniques and asset allocation might perform compared with the "governments only" strategy (see Table 1).

Table 1 includes a wide range of expected annual returns and projects these results to the year 2070, starting with the actual assets of $280.7 billion in the system at the end of 1991. The table projects 15 separate hypothetical results reflecting the effects of three different economic conditions and five different compound rates of return on the portfolio. These projections are compared with

Table 1. Projected Social Security Assets in 2070 (in trillions)—Ending Assets Based on Economic Assumptions

	I	*II*	*II*
S.S. Trustee Projections	$20.5	exhausted in 2036	exhausted in 2019
Projections Based on Assumed Rates of Return:			
6.0%	$141.0	$ 30.1	exhausted in 2030
7.0%	269.9	89.8	exhausted in 2036
8.0%	517.2	217.0	exhausted in 2052
9.0%	991.4	480..4	$ 71.3
10.0%	1899.0	1015.4	296.5

Notes: The economic assumptions in this table involve the government's projections of changes in the number of workers, price inflation, real-wage growth, benefit payments, administrative expenses, and payments for vocational rehabilitation.

Source: Perez and Hammerbacher (1993).

the projected assets of the present trust funds as set forth in the Board of Trustees' 1992 annual report (Federal Old-Age).

Only under the most optimistic assumption (Alternate I) does the social security assets (using the governments-only investment policy) actually survive for the entire 78-year period; under the less optimistic assumptions, the present system falls into deficit in 2036 (Assumption II) and as early as the year 2019 under the most pessimistic assumption (Assumption III).[2]

On the other hand, the flexible asset allocation projections produced positive results in all but three of the 15 projections, far exceeding the results projected by the trustees for the present social security funds. Further computer simulations indicate that a portfolio with at least 40% allocated to common stocks, with the balance in government securities, would remain solvent until 2070 under all three economic assumptions.

The projected rates of return in Table 1 are realistic and could be achieved if the portfolio were diversified into stocks as well as bonds. For example, assuming an asset allocation of one-third each in stocks, bonds, and cash equivalents, James Farrell (1989) forecast an 8.6% per year return over the decade of the 1990s. Moreover, according to Ibbotson Associates, common stocks achieved a 14% rate of return during the 50 months ending in December of 1991, compared to 10% for government securities and 11% for corporate bonds (see Table 2). Over the 50 years ending in 1991, common

Table 2. Past Rates of Return and Standard Deviations

	50 Months Ending 12/31/91		*1941-1991*	
Security Type	*Mean Return*	*Standard Deviation*	*Mean Return*	*Standard Deviation*
T-Bills	-0.01%	10.0	3.4	3.1
Government Securities	10.0	4.1	4.6	5.7
Corporate Bonds	11.0	3.4	5.3	5.6
S&P 500	14.0	3.8	15.6	22.4

Source: Ibbotson Associates as updated by authors.

stocks averaged 15.6% per annum, three times the return on corporate bonds and government securities.

COMPARATIVE PERFORMANCE OF CORPORATE PENSION PLANS

Corporate pension plans have gone through a learning process of their own. Before the passage of the Employee Retirement Income Security Act of 1975 (ERISA), corporate pension plan asset allocation between equities and bonds was volatile and haphazard, ranging from 15% in stocks in the early postwar years to nearly 75% in the early 1970s, falling sharply thereafter to 45% as a result of the severe bear market in equities in 1973-1974. Later, the equity ratio dropped even further just as the bull market in equities got under way in the mid-1970s, resulting in the funds' investments being frequently "whipsawed" by the market.

This excessive switching caused corporate pension funds as a group to perform poorly in the volatile markets of the 1970s according to Dennis Logue's (1989) comprehensive study of investment performance of corporate plans—mainly related to timing-induced turnover. The result: performance of corporate pension plans trailed the comparable composite market index of bonds and stocks during the 1970s and early 1980s, producing an average return of 7.7% per year versus 8% for the composite market index during the 15-year period from 1968 to 1983.[3]

Performance has improved markedly since then, as pension funds have adopted more modern asset allocation strategies. According to data supplied by the Employee Benefit Research

Institute, pension plan performance produced an annual average return of 15.3%, matching the composite market index for the most recent seven-year period ending 1991.

A critical assumption of asset allocators is that riskier common stocks will provide higher returns than less risky debt investments over the long term. Proponents point to studies which confirm that over 90% of long-term performance is attributable to the overall strategic allocation of funds. Accordingly, asset allocation models balance the risk/reward tradeoffs among stocks and bonds and establish asset mix parameters to govern fund investments over five-and 10-year periods.[4]

In its most modern form, asset allocators have developed tactical models to which pension funds are shifting increasingly. Tactical strategies rely on computer-run dividend discount models that evaluate a variety of critical market and financial data to project the expected return from stocks compared with bonds and, therefore, where to allocate a fund's money. Within the framework of the strategic asset allocation plan, the tactical asset allocation decision determines the "tilt" to the asset mix.

While tactical asset allocation strategies tend to underperform the market in rising markets, they significantly outperform the market in falling markets, producing an overall net improvement over a complete market cycle. Tactical programs have been available for two decades, with the oldest, Mellon Capital, achieving an annual return of 15.7% for its model versus 12.7% for the Standard & Poor's 500 stock index over that period.

TIME REDUCES EQUITY RISKS

Actually, the inclusion of equities in the social security portfolios is not as risky at it seems. Under all three of the trustees' economic scenarios, social security will produce net cash inflows, for at least the next 10 years under the most pessimistic economic scenario, and over the next quarter century under the most optimistic. These cash inflows will be sufficient to meet applicable benefit payments in the next two decades, with the excess available for investment in stocks and bonds.

However, despite their superior long-term record—averaging 12.2% annually since 1926, nearly three times that of bonds—the

Table 3. Range of Common Stock Performance Returns (1926-1992)

	1-Year Periods	*5-Year Periods*	*10-Year Periods*	*15-Year Periods*	*20-Year Periods*	*25-Year Periods*
High	54.0	23.9	20.1	18.2	16.9	14.7
Low	-43.3	-12.5	-0.9	0.6	3.1	5.9
Spread*	97.3	36.4	21.0	17.6	13.8	8.8

Note: * Percentage difference between the high and low performance.

Source: Calculated from data provided by Ibbotson Associates.

stock market is subject to wide swings, up and down, in any given year. Be that as it may, annual market swings tend to cancel each other out, making common stock investing prudent for long-term investors. A study of equity returns since 1926 by the Vanguard Group, the mutual fund family, reveals the remarkable reduction in the volatility of returns (risk) that can be achieved if stocks are held over long periods through good times as well as bad times (see Table 3).

On a one-year basis, the Vanguard study found a 97.3% spread in annual returns from the highest annual return to the lowest return since 1926 (+54% for the best period in 1933 contrasted to −43.3% for the worst period in 1931). However, the difference in annual rates of return dropped sharply as the holding periods lengthened. For 25-year holding periods, the spread between the best and worst periods dropped dramatically to just 8.8% (+14.7% for the best period compared to +5.9% for the worst period).

ALTERNATIVE INVESTMENT PROCEDURES

Carolyn Weaver, in testimony before the Social Security Advisory Council, analyzed several approaches to converting social security to a flexible stock-bond investment system. The first approach she analyzed would have the social security trustees, or some other government board, managing directly a mixed portfolio of stocks and bonds. The Congress would have to enact legislation directing the trustees to adopt a flexible asset allocation program for the investment of the trust funds along the lines of private corporate pension funds. Weaver notes, however, that there are major problems involved with the trust fund actively managing its own portfolio. Operating under a defined benefit plan such as social security, rules would need to be established to maintain minimum reserves against future benefits.

Congress would need to establish rules along the lines of the existing ERISA regulations, which embody the "prudent man" rules of investing. Moreover, the trustees would need to build up an internal investment staff to manage the fund's investment portfolios. As with private defined-benefit pension plans, the social security actuaries would have to monitor future trends against past investment performance to adjust their actuarial assumptions in the light of changing conditions. In addition, a policy of investing social security reserves in private securities would force the government to make difficult decisions about how to exercise the right to vote in corporate elections that equity ownership confers.

Weaver questions whether a government entity controlling such an enormous portfolio could make investment decisions in the same manner as individuals or private portfolio managers. The threat remains that investment decisions would be politically skewed, with politically favored projects receiving an unwarranted flow of financial resources.

To avoid control problems, Weaver discussed restricting the trust fund's investment to indexed mutual funds of common stocks and bonds. A number of financial service firms now offer index funds; these include the Wells-Fargo bank, the Mellon bank, and the Vanguard Group as well as other banks and mutual fund organizations. Undoubtedly, the market for such vehicles would expand if the trust funds became major investors in index mutual funds. Since the individual index funds would be independent entities, the investments would be shielded from political pressures and the problem of voting in corporate elections would be avoided. However, it probably would be advisable that the trust funds spread their investments across a large number of index funds to dilute any potential conflicts and excessive concentration in any one vehicle.

On the other hand, the social security system could maintain proprietary index funds, utilizing its bank of computers to allocate the fund's assets automatically among individual securities in line with the market index utilized. But the trustees would still be confronted with the problem of how to vote the stock of the companies held in its portfolio on corporate resolutions or proposals. Clearly, the role of the social security trustees would have to be changed by Congress to strengthen the independence of the system along the lines of the Federal Reserve Board, with trustees appointed for long staggered terms and with government representation held to a minority.

CONCLUSION

After weathering the major crises experienced during the transitional years of the 1980s, a fresh start is now occurring for social security, with surpluses forecast over the next two decades. Modern security research has demonstrated that the risks of holding equity investments are large over short time periods but decline to relatively small levels when returns are stretched out over long time frames. Moreover, over long time frames, common stock returns have more than tripled returns on bonds. Since the social security trust funds will have annual surpluses for the next 20 years or more, the timing is ripe for the introduction of a flexible investment program for social security, whatever form it takes in the future. By adopting a flexible allocation system, Congress would ensure that social security would survive the economic fluctuations of the next century and deliver decent retirement benefits at affordable cost for participants.

NOTES

1. All of the trust fund's holdings of treasuries are in nonmarketable special issues carried at par value with an average interest coupon currently of about 8.7%. If the trust funds were permitted to convert these special issues to marketable treasuries, these holdings would be worth 16% more than their par value—about $50 billion. Of course, if long-term interest rates in the market should rise sharply in the future, this would cause a decline in the equivalent market value of the trust's holdings of government securities.
2. Under the most recent projections, the system falls into default in 2029.
3. The composite index is weighted 50% for the Standard & Poor's 500 Stock Index, 40% for Salomon Brothers High Grade Corporate Bond Index, and 10% for the annual return for Treasury Bills.
4. The traditional calculation of portfolio return and risk depends upon the correlation among the returns, as well as the weights. Constructing portfolios consisting of different types of securities—for example, bonds, stocks, and cash

equivalents—demonstrates the benefits of asset allocation in smoothing out and improving long-term performance. In effect, the weighted average of the variations in the returns of each security in an actual portfolio will be less than the variation in the returns of the individual securities actually used in that portfolio. Therefore, putting many different securities with different risk variables into a portfolio decreases the risk.

REFERENCES

Aaron, H., et al. 1989. *Can America Afford to Grow Old, Paying for Social Security*. Washington, DC: The Brookings Institution.

Boaz, David 1990. "Privatize Social Security." *New York Times* (March 21): A27.

Employee Benefit Research Institute (EBRI). 1984-1992. *EBRI Quarterly Pension Investment Report* (selected issues). Washington, DC.

Farrell, James. 1989. "A Fundamental Approach to Superior Asset Allocation." *Financial Analysts Journal* (May-June): 32-37.

Federal Old-Age and Survivors Insurance and Disability Insurance Trust Funds, Board of Trustees. *Annual Report* (selected years). Washington, DC: U.S. Government Printing Office.

Genetski, R. 1993. "Privatize Social Security." *The Wall Street Journal* (May 21).

Greenwich Research Associates. 1977-1990. *Large Corporate Pensions: Report to Participants* (selected issues). Greenwich, CT: Greenwich Research Associates.

Haanes-Olsen, L. 1990. "Investment of Social Security Reserves in Three Countries." *Social Security Bulletin* 53(2, February).

Ibbotson, R.G. and R.A. Sinquefield. 1982. *Stocks, Bonds, Bills and Inflation: The Past and the Future*. Charlottesville, VA: The Financial Analysts Research Foundation.

Logue, D., et. al. 1989. *The Investment Performance of Corporate Pension Plans*. Westport, CT.

Malley, S. and R.C. Perez. 1983. "Asset Allocation and Social Security." *Financial Management* (Spring): 29-35.

Myers, R.J. 1991. "Pay-As-You-Go Financing for Social Security is the Only Way to Go." *Journal of the American Society of CLU & ChFC* (January): 52-58.

Perez, R.C. and I. Hammerbacher. 1993. "Looking Towards a Sounder Social Security System." *Review of Business* [St. John's University] (Spring): 30-34.

Weaver, C.L. 1990. Testimony before the Social Security Advisory Council, March 8.

________. 1993. "Baby-Boom Retirees, Destined to Go Bust." *Wall Street Journal* (August 26): A10.

Whalen, C. 1991. "Mess With Social Security; Change it From Ponzi Scheme to Private Pension Fund." *Barron's* (March 4): 10.

PART IV

PROPOSALS FOR PARTIAL PRIVATIZATION

THE KEY ISSUES IN THE PRIVATIZATION DEBATE

Yung-Ping Chen

INTRODUCTION

I would like to comment on some of the key issues that surround proposals to replace fully or in part the social security program with mandatory, individual retirement savings accounts.

FREEDOM OF CHOICE

The advocacy for privatizing social security is basically concerned with the freedom of choice in the provision of retirement income. By freedom of choice, I mean more than the choice in the mode of investment of the funds involved. The central question is: who is responsible for providing retirement income? In a three-legged approach, social security is designed to provide a floor of income protection, to be supplemented by private pensions and personal savings, with public assistance or welfare as a safety net. The proponents of privatization argue for eliminating or restricting the role of social security. They believe in giving individuals the rights and responsibilities to invest their own retirement funds in the form of mandatory individual retirement savings accounts (IRSAs).

Since the IRSA holders are expected to direct investment of the funds involved, they assume the risk of losses and, of course, reap the benefit of profits.

Are people in general able and eager to manage their IRSAs? What proportion of the population may be assumed to have the financial acumen to self-direct their investments? What opportunity cost may be incurred if people are required to manage their own IRSAs? It may be suggested that individuals do not need to invest their own funds and money managers can do it for them? If so, then how much freedom are people getting when they opt out of social security? What price is paid for this freedom? And what is the role of society in cases of investment failures?

DEFINED BENEFITS VERSUS DEFINED CONTRIBUTIONS

The privatization debate also revolves around the comparative advantages and disadvantages of defined-benefit plans and defined-contribution plans. Social security, like many corporate pension plans, is a defined-benefit plan. IRSAs are defined-contribution plans. In the private pension field, there has already been a noticeable increase in defined-contribution plans.

Defined-contribution plans do not guarantee a specified level of retirement income. Under those plans, the worker, alone or with his or her employer as well, accumulates savings over time. But the key question is: how much lifetime annuity may be expected at the time of retirement from this total accumulation? This question is important because it addresses the concern over adequacy of retirement income. For example, many workers "cash out" their balances in the defined-contribution plans when they change jobs, thus diminishing their savings for retirement. An additional serious concern, for both defined-contribution and defined-benefit plans, is whether or not inflation is taken into account.

RATES OF RETURN

Most advocates of privatizing social security assume that the interest rates earned by the investable funds will be high. However, like all markets, the financial market has two sides: supply and demand. If we assume that creating IRSAs will inject, by some advocates' estimates, about $200 billion or more annually into the market, there will be an increase in the supply of investable funds to that extent. Unless there is a commensurate increase in the demand for investable funds, market forces will lower the rate of interest. Can the interest rates be assumed to be high over time? This is a key issue because it bears on the rates of return on IRSAs.

Is it realistic to believe that the real rates of return on IRSAs will be 8% or 9% on a steady basis, as believed by some? Yet, IRSA proposals depend on such an assumption. Even if stocks averaged these high rates over a long period of time, rates of return would vary by individual and by generation. In fact, financial planners often advise their clients, before retirement, to shift from stocks into more stable investments yielding lower returns.

Another factor affects the rates of return. For example, one proposal would give participants full income tax credits for contributions to IRSAs. Presumably, when people receive income from their IRSA accounts, they would have to pay taxes on it, and therefore the rate of return to these IRSAs would have to be adjusted downward by the income tax liability.

COMPARABLE BENEFITS TO SOCIAL SECURITY?

Social security provides retirement, survivorship, and disability benefits in a single package. No private insurance carrier offers an equivalent policy. Typically, advocates of privatizing social security point to higher retirement benefits that could be offered by IRSAs. Some of these advocates do attempt to provide for survivors benefits and disability benefits by incorporating life insurance (or, more accurately, survivor income benefit insurance) policies and disability income policies. However, they often illustrate how they would provide these benefits by using the premiums charged by private insurance carriers for these policies. A major problem is that the underwriting requirements that private carriers impose enable them to charge lower premiums. Moreover, any analysis of disability benefits must recognize that not all occupations are insurable by private insurance and that, among the insurables, premiums for the same benefits differ among occupational classes.

INCOME REDISTRIBUTION

When part or all of social security is converted into IRSAs, the effects on income redistribution must be recognized. The feature of social adequacy under social security (i.e., the transfer to low-income earners) is reduced or lost under IRSAs. Unless we argue that society will allow some of its citizens to live in squalor or destitution, then there is cost to society to provide for these people. The issue, then, is whether or not the welfare element in social security is inferior to some other type of transfer payments. These important questions need to be resolved: Should we change from social security to IRSAs so high-income earners will get higher returns on their savings and low-income earners will not receive their disproportionately greater benefits? If so, will we raise taxes to provide more welfare benefits to low-income individuals? If yes, is everyone better off as a result?

ACKNOWLEDGMENT

This paper is based on part of the testimony presented by the author at a hearing on proposals for alternative investment of the Social Security trust fund reserves before the Subcommittee on Social Security, Committee on Ways and Means, U.S. House of Representatives, October 4, 1994. A similar speech was given at the Middlebury Conference.

INDIVIDUAL SOCIAL SECURITY RETIREMENT ACCOUNTS

John Edward Porter, Member of Congress

I believe that we are dealing with the economic future of young people in America. I start with the premise that we have a national debt of $4.5 trillion which is going up, up, and up. Even though we have a plan to reduce it, it is still increasing. I often translate the national debt into what it means to a young person entering the work force in the United States today. If you are an average young person starting out today, you are being handed a bill by the government for $200,000 which you will have to pay throughout your lifetime just to pay your share of the interest on the debt. This amount does not include the cost to government for defense or welfare or transportation or agriculture or anything else: this is just to pay your share of the interest on the $4.5 trillion national debt.

That is bad enough. However, we are also stealing the social security system of our young people in the United States because we are stealing the social security reserve from which their benefits will be derived in the future. Congress raised taxes in 1983 in order to put into place a reserve that would build throughout the next 30 to 40 years to have available funds so that we would not have to decrease benefits in the future when there will be more retirees and fewer workers to support them. The baby boomers who are retiring in about 2015 are going to look at this and say, "We are all set."

But they are not going to be all set, because every day we are stealing the social security reserve by spending it on current consumption. I call all of this "fiscal child abuse," in violation of the intergenerational equity that has always been a principle of life in the United States. Congress is spending the reserve—and, by the way, do not ever call it a surplus. It is not a surplus. It is a reserve to cover deficits, and every day that passes is a day that young Americans are further in the hole economically.

My primary interest has never been to privatize the social security system. It has, instead, been to protect the social security reserve from Congress. There is simply no way to keep Congress from spending the reserve as long as it has a chance to reach it.

So I ask myself, "What kind of mechanism do we need to put the reserve—the part that's not needed for current benefits—out of the reach of Congress? Where should we put it?" In my judgment, we ought to put it in the hands of those who ultimately need it for their retirement and who put it into the system in the first place. If that can be done, we will not only protect the future of the social security system but also ensure intergenerational equity by keeping the system, at least to that extent, strong.

As a byproduct of that, one could say, "We will have created a situation where you will be partially privatizing the social security system." I think that is true. I also believe that once you start that process, once you put into place a system that is like the plan that I have proposed to create Individual Social Security Retirement Accounts, and once people experience it, they will like it and want more.

One can, in my judgment, design an ideal social security system from scratch. One says, "OK, I have all the resources I need; I will design a system that is fully funded, fully vested, and that is run by an individual, not a government." I realize that no such system could have been devised in the middle of the Great Depression, but if we could have devised one at that time, it is the kind that I would have devised.

If we were in the process of privatizing social security, and if we were to begin with a plan based on Individual Social Security Retirement Accounts, it would probably take 50 or 60 years to do so. You would obviously have to buy out the present system in order to do it and, at the same time, create a fully funded system. That would take a very long time to accomplish.

But if we begin with an Individual Social Security Retirement Account system, starting in the next fiscal year, we could end up with a fully funded, fully vested social security system by the year 2050. Children born today could receive, upon retirement, all of their benefits not from the government but from funds that they have earned and invested and seen grow throughout their working lifetimes. History tells us that the benefits individuals would receive would be greater than they receive under the present system. They would be guaranteed to receive those benefits, because the government could not change the rules in the middle—and we all know that government is all too willing to change the rules in the middle of the system.

How would such a system work? My plan calls for a 2% cut in the social security tax: 1% from the individual and 1% from the employer. This cut, which would represent the reserve not needed to pay current benefits, would be refunded annually and directly into Individual Social Security Retirement Accounts (ISSRAs) owned by every single American worker. So, we would effectively take a portion of the social security tax out of Congress' reach and instead put it back into the hands of individuals.

These accounts would be similar to IRAs, funded by the worker and held by a trustee. This trustee would be a bank, an insurance company, a broker, or any other money manager. The funds would be invested as the worker directed within defined parameters of safe investments; time deposits, government obligations, AAA corporate bonds, certain mutual funds, and similar nonspeculative investments that would allow the money to be saved and invested and grow as a nest egg for the future.

The trustees would be required by law to abide by the investment guidelines and would only be able to pay the money to purchase an annuity when the owner reached retirement age. These annuity benefits would then supplement the individual's adjusted social security benefit. By doing this, we would accomplish the following:

1. It would prevent Congress from using the reserve to cover current deficit spending. Senator Moynihan was right three years ago: he wanted to cut the social security tax so that the reserve could not be stolen. The Senator had the right diagnosis but the wrong prescription. What we should do is cut the social security tax and

give this refund back to the people to save and invest. The system I am proposing is one of forced savings. This would protect the reserve for future retirement benefits. as it should be.

2. It would make every American worker an investor in our economy. Every single worker in the United States who paid social security taxes would have an ISSRA. It would give them a tangible stake in the success of our economy.

3. Americans who have never saved a dime in their lives would have savings that would be theirs, that they would manage, and that would grow and be available as part of their retirement. And, if the entire system was ultimately privatized, they would see all of their savings in their own hands and building toward the day of their retirement.

4. It would give every worker an economic stake to pass on. Today, if you die prior to becoming eligible for your social security old age benefits, those benefits are gone, except for survivors' benefits in some cases. But, under my proposal, if you died prior to retirement age, the funds accumulated would be part of your estate because you would own them and you could leave them to your family and to your children.

5. This proposal would put $3 trillion, in 1990 dollars, or at least a very substantial part of that, into private sector investments. This infusion of capital, coupled with an expected drop in the deficit since Congress would not have the reserve to spend, should help drive down interest rates and speed future economic growth.

6. It would create the basis of a completely portable, fully funded, and fully private pension system. In other words, if I were a worker directing part of my social security into an ISSRA with every paycheck, I would go to my employer and say, "Forget the pension plan. I want my share paid into my ISSRA account." Years later, when I was about to retire, I would not have to worry about whether the company's pension plan had been mismanaged or stolen or gone broke. No, I would have the money in my own hands. I would have invested it and I would know that it was available for my retirement.

7. Finally, we would have created not only the basis but the experience of a privatized public social security system. And again, I believe that if you create that experience, you will create the demand ultimately for a fully privatized system. Workers would embrace it. They would find something that they could really relate to, and they would, I believe, demand that it became more and more privatized.

Now, if this is such a good idea—and Malcom S. Forbes, Jr. and many others said that it is a good vision for the future of the United States—how do we get there? Like everything else, one starts knocking on a door and keeps knocking until that door opens. What are the strategies?

First, do not start by criticizing the present social security system. That is the absolutely worst thing anyone can do. I believe that the social security system in our country has been a big success. It has largely eliminated senior poverty in the United States, and it ought to be something that is great not only for previous generations and this generation, but also for all generations of Americans. I support social security very strongly.

One can, however, criticize Congress for stealing the reserve, because that is what is happening. You can criticize the idea of means testing, which could be the only solution for the future of social security, ultimately turning it into just another welfare program, especially when we could instead give people a stake in our society and not a handout.

But we should not call for immediate passage of my legislation. I do not call for it, unless I do so as a precursor to where we ought to go. A short while ago, if you breathed the words "social security" in a room full of politicians, you would have found yourself alone. We are getting better. Today, you would not be entirely alone. There are a few people with courage who are willing to stay around and talk about it. In fact, the Chairman of the Ways and Means Subcommittee on Social Security held hearings in September of 1994 on the management of the Social Security Trust Fund reserve. That is real progress. Three or four years ago, nobody would have dared to touch the subject.

It is up to the experts to create a climate for examining the future of social security and for protecting the reserve. People have to sound the alarm that Congress is mismanaging the reserve and make clear what this mismanagement will mean to the future of retirees in our country.

We need to get current social security recipients on our side. Nothing energizes senior citizens more than social security, and every politician knows this. They are concerned about the future of social security, not just for themselves but for their children and their grandchildren as well. If you sit down with the people from the American Association of Retired Persons (AARP), you think,

"Well, here is a lobby that really is out for their people." But AARP does not think of their constituency as just people who are seniors today. They think of their constituency as people who will be seniors tomorrow—in other words, every one of us. They care very deeply about this problem with the social security reserve.

We need to organize young people as well. Ten years ago, I organized a group called SEND—Students to End National Deficits—to send a message to Congress. It did not get very far, but everything one does makes a difference. I believe in the firepower theory of lobbying: fire out a lot of different bullets and some of them will hit the mark. One keeps on these issues day after day. Get the Bipartisan Commission on Entitlement and Tax Reform involved by getting it to think in terms of the solution, perhaps a solution like the Individual Social Security Retirement Account plan. Ask this Commission: "Can you see another alternative to means testing to have a social security system that would be viable in the future, as viable as the one is today for present seniors, when our children are grown and have reached retirement age?" I believe they would answer "Yes, there are other alternatives; we do not need to do just that."

We cannot try, however, to go out and sell the idea of privatizing the social security system. We have to go out, rather, and talk about what needs to be done to make the present system a viable system in the future and what needs to be done instead of means-testing the system. In this respect, I think we can very easily talk about an Individual Social Security Retirement Account system that supplements the present social security system and saves the reserve from a Congress that would spend it, and is spending it, every single day.

There is very strong resistance in Congress toward giving up over $3 trillion in assets, especially since that is money that is currently being used to help finance deficits. I believe Congress is very vulnerable here and can easily be shown to be irresponsible on this issue. We can hit them hard for not protecting the Social Security Trust Fund.

People also like the concept of an Individual Retirement Account. It is something that they understand and that very readily appeals to them. There is very strong support in the country for that kind of concept, and I think all Americans could see how it could apply to social security and protect the reserves.

So, is all of this possible? With vision and commitment, I believe anything in America is possible. I believe, however, that the experts need to be in general agreement on the problem and more or less agree on a direction to take in order to solve it. It seems to me that we could come to a commitment that change is necessary and that we can change social security and make it an even better system for the young people of the United States and for future generations. It is an excellent system now, but if we do not do things today to make certain that it is a better system, or at least as good a system tomorrow, then it will not really exist in the way it was originally conceived. That, I believe, would be a tragedy for this country. So I encourage everyone to come together on a plan and let their voices be heard.

REFERENCES

Forbes,. March 5, 1990.

A PRIVATE OPTION FOR SOCIAL SECURITY

Peter J. Ferrara

Any good economic analysis begins by specifying the assumptions. So let's do that here. Assume that I am President of the United States.

Here is my proposal.

Workers and their employers would be allowed to contribute an amount up to 20% of the employer and employee OASI taxes for each worker to an expanded "Freedom IRA" for the worker. The contributors would receive a 100% income tax credit for such contributions but would continue to pay their social security taxes in full. As a practical matter, workers who exercised the Freedom IRA option would have their social security taxes offset by the income tax credits to the extent of their contributions.[1]

However, each worker could have his social security retirement benefits reduced proportionally to the extent of such Freedom IRA contributions. Maximum contributions over an entire career would reduce retirement benefits by 20%. Lesser contributions would reduce retirement benefits less under a proportional formula.

The Freedom IRA contributions would be invested under the same rules as for IRAs today. They would accumulate with tax-free returns. Withdrawals before age 59½ would be prohibited. In retirement, these contributions would pay benefits that would likely more than make up for the reduced social security benefits. Workers could take their benefits in the form of an annuity guaranteeing them certain benefit payments for life. Or they could take their benefits through periodic withdrawals, subject to some limitations to avoid dissipation of the funds too rapidly.

As an additional component of the reform, the SSI program would be replaced with a guaranteed minimum benefit for all that would effectively increase benefits to the elderly poor by 20%.

Workers would also be completely free to continue to rely on social security in full and reject the Freedom IRA alternative.

Now, assume the income tax credits would result in an annual revenue loss of $40 billion, with about 90% of workers exercising the Freedom IRA option. The President proposes in his budget to cut other government spending by $40 billion per year to offset the revenue loss.[2]

The President is feeling bold since his party controls both houses of Congress. Over time, the revenue loss under his plan would be offset by reduced social security expenditures as workers retired relying less on social security and more on private IRAs. Eventually, these reduced social security expenditures would completely offset the revenue loss.

This proposal had the following beneficial effects:

- Social security financing would be unambiguously strengthened. Payroll tax revenues into social security would be maintained in full. But over the years, the program's expenditures would be reduced as retirees substituted private IRA benefits for social security benefits. Expanding the private option further over time would completely eliminate the long-term financing gap of the program and even allow room for major payroll tax cuts.
- Workers would be able to get higher investment returns on their funds through the private IRAs. This would result in much higher benefits for the same payment amounts.
- Workers who exercised the private option would also likely feel more secure because they would be free of social security's long-term financing problems and the insecurity of social security's pay-as-you-go system; they would be backed up by a fully funded reserve of capital investments in the private system.

- National savings would be increased by close to one-fifth the size of social security retirement benefits. This would produce more rapid economic growth, higher wages, and more jobs.
- Workers would have much greater freedom of choice and control over their retirement. They could choose the investments for their Freedom IRA funds and the benefits that such funds would pay in retirement. They would have the freedom and flexibility to tailor individual packages of investments, benefits, and insurance coverage to suit their personal needs and preferences. They would also have much greater freedom to choose their own retirement ages, and the time when the Freedom IRAs would start paying retirement benefits. They could start withdrawals any time after age 59½, as with regular IRAs today.
- Equity would be improved as each worker would receive in benefits through the private IRAs what he or she paid in contributions, plus market interest, on an actuarial basis. Under social security, by contrast, two workers paying the exact same taxes into the system over their entire careers can receive radically different benefit amounts (see Ferrara 1980, ch. 6).
- Minority workers with shorter life expectancies, who as a result receive much lower returns through social security, could avoid this problem through the Freedom IRAs. They could retire earlier and use their accumulated funds for support, or pay themselves higher benefits during their expected shorter period of life after the usual retirement age and leave the remaining accumulated funds at death to their children or other heirs.
- The accumulation of national wealth would be more equally distributed as the accumulation of funds in each worker's Freedom IRA would be more equally distributed than the current distribution of wealth. In the process, workers could each develop a more direct ownership stake in the nation's business and industry.
- The poor would be greatly benefited as well. Even career minimum-wage workers would be able to get higher retirement benefits through the private invested system. They would also receive more in benefits for work earlier

in their lives, when the working poor start regular work, rather than less as under social security. That is because the earlier contributions under the private system have more years to earn investment returns, whereas they count little if at all in the calculation of social security benefits. It is the poor who are most in need of the higher retirement benefits and improved economic opportunities that would result from the reform. The personal wealth each worker would accumulate through the private system would provide special opportunities for the poor to break out of the cycle of poverty by giving them control over some capital. Finally, the poor would be backed up through a guaranteed minimum benefit.

- There would be no social security benefit cuts for today's elderly or for those who continued to rely on the program in the future. Instead, their benefits would be more secure, as social security financing would be strengthened.
- Those who wanted to continue to rely on social security completely and have nothing to do with the Freedom IRAs, would be perfectly free to do so.

While the President was initially told that such reform would force current workers to pay twice for their retirement, it became clear under his proposal that this was not the case. The issue here is: what are the proposed net new costs of the reform and what are the proposed net new benefits for the first generation of workers under the reform? These workers would be paying $40 billion each year into the Freedom IRAs, but this would be entirely offset by $40 billion in income tax credits. Present consumption would be reduced by $40 billion due to the spending cuts to finance the income tax credits, but savings would increase by $40 billion each year as a result of the payments into the Freedom IRAs. Of course, any savings increase of $40 billion, no matter how it comes about, involves a cost of foregone present consumption of $40 billion.

The question, then, is whether the returns to that increased savings, and all the other benefits of the reform, are worth the cost of the saving increase—foregone present consumption equal to the amount of savings increase. The savings increase would produce the same full returns as any other savings increase, which is the full, *before tax*, real rate of return to capital. However, the first generation of workers under the proposed reforms would also forgo social security benefits that they would otherwise have received for their payment of social security taxes. That does not mean, however, that the savings increase must be a bad deal for the first generation of workers. As an empirical matter, the full before-tax real rate of return to capital produced by the increased savings minus the foregone social security benefit is still greater than the after-tax real rate of return to capital that workers receive on their savings today. So we cannot say a priori that the net greater returns that workers would receive on the greater savings are not worth the cost of those savings.[3]

Of course, we cannot say a priori that the net returns on the savings increase and the other benefits of the reform must be a good deal. It is a matter of the individual preferences of workers and voters. All that policymakers can do is exercise their judgment about whether the reform would be desirable overall and, ultimately, put the issue before the voters.

This is all the more so because the reform would provide many additional nonmonetary benefits that cannot be quantified. As discussed above, workers would have much greater freedom of choice and control regarding their retirement. They would also be free of social security's funding problems and insecure pay-as-you-go system. As Carolyn Weaver (1985) has pointed out, workers would not be concerned about foregoing social security benefits that they feel they are probably not going to get anyway.

Workers also would value the immediate opportunities presented by a more rapidly growing economy, with more jobs, better wages, and expanded business opportunities resulting from the increased savings. The improved equity and new advantages for the poor and minorities would also be valued.

Note, however, that the long-advocated view of Harvard economics Professor Martin Feldstein, and many others, that social security should be fully funded is based precisely on the judgment that the benefits of a reform such as the President's are well worth the costs. The President's proposal simply involves fully funding social security in the private sector rather than through the public sector. But in both cases, the costs of the transition to the new system are the same. These costs do not involve the first generation paying twice for their retirement, but they do involve paying for the cost of the increased savings from shifting from a pay-as-you-go to a fully funded system. And the question in each case is the same: whether the benefits of the increased savings and other advantages of the reform are worth the costs of making that savings. Indeed, fully funding social security through the private sector would result in many additional benefits, described above, that would not result from fully funding social security through the public sector.[4]

The President also suggested that over time, his proposed reforms should be expanded. Eventually, workers and their employers should be able to contribute up to 100% of the worker's OASI taxes to a Freedom IRA in return for offsetting income tax credits. Future retirement benefits would then, again, be reduced proportionally for each worker to the extent they exercised this option. Workers should also eventually be allowed to substitute private life insurance for social security's pre-age-65 survivors benefits. They should eventually be allowed to contribute additional funds up to the amount of disability insurance taxes for the purchase of private disability insurance to substitute for social security disability benefits. And they should eventually be allowed to contribute additional funds for private savings and insurance to substitute for Medicare. Ultimately, workers would have complete freedom to choose how much to rely on social security and Medicare and how much to rely on private savings and insurance.

What was the reaction to the President's proposal:

- Young workers overwhelmingly supported it, as they saw tremendous benefits for them and did not believe they would receive anything from Social Security anyway.
- Higher income people of all ages saw how they could get much higher returns through the private sector and, consequently, immediately supported it. This included those working in the critical news media.
- Lower income people provided surprising support for the proposal because they saw it as the only way they could get control over some capital. The reform also provided them with the increased benefits that they most need.
- A surprisingly large bloc of voters supported the reform because of the freedom and control it gave them over their own funds and retirement.

- The investment community saw the proposal as creating a big new market for them, so they provided strong support.
- The elderly were not hurt by the reform so they did not oppose it. In fact, they supported it as providing better opportunities for their children. While certain demagogue groups tried to scare the elderly regarding the reform, the President was able to command national media attention to defend it against their attacks. So they were not successful in cutting off national debate.

In passing the proposal through his committee, the House Ways and Means Chairman observed that this was not really so radical a proposal after all. It simply offered workers a tax credit for private IRA contributions tied to future social security benefit reductions. What better way could there be to gain control of entitlement spending, he asked.

But the Chairman of the Senate Finance Committee had an objection. He opposed trying to offset the income tax credit revenue loss with budget cuts. He argued that President Ferrara had already slashed spending enough in his first term when he proposed three consecutive balanced budgets for the first time since the 1920s, while enacting a flat rate tax of 15%.

A student of Milton Friedman supported the Chairman in testimony before the Committee. Just borrow to cover the income tax credit revenue loss, he recommended, because this is only a one-time transition cost. (In the long run, the revenue loss would be offset by the reduced social security expenditures resulting from workers relying on their private benefits instead). In doing so, he argued, you would only be issuing explicit government bonds to recognize the implicit debt that already exists in the unfunded liabilities of social security. In other words, he said, do not try to fully fund the past liabilities of the social security system. Just fully fund new retirement liabilities and over time, as the old liabilities are paid off, you will still eventually reach a fully funded system, although much more slowly.

The economist explained further that social security's pay-as-you-go system was begun by effectively issuing government debt to current workers, by promising to pay them future benefits, in return for the then-current taxes that were used to pay current benefits to the elderly at that time. To end that system and shift to a fully funded system, you would stop effectively issuing new debt to today's workers for their taxes and effectively allow them to use their payments to fully fund their future benefits. You would then issue explicit debt to fund the past obligations of the system that had already been built up. Existing unfunded liabilities would then be frozen in place and new retirement liabilities would be fully funded. This result would be achieved by simply borrowing to cover the income tax credit revenue loss until that loss was offset by reduced social security expenditures resulting from workers relying on the private benefits instead.

This view carried the day, and the President's proposal passed on these terms. This meant that savings grew much more slowly over time than would have occurred under the President's original proposal. Net savings were increased as social security expenditures were reduced due to workers relying on the private benefits. This was very small at first. But the increased savings also generated new net tax revenues that helped to offset the income tax credit revenue loss, adding further to new savings. These two factors would have completely offset the revenue loss by the end of the first working generation, producing a fully funded system thereafter. But another factor greatly accelerated the savings increase. The higher reported government deficits due to the income tax credit revenue loss created pressure for more government spending cuts to balance the budget. This pressure caused about 50% of the revenue loss to be offset by spending cuts, producing a much greater savings increase and a fully funded system much sooner.

Once the President's proposal was enacted, the people loved it, for all the reasons discussed above. As a result, the President's party controlled the White House and the Congress for another 40 years.

NOTES

1. The employer could make contributions for a worker only with the consent of the worker. The worker and the employer could contribute up to the maximum allowed for a worker in whatever relative shares they agreed. The tax credit would go to each to the extent of their relative contributions.

2. Any increased spending due to replacing SSI with the higher minimum benefit would also be offset by cuts in other government spending.

3. This same analysis applies regardless of the taxes that may actually be assessed on to the capital returns earned on the Freedom IRA investments. These taxes would generate net new revenues from the net new Freedom IRA savings, which would offset costs that would otherwise by borne by taxpayers. The full monetary benefits resulting from the net new Freedom IRA savings are measured by the full before-tax real rate of return to capital.

4. The only time the first generation would pay twice for their retirement is under the policy advocated by many defenders of the status quo of social security. They argue that payroll taxes should be maintained higher than necessary to fund current benefits, in order to build up a substantial social security trust fund that would be used to finance the retirement benefits of the baby boom generation. But this proposal would not result in any increased savings, because the extra payments into social security would make the federal deficit look smaller than otherwise, leading to more federal spending on other programs, which would effectively dissipate the extra social security payments. While paying more into social security than necessary, therefore, this generation would not receive any of the advantages of increased savings. They would effectively only be paying twice for their retirement, once through the funds necessary to maintain the pay-as-you-go social security system and once through the additional sums exacted from them to fund their own future retirement benefits.

REFERENCES

Ferrara, P. 1980. *Social Security: The Inherent Contradiction.* Washington, DC: Cato Intitute.

Weaver, C.L. 1985. "The Economics and Politics of the Emergence of Social Security: Some Implications for Reform." In Peter Ferrara (ed.), *Social Security: Prospects for Real Reform.* Washington, DC: Cato Institute.

CONTRIBUTORS

Barry Bosworth is a Senior Fellow in the Economic Studies Program at the Brookings Institute in Washington, DC. He received his Ph.D. from the University of Michigan in 1969. His research has concentrated on issues of capital formation and saving behavior.

Yung-Ping Chen holds the Frank J. Manning Eminent Scholar's Chair in Gerontology at the University of Massachusetts Boston. Previously, he was the Frank M. Engle Distinguished Chair in Economic Security Research at the American College in Bryn Mawr, Pennsylvania. He is a fellow in the Gerontology Society of America and a founding member of the National Academy of Social Insurance. He has authored or edited several books, including *Social Security in a Changing Environment* and *Checks and Balances in Social Security*. He is a frequent contributor to scholarly journals and Congressional hearings. He was a consultant and delegate to the 1971 and 1981 White House Conference on Aging.

David Colander is the Christian A. Johnson Distinguished Professor of Economics at Middlebury College. He is the author or editor of 25 books on a variety of subjects in economics. He is currently the president of the Eastern Economic Association and vice-president of the History of Economic Thought Society.

James E. Duggan is currently a senior economist in the Office of Economic Policy at the U.S. Department of Treasury, where he provides research and advice for policymaking purposes to Treasury officials primarily in the areas of social security and health care. His published research includes papers that address both the financial status and distributional effects of social security. Before joining Treasury, he was a senior research economist at the U.S. Department of Labor.

Peter J. Ferrara is an economist at the National Center for Policy Analysis. He is the editor of *Social Security: Prospects for Real Reform* and the author of numerous articles advocating the privatization of Social Security

David Horlacher is the Hepburn Professor of Economics at Middlebury College. He was the section chief of the Population and Development Section at the United Nations from 1980-1992 and has written numerous articles on population and aging.

Robert Myers is currently a member of the Prospective Payment Assessment Commission on the Social Security "Notch" Issue and is an actuarial consultant to several foreign countries. He was Chief Actuary for the Social Security Administration (1947-1970), Deputy Commissioner of Social Security (1981-1982), Executive Director of the National Commission on Social Security Reform (1982-1983), and Chairman of the Commission on Railroad Retirement Reform (1988-1990). He is the president of the International Fisheries Commissions Pension Society and a consultant on Social Security to the National Association of Life Underwriters and The Senior Coalition. He has authored four books and numerous articles on Social Security. He received his LL.D. from Muhlenberg College and his M.S. from the University of Iowa.

Robert C. Perez worked on Wall Street for over two decades before joining the finance department at Fordham University and later at the Iona College Hagan School of Business. He has done extensive research aimed at increasing the investment returns of the Social Security Trust Funds through improved asset allocation. His work in this area has been published in scholarly journals and the financial press. He has also authored five books on various financial topics. He holds an MBA and Ph.D. from the New York University Graduate School of Business Administration.

John E. Porter (R-10th) of Illinois is serving his ninth term in the United States House of Representatives. He is a member of the House Appropriations Committee and is chairman of the Labor, Health and Human Services and Education Subcommittee. He also serves on the Foreign Operations Appropriations Subcommittee. Representative Porter has been recognized repeatedly by various groups as one of Congress' most fiscally conservative members. He holds a law degree from the University of Michigan Law School.

David M. Rajnes is a Ph.D. candidate in the Department of Geography and Environmental Engineering at the John Hopkins University in Baltimore, Maryland. His dissertation focus is the reform of old age pension systems in the transitional economies of Central and Eastern Europe. He is the author of several articles on international pension issues.

Marco Santamaria recently joined ING Capital Holdings as a vice president and sovereign risk analyst. Before joining ING, he was a vice president in the Global Bond Research Department of Alliance Capital Management. He has also served as an associate director in the sovereign ratings group at Standard and Poor's and as an economist at the Federal Reserve Bank of New York. In his current and past professional capacities, he has analyzed the impact of Latin American economic and political developments on local and international financial markets. He holds an M.A. from the Johns Hopkins University School of Advanced International Studies.

Kevin Stephenson is an assistant professor of economics at Middlebury College. He holds a Ph.D. from Cornell University and has written several articles on corporate reorganizations.

John Turner is deputy director of the Office of Research and Economic Analysis, Pension and Welfare Benefits Administration, U.S. Department of Labor. He is also an adjunct professor of economics at George Washington University, where he teaches the economics of aging. He formerly worked in the research office of the Social Security Administration. He received a Fulbright Senior Scholar award to do pension research at the Institut de Recherches Economiques et Sociales in Paris in 1994. He has written or edited seven books on pensions and has published more than 45 articles on pension and social security policy. He holds a Ph.D. from the University of Chicago.

Carolyn L. Weaver is a resident scholar at the American Enterprise Institute and director of AEI's Social Security and Pension Project. She has been a senior research fellow at the Hoover Institution and a member of the economics department and research associate at the Center for Study of Public Choice at Virginia Polytechnic Institute. She is the author of *Crisis in Social Security: Economic and Political Origins* and many articles on social security and is the editor of *Social Security's Looming Surpluses: Prospects and Implications.*